IN DUTY BOUND

In Duty Bound

Men, Women, and the State in Upper Canada, 1783–1841

J.K. JOHNSON

Carleton Library Series 227

McGill-Queen's University Press
Montreal & Kingston · London · Ithaca

© McGill-Queen's University Press 2014

ISBN 978-0-7735-4277-8 (cloth)
ISBN 978-0-7735-4278-5 (paper)
ISBN 978-0-7735-8963-6 (ePDF)
ISBN 978-0-7735-8964-3 (ePUB)

Legal deposit first quarter 2014
Bibliothèque nationale du Québec

Printed in Canada on acid-free paper that is 100% ancient forest free
(100% post-consumer recycled), processed chlorine free

This book has been published with the help of a grant from the Canadian
Federation for the Humanities and Social Sciences, through the Awards to
Scholarly Publications Program, using funds provided by the Social Sciences
and Humanities Research Council of Canada.

McGill-Queen's University Press acknowledges the support of the Canada
Council for the Arts for our publishing program. We also acknowledge the
financial support of the Government of Canada through the Canada Book
Fund for our publishing activities.

Library and Archives Canada Cataloguing in Publication

Johnson, J. K. (James Keith), 1930–, author
In duty bound: men, women, and the state in Upper Canada,
1783–1841 / J.K. Johnson.

(Carleton library series; 227)
Includes bibliographical references and index.
Issued in print and electronic formats.
ISBN 978-0-7735-4277-8 (bound). – ISBN 978-0-7735-4278-5 (pbk.)
ISBN 978-0-7735-8963-6 (ePDF). – ISBN 978-0-7735-8964-3 (ePUB)

1. Working class – Government policy – Ontario – History. 2. Men –
Government policy – Ontario – History. 3. Women – Government policy –
Ontario. 4. Working class – Ontario – Social conditions. 5. Men –
Ontario – Social conditions. 6. Women – Ontario – Social conditions.
7. Ontario – History – 1791–1841. 8. Canada – History – 18th century.
I. Title.

HD8109.O532J64 2013   305.5'620971309033   C2013-905278-X
                                                C2013-905279-8

This book was typeset by Interscript in 10.5/13 Sabon.

Contents

Map, Figures, and Tables

Abbreviations

AO	Archives of Ontario
App	Appendix
Bath	Bathurst District
BNA	British North America
Brock	Brock District
CHA	Canadian Historical Society
CHR	*Canadian Historical Review*
DCB	*Dictionary of Canadian Biography*
East	Eastern District
Eng. Can	English Canada
Fr. Can	French Canada
Fr	France
Ger	Germany
Gore	Gore District
HAJ	Upper Canada, House of Assembly, *Journals*
Home	Home District
Hs/SH	*Histoire sociale/Social History*
John	Johnstown District
LAC	Library and Archives Canada
LC	Lower Canada
L/LT	*Labour/Le Travail*
Lond	London District
MG	Manuscript Group
MHA	Member of the House of Assembly
Mid	Midland District
NB	New Brunswick
Newc	Newcastle District

Nia	Niagara District
OAR	*Ontario Archives Report*
OH	*Ontario History*
Ott	Ottawa District
PE	Prince Edward District
Port	Portugal
PP	Provincial Penitentiary
RG	Record Group
Tal	Talbot District
UC	Upper Canada
UE	United Empire Loyalist
Unk	Unknown
USA	United States of America
Vic	Victoria District
West	Western District

Acknowledgments

I am thankful for the assistance, over many years, of the staffs of Library and Archives Canada, the Archives of Ontario and the City of Toronto Archives. I wish to thank the anonymous readers for their thoughtful and helpful comments. I am grateful to Janna Ferguson for her indispensable technical skill in imposing order on an earlier draft of this book, to Michael Vickers for answering repeated cries for help, for the encouragement and guidance of Philip Cercone and Jessica Howarth of McGill-Queen's University Press and the thorough and skillful copy editing of Stephen Shapiro.

Lastly I wish to acknowledge another longstanding debt, to the influence and example of the late Professor J.M.S. Careless, who first set my feet upon the path of Upper Canadian history nearly sixty years ago.

This book has been published with the help of a grant from the Federation for the Humanities and Social Sciences, through the Awards to Scholarly Publications Program, using funds provided by the Social Sciences and Humanities Research Council of Canada.

IN DUTY BOUND

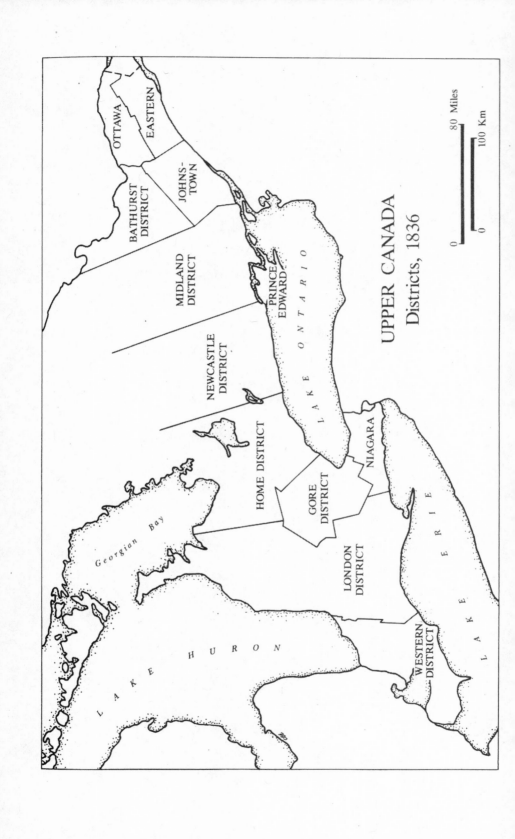

UPPER CANADA
Districts, 1836

Introduction

John Ross Robertson, the indefatigable amateur chronicler of life in early York/Toronto, discovered, on examining a fortunately preserved copy of the first York census of 1805, that there were quite a few people listed there about whom he was able to find no information. "This would seem to indicate," he concluded, "that most of them were labourers or members of the lower ranks of society and on this account there was nothing by which their memories could be preserved from forgetfulness."[1]

This book is about forgetfulness and forgotten people, and the way in which their lives were both forgotten and remembered by the state. Trying to investigate the lives of "the lower ranks of society" has always been difficult, especially in the earlier period of Canadian history, when, as Professor Allan Greer has ruefully pointed out, the "very fragmented and partial nature of the documentation makes research of the distant past into a detective operation: rather than organizing massive information, the historian scrutinizes clues, oblique and problematic indications of reality."[2] In the circumstances it is not surprising that relatively few historians have attempted to write about the plain people of Upper Canada, especially since, until after Upper Canada came to an official end, no census of the provincial population was taken. There is thus no statistical basis for the kind of analysis that historians of later periods were to find so useful in order to reconstruct the lives of individuals, families, and urban or rural populations in particular regions.[3] Fortunately, as some quite recent outstanding examples demonstrate, research on the lives of ordinary Upper Canadians, while difficult and time consuming, can be highly successful. As Elizabeth Jane

Errington found when setting out to write a history of working women in Upper Canada, the problem of finding appropriate sources is in fact more apparent than real.[4] Her ground-breaking book, *Wives and Mothers, School Mistresses and Scullery Maids: Working Women in Upper Canada, 1790–1840*, reflects the use of a very wide range of sources, including letters, diaries, journals, and newspapers, as does her subsequent work on emigrants to Upper Canada, *Emigrant Worlds and Transatlantic Communities: Migration to Upper Canada in the First Half of the Nineteenth Century*. Equally impressive is the work of the historical geographer John Clarke, who for many years has studied and written about the early development of Essex County. His most recent book, *The Ordinary People of Essex: Environment, Culture, and Economy on the Frontier of Upper Canada*, is the result of a prodigious exercise of gathering and expertly analyzing data (including in this case the 1851 census) relating to "everyday settlers" in one corner of Upper Canada from the late eighteenth to the mid-nineteenth century. Upper Canadians who kept or frequented taverns are featured in the work of Julia Roberts, whose highly original book, *In Mixed Company: Taverns and Public Life in Upper Canada*, also uses a wide variety of sources, such as private papers, journals and diaries, government records, and newspapers. *Family Life and Sociability in Upper and Lower Canada, 1780–1870*, by Françoise Noël, is more narrowly based on diaries and family letters and of course goes beyond both the geographical and chronological boundaries of Upper Canada. And it is also possible to find, in recent issues of the journal *Ontario History* and elsewhere, a range of articles which, in different ways, touch on the lives of ordinary Upper Canadians.[5]

So John Ross Robertson has been proved wrong. Forgetfulness is not the necessary fate of all of the ordinary people of Upper Canada. This book, by exploring the relationship between the people of Upper Canada and the Upper Canadian state, is an attempt to expand even further the boundaries of what can be known about the lives and experiences of the Upper Canadian population throughout the period and throughout the province. There are in fact still some largely unexplored sources from which at least partial evidence relating to a great many commonplace lives can be extracted, sources which often allow the people involved to speak for themselves. The government of Upper Canada itself compiled and preserved surprisingly large bodies of official records which concern quite humble people, particularly in petitions submitted to the lieutenant governor.

Petitions, as generally thought of today, that is documents bearing a great many signatures gathered to lobby for, or protest against, something that has been done or may be done, were certainly commonly submitted to the government in eighteenth- and nineteenth-century Upper Canada[6] but such petitions bear little or no relationship to the kinds of petition under discussion here. These were mostly personal petitions, in which an individual directly addressed the representative of the Crown. Collective petitions, then as now, demand; personal petitions of the past were closer to begging. The point is that in the pre–responsible government era in the British colonies, the governors and their advisors actually had quite a bit of real power and could grant, or deny, many individual requests, whereas nowadays petitioning the lieutenant governor of Ontario would be about as effectual as throwing a note in a bottle into the ocean. These earlier petitions were very numerous and each one contained some personal information about a person at the time the petition was written. Because there are so many of them and because they can be sorted into a number of main categories, petitions have the advantage of providing some information about individuals while also providing an opportunity for collective analysis. And since, as shall be seen, petitions were the principal way in which Upper Canadians approached and were responded to by the state, they help us to understand the circumstances and needs which prompted Upper Canadians to approach the executive government or the legislature; the way in which, and the extent to which, people interacted with their government; what they knew about the workings of government; and the ways in which they used their knowledge.

All those personal petitions were received, and fortunately preserved, by the government of Upper Canada, because Upper Canadians were following a custom and exercising a right enjoyed by British subjects for a very long time. England's Bill of Rights of 1689 gave formal sanction to a practice that was then already of ancient origin; the right of an individual to petition the Sovereign: "It is the right of the subject to petition the King, and all commitments and prosecutions for such petitions are illegal." The petition had become a standard device by which a subject could make some request of the monarch. Legal historians have divided such petitions into two types: petitions asking for something to which the petitioner had a legal claim, and those asking for something as a favour, or "petitions of right" and "petitions of grace."[7]

In Upper Canada petitioning of both kinds began with the Loyalists, even before there was an actual Upper Canada. Instructions issued by the governor from Quebec directed that any application "for grants or parcels of the waste lands of the Crown ... shall be by petition to the Governor in Council." Petitions for land began to pour in from Loyalists wanting land in addition to their original locations, then from prospective settlers from the United States and ultimately from overseas. There was no prescribed form for such petitions but the main ingredients of a successful application quickly became widely known. In general, land petitioners were expected to state their place of birth, previous residence, details of family, and proof of ability to "improve land." They had also to have taken an oath of allegiance. After Upper Canada was created as a separate province in 1791 and John Graves Simcoe assumed the office of lieutenant governor the following year, some other necessary qualifications and disqualifications were officially added. Petitioners were informed that no one was to have land "but those whose loyalty, industry and morals shall appear to entitle them to his Majesty's Bounty." As well, only those "professing the Christian Religion and ... who can adduce satisfactory vouchers of their having paid obedience to the laws, and led a life of inoffensive manners ... shall in future be considered as qualified to be admitted to the possession of lands." In other words, petitioners had to try to show, with the support of others, preferably magistrates or other leadership figures, that they were deserving people of good background and morals who had the means to become useful and loyal Upper Canadians.[8]

Because Upper Canada began as, and remained, an overwhelmingly rural province, land petitions were by far the most common, but by no means the only, form of personal petition. In roughly descending order by quantity, petitions were also routinely submitted in at least five other general categories: for government jobs; for pardons or ameliorations of court sentences; for pensions; for compensation for damages done by, or work done for, the government; and for relief. Each of these, among other matters, is given separate study in this book.

None of these documents are truly biographical. They provide only episodic entry into a period in a person's life, and of course, since the object of a petition was to get something from the government, they usually included only information that seemed likely to gain a sympathetic hearing. Many such brief appearances in the government's records occur only once. Still it is possible to learn quite a bit about people whose names reappear with some frequency and at least a minimum amount about most others, such as their age, sex, family, place of origin, and location in Upper Canada. And every document yields some information about how a man or woman at a particular time came to be an entry in the government's files; about why they felt qualified for a land grant or a job or compensation or a pension they did or did not get; about how they had got into, and sometimes got out of, trouble with the law; about whether they sent their children to the state-aided schools; about what calamitous circumstances had reduced them to begging for relief; and much, much more.

Petitions then provide the major source of evidence used here concerning various aspects of the lives of ordinary Upper Canadians, but because some men, and especially women, probably never submitted petitions at all, and also because this book is concerned not only with Upper Canadian people but with the Upper Canadian state, it makes use of a wide variety of other government records. Documents from the courts and penal institutions, the administration of the pension system and of the schools, government employment, finance, and the deliberations of the executive council and the legislature have all been used to flesh out the nature of the people's relationship with the state and to clarify how the several government agencies actually worked, for, or against, the interests of the population. The connection of the people of Upper Canada to their government was not maintained only by constant petitioning, whether successful or unsuccessful. In the case of their involvement with the common schools for instance, as parents, students, teachers, and trustees, petitioning was hardly involved at all. A complete list of government records which have been consulted can be found in the bibliography.

Obviously Upper Canada, as a colony of Great Britain, was not a "state" in the full sense of an organized political community with sovereign powers, but a dependent state, whose actions could be reviewed and even nullified by the Imperial government. As a consequence the limited Upper Canadian state discussed here refers in most cases to the basic apparatus of government and administration;

that is, to the executive, the legislature, the judiciary, and the provincial and local public service. For practical purposes this was the state which the men and women of Upper Canada interacted with, and whose workings they had to try to understand and to cope with, for good or ill. But even in colonial Upper Canada where changes, if they were made at all, were unlikely to be rapid or dramatic, the institutions of the state were never entirely static. Laws and regulations having been put in place, they were often later amended or even discarded. New procedures were introduced, in part because the imperial government began to demand factual information about what was actually going in its colony. In the fifty-year Upper Canadian period, the personnel of the public service saw inevitable change and some modest expansion. Even more obvious than the growth of the central provincial government in the capital of York/ Toronto was the expansion of local government, as new districts, increasing from four to twenty, with new sets of officials had to be periodically created to keep up with the increase in population. So the Upper Canadian state, in even its most rudimentary form, cannot be understood as simply the sum of its parts. But can the Upper Canadian state be seen as something more than an undeveloped entity slowly and reluctantly groping its way forward?

For some time a number of historians and historical sociologists have argued, from a variety of theoretical perspectives, that "the state" cannot be viewed only as an institution but as a "process," a process of "state formation" by which central authority, including government institutions, "became more effective agencies of coercion and administration, taking fuller control of civil society and penetrating into previously neglected corners of the social formation."[9] The origins of state formation in England have been detected by historians as early as the medieval period, but most Canadian historians have found evidence of a similar phenomenon only in the 1840s and 1850s,[10] coinciding, in the opinion of Bruce Curtis, the foremost student of state formation in the Canadas, with the emergence of executive government power and state control of education. In the case of Upper Canada, Curtis argues that before the Union of 1840 the administrative capacity of the state was too limited to permit any real attempts to establish successful dominance of the population.[11] Since this book deals with the Upper Canadian state in relation to its people in a number of areas, it presents an opportunity to examine that relationship at points where people and state regularly intersected, where ordinary Upper Canadians approached agents of the state seeking land, employment, compensation, pensions, pardons, schooling, and relief, and to ask whether evidence of growing coercion and effectiveness on the part of the state can be discerned. Though some scholars have argued that during the 1830s increasing official attention paid to the problems of crime, lunacy, and poverty represented "the birth of a technocratic state" in Upper Canada,[12] it is the contention of this book that Professor Curtis has got it largely right. Before 1840 the history of the Upper Canadian state provides little evidence of a burgeoning "colonial leviathan," steadily increasing its sway over the population.

If relatively few historians have taken up the task of exploring the fate of "the lower orders" in Upper Canada, even fewer have written about the Upper Canadian state, even from a purely institutional or bureaucratic point of view. There is no Upper Canadian equivalent of J.E. Hodgetts's *Pioneer Public Service: An Administrative History of the United Canadas, 1841–1867*, which begins when Upper Canada comes to an end. It is sad to say that one of the only good general discussions of the organization and functions of the provincial government remains the chapter on "The Government of Upper Canada," in Aileen Dunham's *Political Unrest in Upper Canada*, first published in 1927. The single aspect of the Upper Canadian public service to have been much written about has been the matter of the imperial and provincial government policy concerning the distribution of land[13] but the actual working of even that system was unexplored until the completion of the MA and PhD theses by David Moorman, "The District Land Boards: A Study of Early Land Administration in Upper Canada, 1784–1794" and "The First Business of Government: The Land Granting Administration of Upper Canada." An indispensable guide to government offices and officeholders at the provincial and local levels can be found in F.H. Armstrong's *Handbook of Upper Canadian Chronology*, but again the actual day-to-day operations of most government offices and departments has remained something of a mystery. Sadly, shedding adequate light on this subject would require another and different book. This one can only claim to begin that task in a very preliminary way. Figure 2 provides a skeletal version of the main features of the Upper Canadian bureaucratic state, and its principal components and their responsibilities are briefly described in chapter 2.

The only history of Upper Canada as a separate province that has ever been written, Gerald Craig's now somewhat dated but still admirable *Upper Canada: The Formative Years* dealt, as one would expect, with major themes such as war and rebellion, immigration, settlement, politics, and the economy, but in his preface he wrote that there was really "a deeper and more lasting story" which was "the hard work done by many thousands of plain people to clear the land, to build farms and towns, to improve communications, to adapt political, religious, and educational institutions to their own needs."[14] Quite a lot of the deeper and more lasting story of the plain people of Upper Canada can be read in the bits and pieces of the public record that have survived since 1841.

I

Getting Land

PART I

When the area that was to be Upper Canada became British by virtue of the Treaty of Paris of 1763 it was entirely undeveloped as a European agricultural colony except for a small French-speaking community which had crossed the river from Detroit. Otherwise the land was the home territory of a number of groups of native people. This situation changed abruptly with the outbreak of the American Revolution. As early as 1781, English-speaking Loyalists were beginning to settle in British territory on the west side of the Niagara River. When the Revolution ended, the real Loyalist influx began. Around 7,000 people who had been on the losing side, many of whom had also lost their property and most of their possessions, were allowed by the colonial government at Quebec to take up land along the north shore of the St Lawrence River so that they could start over. So began the process of land distribution in Upper Canada.

The way in which the imperial and colonial governments organized the disposal of public lands in Upper Canada has been the subject of a long series of investigations. There may in fact be more reports, books, theses, and articles dealing with Upper Canadian land policy and administration than with any other Upper Canadian topic. Without exception, everyone who has looked closely at the question has come to a single conclusion: the system was a disaster.

The Earl of Durham, in his famous *Report on the Affairs of British North America of 1839*, was the first to officially condemn "the general mismanagement" of the land administration in Upper Canada. More recent writers have seen no reason to disagree.

The first of a succession of twentieth-century scholars, G.C. Patterson, pointed out many "defects of the land system" and "evils" which required "years in the removing." Alan Wilson wrote of government "ineptitudes" and Lillian Gates of "inefficiency and favouritism." Colin Read found that Upper Canada suffered from a "profligate" land policy by which the government "squandered the province's patrimony." The most recent and most thorough examination of the administration of land policy in Upper Canada, by David Moorman, has concluded that it was marked by "administrative confusion."[1]

The litany of the serious problems within the land system has been repeated over and over, and need not be restated in detail. The administration was inefficient and disorganized, operating with an antiquated and decentralized system of record keeping. Surveys were sometimes faulty and the method eventually adopted for paying for them was ill-advised. The creation of Crown and Clergy reserves slowed economic progress, dispersed settlement unduly, and caused political and religious discontent. Enormous amounts of land were allowed to fall into the hands of absentee owners and speculators, which also hindered progress by deferring local tax revenue and by keeping the land out of production until it had acceptable value, which in many cases meant until well after the Upper Canadian period. Above all, land-granting policy was ridiculously slanted in favour of "privileged" individuals and institutions. Lord Durham believed that "perhaps less than a tenth" of Upper Canadian land had been given to real settlers. Colin Read's modern recalculation is only a little more generous. His figures show that of the 13.7 million acres of Crown land disposed of by the government up to 1838, 2.1 million, or about 15 per cent, went to ordinary settlers. David Wood's case study of Essa Township, surveyed in 1820, found that initially "60 per cent of the township was held by absentees ... and 28 per cent was in Crown and clergy reserves. The 12 per cent that was available to *bona fide* settlers was largely pushed to far reaches of the township by the land of non-residents."[2]

Part of the problem was that land policy was meant to do a number of different things at once, most of them contradictory. Of course the members of the executive government wanted the land settled in a rational way by the right kind of successful, hard-working farmers, but they also pursued the impossible dream of creating a colonial landed aristocracy in a wilderness by giving excessively large grants to military officers, government officials, and other people deemed worthy of favour. It was intended that land would be reasonably accessible to *bona fide* settlers, but the government also wanted the distribution of land to produce revenue, so that the "free grant" system was never actually free of fees or direct cost to non-privileged applicants and the largely unused and resented reserves were also a failure as a source of rental revenue. David Moorman is of the opinion that the one measure which would have provided the government with an adequate income and encouraged actual settlement, the imposition of quit rents, was too hastily and foolishly abandoned from "ignorance, neglect and sanguine expectations of rapid development."[3]

Despite the complications and contradictions within the system and the assorted barriers to accessibility, the province eventually got settled and people came to own land, and at a rate of individual ownership which by 1871 compared favourably with that of the adjacent American states.[4] In other words, ordinary people eventually got access to most of the land that was originally given away by the Crown, although most of them had to buy it from other people. Still, even during the Upper Canadian period itself, many thousands of immigrants to the province, the vast majority of whom had no pretensions to rank or distinction, were collectively granted over two million acres of land, began to develop it, and, in a good many cases, even got title to it. So how was the land that was available acquired from the government?

Before individual ownership of the land was even a possibility, the Crown's right to it had first to be negotiated. Territory for settlement was obtained as needed by a series of treaties and surrenders, a process by which the native people were systematically dispossessed of their accustomed space on disadvantageous terms, although that was not a concern of the newcomers who came to clear the forest. Once the Crown had title to the land it could be distributed as the government saw fit, a procedure that began in earnest with the Loyalists in 1784. Most of the Loyalists who came to settle in Upper Canada were quite ordinary people, but within the framework of official land policy as it ultimately developed they received decidedly special treatment. They did not have to ask for land; it was given to them as compensation for lost property and as a reward for their support of the Crown in the Revolution. They did not have to search for a likely location; it was simply assigned to them. Through a series of astute

manoeuvres and complaints on the part of former Loyalist officers
the minimum amount of land to which they were all entitled was
increased from fifty to 200 acres and a similar amount was granted
to their children, male and female. Their land grants came with few
conditions attached. Quit rents were first waived for a ten-year
period and then were never reimposed.[5]

It was only with the arrival of more would-be settlers, at first
mostly from the former Thirteen Colonies and later from the United
Kingdom, that complications arose and Upper Canada's notorious
land policy began to take shape. There had been no need for the
government to pick and choose among the Loyalists, to give land to
some and withhold it from others, or to impose conditions on their
grants; all were assumed to be equally worthy. The newcomers presented a problem of distinguishing between those who were deserving of land and those who were not, and if deserving, of how much,
and on what terms? But that was the government's problem. From
the point of view of the land seekers, the question was: what did they
have to do to get a share of "the waste lands of the Crown"?

In 1788 the new settlements in what was still the western part of
the Province of Quebec were divided into four administrative districts, originally called Lunenburg, Mecklenburg, Nassau, and Hesse,
and centring on Cornwall, Kingston, Niagara, and Detroit (then still
British territory). For these districts the first set of regulations for the
granting of land were issued the following year and, to keep applicants on their toes, frequently amended in the years that followed. A
basic requirement was that each "application shall be by petition to
the Governor in Council," in other words no one was to have land
without formally asking for it, and the petitioner had to justify the
application on the grounds of his or her "merits or pretensions."
Fortunately the petitions did not actually have to go to the Governor
in Quebec unless the applicant wanted more than 200 acres, for in
1788 land boards were appointed in each district to interview potential grantees, requiring only attendance at a meeting of the board in
the district of their intended settlement. The regulations were printed
in large quantities, 500 copies at a time, for the use of the boards, but
were also "to be made public in their respective districts." The boards
were to "give free and easy access to petitioners" by holding "peri-
odical" meetings at stated times, "made publicly known." If the
board which met at Detroit was typical of the others it can be said
that a genuine attempt was made to communicate with the public,

though in its case not always with complete success. This board met at least weekly and sometimes for several consecutive days in such places as the house of one of the board members, beginning at the civilized hour of eleven o'clock in the morning. The board initially directed that the regulations and also "Models of Petitions for lands" be sent in both French and English to "the principal loyal settlers in this District" to "be dispersed among the settlers." The board later discovered that their orders had not been followed by their secretary, Thomas Smith, who had set up a little business for himself, telling applicants that "Petitions would only be received by the board in a certain form ... which nobody had but himself," and charging as much as £14 to prepare individual submissions for land. The conscientious board issued a second complete set of instructions in "a circular letter to the principal settlers." So far as the acceptable form of petition was concerned it appears to have become common knowledge very quickly, for from the beginning land petitions all followed roughly the same format. Upper Canadians quickly became adept at petitioning, not only to get land but for many other reasons, as shall be seen.[6]

Even if the communication system worked well, the petitioners faced a fair number of bureaucratic hurdles on the way to becoming independent landowners. Though in some cases boards allowed petitioners to be represented by "someone authorized to answer for them," the use of agents was not provided for in the instructions, and at all times the official preference was for the applicants to appear in person. Petitions were supposed to be considered in the order in which they were received "where there is no special cause for a different course of proceeding," so petitioners had to attend the meetings of the boards but wait around until their turn came, possibly at a later meeting. Petitioners typically faced a panel of at least three examiners, usually former Loyalist officers. The criteria by which the boards made decisions boiled down to two: loyalty and character. Was the applicant genuinely attached to the British Crown and Empire and a person of passable moral and religious standards? In most cases apparently the answer was yes. According to David Moorman the boards "had no interest in probing the character of the settlers too deeply," because they wanted their districts to grow and prosper and did not wish to discourage immigrants from the United States from coming to the province. Entries such as that for Humphrey Waters – "refused as being Himself and family of bad fame" – are rare. Moorman gives the example of a board that met at Adolphustown in 1792–94 which rejected only four of 271 petitions. For most people, appearing before a board was evidently not a harrowing ordeal.[7]

Successful newcomers went immediately from being nobodies to possessors of official documents. The boards issued slips of paper to grantees which were licences of occupation. The prospective settler then had to seek out a provincial deputy surveyor who assigned a specific lot and wrote out a "location ticket" for 200 acres on which the township, concession, and lot number were specified. The settler was then supposed to make another trip to the board to register the assigned lot so that it could be recorded as occupied. Actual settlement could then begin and was in fact supposed to take place within a year on (theoretical) pain of losing the lot.[8]

Those first pieces of official paper were initially just improvised documents, written on whatever the board clerk and the surveyor had at hand, containing the settler's name and lot number. Inevitably, as in all bureaucratic procedures, the system became more regularized and standardized so that the location tickets became more elaborate, on printed forms, with requisite blanks on which were filled in not only the settler's name and the plot's location but the settler's place of birth, the settlement duties to be performed on the lot, the rights of the heirs in the land, and the restrictions applying to the transfer of the land to someone else.[9] This last part of the document, concerning restrictions on how the settler could dispose of the land, was immediately and cheerfully ignored by a large proportion of settlers, thereby creating a fine mess for the government and the settlers alike, a mess which requires a brief digression to explain.

The procedure that was supposed to be followed was that the settler, having successfully begun actual cultivation, would get witnesses and a magistrate to attest to this fact and then apply for a deed or patent from the Crown. Only with the issuing of the patent would real legal ownership of the land by the settler begin, and with it the right to sell, give, or will the land to somebody else. The problem was that a very great number of settlers did not bother with the last step in the process – getting the deed.

Why would people fail to acquire that precious attribute, legal possession of their own land? For one thing, getting a deed was not all that easy. Before 1792 the necessary documents had to be sent to Quebec to be approved by the executive council. That approval would then be announced in the *Quebec Gazette*, an official organ not widely available in the backwoods, but if word did reach the settler the deed had to be picked up at Quebec in person or by someone acting as an authorized agent. When Upper Canada came into existence the deeds had only to be got from the new capital at York, but the government compounded the problem by issuing no patents at all between 1792 and 1796 while a schedule of fees was being worked out. Further disincentives were added by expecting the fees to be paid in cash, not readily available to struggling settlers, and by a bewildering amount of red tape, of which more later.[10]

Understandably settlers ignored the provisions of the law. A deed to land had no immediate practical value. It did not hasten the task of clearing the land or make it more productive. The settler had a document which showed that he or she had been granted a particular lot, furthermore, it was a document which other people were willing to consider valid proof of ownership. Location tickets were readily exchanged, devised, bought, and sold as if they were Crown deeds. So began a bureaucratic and legal nightmare. Property passed to new owners, or to a succession of owners, or within families, to which no legal ownership had ever existed. To quote a scholar of the subject "by the mid 1790s property rights were in such chaos and confusion that remedial action was imperative." The abuse was so widespread that the government was forced to create a kind of court of equity called the Heir and Devisee Commission to adjudicate claims to land "where no letters patent had issued to the original nominees of the Crown, their heirs, devisees or assigns." This legal sorting-out process, involving commission appointees and staff on the one hand, and claimants and their lawyers on the other, continued to plague the system for many generations. The original commission was established in 1797 but its work was not finally wound up until 114 years later, in 1911.[11]

The buying and selling of documents whose status was quasi-legal at best also contributed greatly to the problem of speculation and absentee ownership. People who had the means, the time, and the knowledge were able to buy up, at bargain prices, thousands of acres in entitlements to land from grantees who did not want or need the land, or simply wanted some ready money. "Loyalist rights" were particularly popular as a speculation because they could be turned into patented land without fees or conditions. Lillian Gates compiled a list of seventeen prominent Upper Canadians who had acquired a total of 296,874 acres in Loyalist rights prior to 1818, led by Colonel John Crysler, MHA, himself a Loyalist, with 60,200 acres.[12]

The procedures involved in the "remedial action" caused by the exchange of unofficial land documents were neither speedy nor simple. The Heir and Devisee Commission originally moved around the province hearing appeals but after 1805 met only in York / Toronto and only once a year for two weeks, so cases which were deferred had to wait a year. Notice of claims had to be posted at least thirty days before the commission met and claimants had to produce a wealth of documentation "such as land certificates, deeds of bargain and sale, mortgages, birth, marriage or death notices, affidavits sworn before a commissioner for the taking of oaths, family letters, receipts, or any other type of evidence." In other words, the remedial apparatus cost both the government and those who ultimately sought legal title to land a great deal of unnecessary time and money. Still it is probably pointless at this distance to try to assign blame to either side for the fact that the rules were so easily and almost universally broken. No doubt the grantees should have followed the regulations, and no doubt the government could have made it somewhat easier to do so, or been more vigilant in enforcing the rules, but as David Moorman has pointed out, for a long time in the new settlements the government was not really in a position to enforce much of anything. At any rate, rather than smooth the path to legal land ownership the administration over time steadily created additional hurdles and discouragements which made the situation worse.[13]

In 1791 the new Province of Upper Canada came into official existence and the following year Lieutenant Governor John Graves Simcoe arrived to take executive charge of it. Under his leadership an inevitable further process of bureaucratization and centralization got under way. Simcoe took an active interest in land policy. He increased the number of land boards in 1792 to speed up land granting but was still impatient with the rate at which they were advancing settlement, so he concurrently embarked on a pet settlement scheme of his own – personally granting whole townships to prominent "leaders" who were supposed to bring large numbers of "associates" with them to quickly fill up the vacant lands. (He was hoping especially for an influx of settlers from Connecticut.) The abject failure of this plan has been described often enough. The leaders almost always turned out to be ambitious speculators looking to get their hands on large quantities of land and the associates to be few or fictitious. While Simcoe remained in office he did not give up on this naive scheme, which was quickly scrapped as soon as his back was turned, but he did give up on the land boards. In 1794 they were abolished. The power to make basic land grants was transferred temporarily to the district magistrates and in 1796 centralized entirely within the bureaucracy at the provincial capital. From then until 1819 the road to all land grants began at the governor's Executive Council.[14]

While the land boards operated at a local level petitioners made a relatively short trip, or trips, to the board's location. If some problem arose with the lot they had been assigned they could simply go back to the board to ask to have it sorted out. Under the new arrangement, everyone wanting land, with the exception of those within handy reach of York, had to make a much longer and more expensive journey. Despite this fact the Executive Council continued to insist that if humanly possible applicants for land appear in person to have their loyalty and character assessed. Agents were at first reluctantly permitted but if the council had doubts about an applicant, or suspected fraud, a personal appearance was insisted upon. In 1804 agents were banned altogether to prevent "gross fraud." In 1806 exceptions were again allowed but only where "the agent is known" to members of the council.[15]

Some few cases of actual fraud did come to light, but it is difficult to see what was gained by such close scrutiny of the petitioners, for on the whole the council proved no more rigorous in weeding out bad apples than the land boards had been. Moorman cites a single meeting of the council on 21 July 1797, at which 182 applications were dealt with and approved, with no rejections or referrals.[16]

It is worth pausing here for a moment to consider the unusual implications of the executive council's paranoia. Meeting the members of the council face to face meant that the process must not only have been daunting, even terrifying, for many applicants, but was also extraordinarily personal. Applicants for land, most of them of humble background and education, found themselves being cross-examined on the claims in their petitions by the most senior and powerful officers of the Upper Canadian government. Many thousands of Upper Canadians went through this experience. Here the state and the people were definitely not abstract entities, not at arm's length from one another, but in the same room together, a situation unique to its time which now seems almost inconceivable. If a modern comparison might be suggested, it is as if, in order to get something that the government pretty routinely hands out, such as an old age pension, all applicants were interviewed by the prime minister and the cabinet, having first of course travelled to Ottawa at their own expense.

The Executive Council members did have their reasons for insisting on personal attendance and did reject some applications, as shall be seen, but it must also be said that their decisions were sometimes high-handed, arbitrary, and even bigoted. The council quickly developed a healthy sense of its own importance. An entry in the minutes of 1797 for a man named Caleb Forsyth reads "the petitioner having expressed a contempt for the board, no lands to be granted to him," and another for Angus Macdonell MHA, "When the Petitioner learns to address this board with the respect he ought to pay to the Executive Government of the Province his petition may be attended to." The council also kept a sharp eye out for prospective grantees they considered undesirable. By a proclamation of 1794 land in Upper Canada was to be given only to qualified persons "professing the Christian Religion." On this basis the petitions of Levy Solomons and Moses Hart were both rejected, though Solomons had been a resident of Upper Canada for two years. Moses Hart, part of a prosperous clan of Lower Canadian Jewish merchants, had bought quantities of military land rights from discharged soldiers and non-commissioned officers and wanted to take up the lands in Upper Canada. His petition was "not recommended." George Wright, "a free mulatto," and Adam Lewis, "a black man," were also refused land. On occasion the council refused to grant land on other grounds, including age and size. John Hutchinson Newell failed his examination by the council "being only eighteen and small."[17]

In most ordinary cases initial approval of an application for land seems to have been fairly routine, but that was just the beginning of a series of official procedures which can only be called bewildering. Rather than streamlining the process the administration made getting land, especially meeting all the requirements necessary for actual legal ownership, slow, highly inconvenient and increasingly costly. David Moorman estimates that after land granting became part of the duties of the provincial public service, just getting a location ticket meant a trip to York "lasting a month or more." Why?[18]

The Executive Council was the first bottleneck. Though land matters were a major concern for the council members, they were only a part-time concern, for they had a lot of other affairs "of state" to occupy their time. Before 1815 the council held only *ad hoc* meetings on land business, "based on the convenience of the councillors." After 1805 the council met as a land committee once a week and only in the afternoon. In 1819, according to John Strachan, then a member of the Executive Council, the council met to hear land petitions only "every second Wednesday" so just getting through the door of the council chamber could take some time. Then the real paper chase began. Each file had to be seen and approved, or not, by a great many officials besides the executive councillors: the lieutenant governor himself, the civil secretary, the clerk of the council, the attorney general, the surveyor general, the provincial secretary, the surveyor of woods, the auditor general, and the receiver general. Whether the involvement of so many functionaries was really essential is a good question, but from their points of view there was at least one good reason why they needed to examine each file. Most of them received a fee, paid by the applicant, for certifying the relevant documents as they passed from office to office. These fees were first imposed in 1796 at the rate of £5-1-2 on each 200 acres. Fees were increased to £5-11-0 in 1798, to £8-4-1 in 1804, to £16-17-6 in 1819, and to £30 in 1820. So many protests were raised about this final steep increase that in 1824 the imperial government ordered the fees rolled back to £16-17-6. David Moorman provides a breakdown of the shares of the £16-17-6 in fees received after 1804 by the officeholders as: surveyor general, £1-7-6; lieutenant governor, £1-1-0; provincial secretary, £0-12-6; provincial registrar (actually the same person holding both offices), £0-12-6; clerk of the council, £0-12-6; attorney general, £0-12-6; receiver general, £0-7-6; surveyor of woods, £0-5-0. To provide some context for these sums, on every 100 grants of the minimum 200 acres made, the surveyor general collected £137-10-0; the lieutenant governor, £100-5-0; the provincial secretary and registrar, £100-2-10; the clerk of the Executive Council and the attorney general, both £62-10-0; the registrar general, £37-10-0; and the surveyor of woods, £25, in addition to their regular salaries. In the years 1804–06 there were an average of 488 petitions per year, so at that time they would all have collected nearly five times that much in each year.[19]

It might be helpful at this point to provide a summary of the steps a petitioner was obliged to take, including paying fees, on the way to his or her possession of a land grant. This was usually done in three stages.[20]

Stage 1

The petitioner took the oath of allegiance before a magistrate or someone else authorized to administer the oath, for which a fee was paid, and received a certificate which was attached to the petition.

The petitioner sent, or took, the petition to the Executive Council office, where it was entered in the records by the clerk. The clerk sent it by messenger, a servant employed by most government offices, to the lieutenant governor's office for initial approval. The petition was sent back to the clerk of the council to await the council's judgement when it was the petitioner's turn to have the case heard (figure 1, steps 1–3).

It is not entirely clear how the petitioner learned when an interview was to take place, presumably by regularly pestering the door-keeper of the council office for information. When the candidate did pass the oral examination the petition was sent again to the lieutenant governor for his approval of the council's decision and sent back to the clerk of the council, who issued an order-in-council, or warrant, for land. The petitioner then had three days from the date of the order-in-council to come back to the council office to get a transcript of it (figure 1, steps 4–6).

The petitioner took the transcript to the receiver general's office and paid the fees. The receiver general recorded the payment and made out a receipt which was sent to the clerk of council. The clerk prepared another order-in-council for the attorney general, permitting him to issue his fiat (a legal order or authorization). The file, now bearing the approval of the receiver general and the attorney general, was sent to the surveyor general. After the file got to the surveyor general's office the petitioner went there, during the staff's hours of ten and three, to choose a location from among the lots then surveyed and available for settlement. The surveyor general prepared a location paper containing the grantee's name and an exact description of the size and location of the grant (figure 1, steps 7–11).

Stage 2

At this point, with a copy of the location paper in hand, the ordinary successful grantee got off the bureaucratic treadmill for the time being, because to go further in the process and to qualify for a patent it was necessary to perform the specified settlement duties: clearing a minimum amount of land and part of the roadway in front of the lot, and building "a habitable house." This would probably take at least a year. If the grantee did decide to apply for a patent as soon as possible, rather than put it off or not apply at all, written evidence of performance, including a magistrate's certificate, was required.

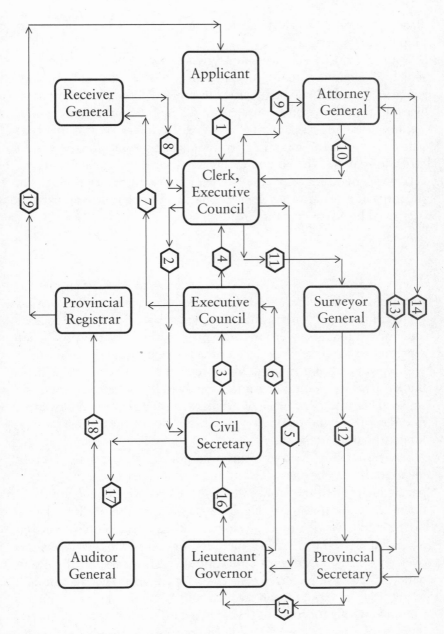

Figure 1   The paper trail: petition to deed

Privileged grantees, whose grants came without conditions, could skip this stage entirely.

For the majority who were non-privileged, assuming that the decision was made eventually to apply for a patent and that proof of performance of settlement duties had been obtained, the grantee became a petitioner once more, again taking the road to York with a petition asking for a patent to be issued. No interview was involved this time but there was still a lot of waiting around for the paperwork to be done. The file containing a new order-in-council, plus the receiver general's receipt, the surveyor general's description of the location, and the attorney general's fiat, had to be re-assembled and approved by the lieutenant governor.

Stage 3

The Provincial Secretary's office now "engrossed" the patent, that is, produced an elaborate legal document in large ornate letters, written on parchment. The patent still had to go back to the attorney general and the lieutenant governor for their signatures, to the provincial secretary to have the Great Seal of the Province attached, and to the auditor general and the provincial registrar to be entered in their books, at which point it was finally ready to be collected by the petitioner. This whole sequence of events was supposed to take twenty-one days from the order-in-council, but could take considerably longer (figure 1, steps 12–19).

The business of land granting was not designed for the convenience of land petitioners. The machinery of government moved at a pace which suited the work habits of the executive councillors and the other senior officers of the public service and as a result backlogs in the paper work often developed. When Lieutenant Governor Maitland arrived in 1818 he found the Executive Council "sleeping over an office choked with applications." Petitioners, on the other hand, would have preferred a speedier system, for to get a grant and to get title to it could mean two stays in York of roughly a month, running up bills for food and lodging for at least one person, and in the case of a family just arrived in Upper Canada, for several others. A further inconvenience was the location of government offices. Before 1832, when government activities were finally consolidated in the new government building on Front Street in York, the various offices were scattered all over town. In a report to the colonial secretary in 1804, Lieutenant Governor Peter Hunter complained "that there is not at present a single building here, for any one public Office. The Offices of the Executive Council, of the Secretary, the Register, the Auditor, the Clerk of the Crown and the Courts of Probate and Surrogate [are] all within the private houses of the Individuals who fill those respective Situations, and the Executive Council is obliged to meet in a very small room in the Clerk's house, exposed to the hazard of having their discussions overheard. These houses are all built of Wood, and of course afford slender Security for the public Records." (Hunter had good cause to be concerned about security. The year before five sets of land petitioner's documents had been eaten by mice.) It was not until twenty-seven years after Hunter's report, in 1831, that a guidebook description of York could reflect impending improvement: "The government here appears to be concentrating the public offices under the same roof – a most desirable regulation; for at present they are distributed all over town; and after a person has transacted business at one office, it takes him half a day to find out the next." The "steps" illustrated in figure 1 were not just steps on paper, or even short trips down the corridor to the next office, but annoying journeys of some distance, and for newcomers some puzzlement, through the streets of muddy York.[21]

In 1819 a major administrative change was introduced which seemed to promise land seekers a much simpler, faster, and more convenient procedure. Land boards were re-established in each of the districts, now grown to eight from the original four. A trip to York was no longer necessary either to petition for land or for a patent, for the boards provided a local service, meeting at least once a week at an advertised time and place to interview applicants and handling the delivery of patents, which were sent from York to be picked up by qualified grantees. Each board employed a clerk who could provide information. The boards took charge of certifying the performance of settlement duties. They were even allowed to provide a guide when needed to help newcomers find their lots.

The boards however operated under some important restrictions which made the new system less of an improvement than it seemed. They could only grant a maximum of 100 acres, instead of the 200 acres that had previously been the norm. In the wake of the War of 1812 they were allowed to grant land only to immigrants of British origin, though once again the examination of candidates could be casual and some Americans were assigned locations. In

addition to the normal fees, petitioners now had to pay an extra
7s 6d to the clerk for his services. Patents did not have to be collected
from York, but the paperwork involved in issuing them still took as
much or more time, since the petitioner's documents had to be sent
to York, examined by all the usual officials, and then sent back to the
relevant board.

The boards did not prove popular with people wanting land and
never did a large amount of business. In the end the bulk of their
workload was in assigning land to non–fee-paying military and Loyalist
claimants, a task initially reserved for the Executive Council. Most
petitioners simply followed the familiar path of having their petitions dealt with in York. John Strachan wrote in his guide book,
published in 1820 that "many prefer going to York, the seat of government, and applying to the lieutenant-governor in council, either
in the hope of getting a larger grant of land, from their greater means
to improve it, or from curiosity, or because they think it better to go
to the fountain-head." David Moorman believes that the new boards
were created as much to solve administrative problems as to make
life easier for prospective settlers. It was hoped that the boards could
do what the provincial government found it hard to do at a distance – detect fraudulent (or non-British) applications, supervise the
surveyors, police the performance of settlement duties, and acquire
an adequate knowledge of variations in local land quality.[22]

In any case though the second version of the land boards took
some of the routine granting work off the hands of the Executive
Council and provided a shortcut to land-owning for some applicants, their existence, like that of the first boards, was brief. In 1825
they too were abolished, this time because a fundamental shift in
land-granting policy had taken place. After 1826 Crown land was no
longer to be disposed of by grant, but by sale. As David Moorman
observes, land was no longer conferred for loyalty, but for cash.[23]

The reasons for this change in policy were financial and strategic.
The imperial government wanted to shift more of its costs to the
colonies themselves, the provincial government wanted to increase
its revenues and to keep the disposal of public lands firmly in the
hands of the executive. None of these considerations were of interest
to immigrants and ordinary Upper Canadians who wanted land, or
more land. For them land had never been free and now it was more
expensive than ever. Under the new rules an "upset price," or minimum price per acre at which land was sold at auction was

established which varied, depending on local conditions, from four to ten shillings per acre. Compared with the former fee structure, under which £16-17-6 was paid on a 200 acre lot, the same lot now cost at least £40 and as much as £100 or more. In 1833 the upset price was jacked up even farther, to a range of ten shillings to one pound per acre, or up to £200 for a 200 acre lot.[24]

The system seemed at least to offer direct access to land without having to petition for it or go through a bureaucratic maze. Sadly the new arrangements turned out to be not only more costly but also not much more efficient than the old. An applicant for land had to apply to the surveyor general and pay an initial irksome fee of 2s 2d. Sales were advertised but held in each district only once a year so that a purchaser wanting a particular lot had to wait for it to become available and could still lose it to a higher bidder. Payment could be made in instalments without interest but only if the whole amount was paid off in one year, otherwise interest was charged on payments, initially spread over five years, but reduced to a maximum of two years in 1833. These were hard conditions for most new settlers, especially recently arrived immigrants, to meet. Title to the land could only be applied for after all payments were made and settlement duties completed. There was originally no provision for resident Crown land agents to provide information to "bewildered immigrants." Eventually four were hired for the entire province, on a part-time basis.[25]

Government land sales also were not a success. Relatively few land seekers bought land at the auctions and as a result they produced little revenue. In fact, as Lillian Gates concluded, the system was "a sham," because the government continued to also grant large amounts of land. The new regulations issued by the Executive Council at first left a very large loophole for ordinary applicants. "Grants without purchase" of 200 acres were still to be had by petitioners who declared their intention to "reside upon and improve the same" and agreed to pay a quit rent of 5 per cent of the value of the land for a period of seven years, which on land valued at ten shillings an acre meant paying £5 a year for seven years, after which the land was free. Bought at auction the same land would have cost at least £100 instead of the £35 in quit rent. This overly generous provision was cancelled by the imperial government in 1831. Free grants to discharged soldiers and sailors were also still made until 1834 when they too were abolished, but free grants to militiamen and the children of Loyalists continued to the end of the Upper Canadian period. After the land auctions were instituted, ten times as much public land was still disposed of by grant as by sale. An 1840 committee of investigation found that at the end of the 1830s the Executive Council was, as ever, receiving a great many land petitions, at an average rate of 1,500 per year.[26]

However land was acquired and whether the recipient of a grant of land from the Crown got title to it promptly, or some time later, or quite possibly not at all, the grantee's relationship with government did not end with the occupation of an assigned location. The possession of land implied the payment of taxes on an annual basis to a township tax collector, of an amount determined by a tax assessor, and was, as of course it still is, a continuing financial obligation to the state. The payment of taxes again involved some travel, if only a relatively short trip, though possibly overnight, at a time and place designated by the collector for receiving the required sums from the land-holding residents of the township. The burden of taxation was generally dismissed by contemporary writers as being so light as to be almost negligible. Contemporary writers claimed that there was practically no taxation. Taxes on land were "so trifling they scarcely deserve notice." It was true that the tax regime was far from onerous. Even on arable land, that is land cleared and fit for the plough, the maximum rate was only a penny in the pound, and since for most people land-clearing was a slow and tedious business of only two or three acres a year, the beginning settler especially had no great sum to pay. If after ten years occupation a settler had twenty-four acres in crop, assessed at £1 per acre, the taxes would have been only two shillings, less than the daily wage of an unskilled worker. For the struggling cash poor settler of course even two shillings could be hard to find, but it is probably significant that among the many grievances eventually raised by political reformers in Upper Canada, the issue of taxation was seldom if ever mentioned. What is significant is that hundreds of settlers did not pay their taxes at all. The appendices of the Journals of the House of Assembly in the 1820s and 1830s contain entries for the land of many hundreds of (unnamed) people which was sold by the district sheriffs "to satisfy the assessment in arrears eight years." In the year 1831 for example these printed listings occupy forty-three foolscap-sized pages. Why was so much land simply abandoned by its owners when they could have kept it for a modest annual payment? David Wood's opinion is that sheriff's sales represent a widespread failure of new settlers to make a success of farming – in other words they gave up, in the face of backbreaking work and meagre returns, and no doubt in many cases that was true. But it is also likely that sheriff's sales in part reflected the original unwise policy of granting too much land to too many people. Even the ordinary grant of 200 acres was more land than most people were likely to clear in a lifetime, but land was acquired, often in large quantities, by privileged grantees, speculators, and loyalists and their children, often scattered in townships remote from their home location. Many people probably never set eyes on such land, and it would be not surprising that they lost interest in it and had little incentive to pay taxes on it. In any case it is also not surprising to find that much of the land sold by the sheriffs at auction was bought by people of means and of prominence, including politicians and senior public servants. In 1831, Zaccheus Burnham, wealthy Cobourg businessman and Conservative politician, who had received a grant of 1,500 acres and was awarded 4,970 acres as a survey contractor, bought more land at sheriff's sales in eight townships in the Newcastle District. In the Home District the Reformer Robert Baldwin bought only five properties, but one of these was 200 acres of which he was in fact the registered owner. It is possible that this was a lot he had once acquired and forgotten about until it was listed for sale.[27]

PART II

The foregoing account of the manner in which land and land title was acquired from the government has presented a greatly generalized version of reality. It does not begin to detail the many changes in the regulations which land seekers were bedevilled by, such as when residency requirements and settlement duties were actually enforced and to what extent, who periodically got land by paying full fees, or half fees, or no fees, or the conditions under which free grants of fifty acres were given to "pauper" immigrants. It does not attempt to describe the differing experiences of people in situations only partly in the control of the provincial government, such as those under Colonel Thomas Talbot's superintendence, or in various imperial or privately sponsored settlement schemes. All of these matters, and much more, can be found explored at length in other sources.[28] What this introductory discussion has attempted to do is to show what most ordinary applicants for land went through, most of the time. The focus on the disposal of public land needs now to be narrowed somewhat, not to descend into more bureaucratic detail, but to put a more human face on the relationship between people and government when it came to something as vital as the possession of land. But first, some methodological preliminaries.

Most of the original petitions for land in Upper Canada are at Library and Archives Canada, designated Record Group 1, L3, vols. 1–632. Needless to say there are a lot of them, occupying some 66.7 metres of shelf space. Fortunately the petitions are thoroughly indexed and reasonably accessible. They have both an alphabetical and a chronological organization. They were put into bundles alphabetically by surname and filed chronologically, labelled, for example: A bundle 1, A bundle 2, A bundle 3, etc. The petitions are not in fact in actual alphabetical order within the bundles nor are they in strict chronological order, for the dates on the bundles often overlap, but for present purposes the point is that the petitions of everyone whose name began with a particular letter are all together in one place. It will be apparent that for some letters, such as M or S, there are a great many bundles, containing thousands of petitions, while for others, such as Q or Z, there are relatively few. Which brings us to letter N. There were not all that many petitioners whose names began with N, but for the purposes of some closer collective and individual study, they constitute a handy and manageable number, 503 personal petitions in twenty-four bundles. For purposes of analysis this particular run of petitions has some apparent imperfections. As a sample of the total number of land petitions it is a bit on the small side and might not meet the modern poll taker's standard of a margin of error of plus or minus 3.1 per cent, nineteen times out of twenty, especially since the petitions do not represent a particular moment in time but are spread over more than fifty years (1788–1840). Also the N petitions may not fairly reflect the various national groups among the petitioners: Some of the Scots, for example, so many of whom had names beginning with "Mc" and "Mac," are obviously not going to turn up among them. Be all that as it may, the N petitions do appear to be reasonably representative of what is broadly known about petitioners, and Upper Canadians, as a whole. On the question of nationality, or more accurately, place of birth, the N petitions are not wildly out of line with what was (or may have been) the case in Upper Canada, there being no provincial census birthplace figures prior to 1842. Where the N petitions do not at all

Table 1.1
Origin of "N" petitioners and of population, compared

A. Percentages of "N" Petitioners by Origin								
Ireland	England	Scotland	"Great Britain"	Thirteen Colonies	US	BNA	Germany	Unknown
13.3	5.4	3.6	0.4	1.4	4.2	1.9	0.4	69.3

B. Percentages by Origin – 1842 Census							
Ireland	England	Scotland	US	Eng. Can.	Fr. Can.	Europe	Unknown
16.1	8.3	8.2	6.7	50.8	2.9	1.3	5.6

Sources: LAC, RG 1, L3, vols 381A–86; Canada, Census, vol. 4, 1871, 136.

match the 1842 profile is in the balance between immigrants and the native-born. Among the petitioners, immigrants greatly outnumbered the native-born, rather than the other way around, but that is hardly surprising since the immigrants were the ones who started out with no land at all and were much more likely to petition for it. It is also not surprising to find far fewer women (17.3 per cent) among the petitioners than can ever have been in the general population, but again the N bundles are probably not a bad reflection of reality. A rapid check of a much greater number of petitions (2,301 names) produces gender proportions remarkably similar to those for the N bundles (male, 81.9 per cent; female, 18.1 per cent).[29]

Assuming then that the N petitions may have some validity as a statistical sample of all the land petitions, what can be learned from them? Well a number of things. The figures for place of birth, such as they are, compared to the 1842 census figures, have been summarized in table 1.1. They must be treated with some caution because in only 154 cases out of the total of 503 personal petitions (30.6 per cent) has it been possible to assign a definite place of origin. As well, as can be seen, the number of birthplace identifications varies a lot during the whole period, ranging from seven petitioners out of fifty-nine in 1801–10 (11.9 per cent) to fifty-six petitioners out of 102 in 1811–20 (54.9 per cent) (table 1.2). It is highly likely that in the years before the War of 1812 the number of petitioners coming from the United States was considerably higher than the numbers shown in table 1.1, for quite a few of the petitioners stated that they had been in the province for some time and had brought considerable amounts of goods or livestock with them, suggesting an American origin, but since they did not make a point of saying where they had actually come from they cannot be counted as post-Loyalist

Table 1.2
Origin of "N" petitioners by period

	Ireland	England	Scotland	"Great Britain"	Thirteen Colonies	US	BNA	Germany
Pre-1801	2	2	1	2	6	9	0	0
1801–10	0	0	0	0	1	6	0	0
1811–20	24	11	8	0	0	5	7	1
1821–30	20	4	3	0	0	1	2	0
1831–40	21	10	6	0	0	0	1	1
Totals	67	27	18	2	7	21	10	2

Source: LAC, RG 1, L3, vols 381A–86.
Note: These figures represent only the 154 cases where a definite place of birth is known, or 30.6% of the total number of petitioners. These numbers, broken down by period, are:

Pre-1801: 22 petitioners out of 101 (21.8%); 1801–10: 7 petitioners out of 59 (11.9%); 1811–20: 56 petitioners out of 102 (54.9%); 1821–30: 30 petitioners out of 89 (33.7%); 1831–40: 39 petitioners out of 152 (25.6%).

Americans. In 1812 the government began to refuse to accept land petitions which did not include the age and place of birth of the applicant.[30]

Among immigrants from the United Kingdom the figures coincide roughly with the census figures at the end of the period, though the preponderance of the Irish is even more marked among the N petitioners. The Irish numbers also demonstrate the validity of the now well-established fact that the Irish came early and often to Upper Canada long before the famine migration of 1847.

The overall results of an analysis of the N petitions are summarized in table 1.3. Since the picture which emerges generally bears out the impression that most land petitions were routinely dealt with and were usually successful, it is really the exceptions to the norm which most merit looking into and explaining. To begin with, not all land petitioners asked for land, or more land. Petitions for grants of land predominated (about 75 per cent of the total) but applicants could have a variety of other reasons for petitioning. The largest number of petitions in the "other" category (13 per cent) was for patents to land already granted, though it is worth noting that they by no means match the number of petitions for land itself and that there are no such petitions in the N bundles before 1800, reflecting the period when few patents were issued and the longstanding and widespread practice of treating location tickets as if they were patents.

Table 1.3
Land petitioners in the "N" bundles – general summary

	Number	Percent
Success	392	77.9
Failure	77	15.3
Decision Unknown	34	6.8
Petitions for Land	376	74.8
Petitions for Patent	66	13.1
Other	61	12.1
Male Petitioners	416	82.7
Female Petitioners	87	17.3
Loyalists	33	6.6
Sons of Loyalists	48	9.5
Daughters of Loyalists	72	14.3
Illiterate	74	14.7
Illiterate Males (Total 416)	46	11
Illiterate Females (Total 87)	28	32.2
Former Military	77	15.3
Non-Loyalist Women	15	3
Well-to-do	15	3
Total Petitioners	503	100

Source: LAC, RG 1, L3, vols 381A–86

Some 4 per cent of the petitioners asked the Executive Council to allow them to buy Crown land. Such petitions begin only in 1835 and can be said to suggest two things: the long cherished hope that land could be "free," and the frustrations of getting land under the auction system. Smaller numbers of petitioners had still other kinds of (often unsuccessful) land-related requests, some of which were: to be put on the Loyalist List, which implied free grants of land, to exchange one lot for another, to lease reserved land, to have fees or settlement duties waived, to be granted a mill site or a wharf site, to exchange land for cash, to be granted a specific lot, to be allowed to sell a location ticket, or to have a survey done.

So most petitions were successful but in fact a considerable minority were not. David Moorman, whose research has already been frequently cited in this chapter, gives the impression that very few petitions were ever refused but there are two main reasons why that conclusion must be modified a bit.[31] Moorman looked mostly at early petitions and at petitions for land itself. The greatest number of unsuccessful petitions turn up late in the Upper Canadian period. The overall failure rate for the whole period was 15.3 per cent. In the 1830s it was 26.1 per cent. Most unsuccessful petitions were for patents, not land, and the most common cause of rejection in these cases was that the requirement for "actual settlement," involving some land clearing and three years residence on the land, had not been met. Of course there were a great many other reasons why a petition might be refused: failure to provide sufficient, or any, proof of claims made in the petition, not qualifying for the loyalist list, applying for a lot already granted or reserved, claiming a lot also claimed by someone else, not being considered entitled to extra land, not being of age, applying too late, being a squatter, not being resident in Upper Canada, having to establish a claim under the Heir and Devisee Commission, not being allowed to exchange a lot after the patent had issued, not being permitted to have fees waived or remitted, and a variety of other causes. Sometimes petitions were refused for no stated reason at all.

The cases in which patents were refused because settlement duties had not been performed overlap quite a lot with another sizeable minority among petitioners, former military personnel, who made up 15 per cent of the petitioners. As a rule old soldiers did not make good settlers, even though in the late 1820s and 1830s the imperial government strongly encouraged discharged soldiers to take up land in Upper Canada, including about a thousand disabled out-pensioners of Chelsea Hospital who were induced to give up their *per diem* pensions for a lump sum commutation payment in exchange for emigration to the colony (see below, chapter 6). In the 1830s petitions began to trickle, and then to pour, into the Executive Council office from ex-soldiers who wanted title to their land, in most cases so they could sell it, but from "a broken constitution" or "not being fit to labour" were unable to clear land for settlement or to put in the required period of residence on the still unproductive land. The Executive Council steadily refused to grant patents to these applicants because the regulations were clear. Patents could only be issued if the petitioner actually settled for at least three years on the lot. The land, the council insisted, was given to soldiers so that they could make a living on it "and not as a mere gratuity." So the failure rate among petitioners for patents continued to climb in the 1830s and would have gone higher except that in this case the Executive Council actually underwent a change of heart. So many discharged soldiers who claimed that it was physically impossible for them to tackle the wilderness had "been extremely importunate in urging their claims for deeds" that the councillors confessed themselves troubled. On the one hand, if deeds were given to such applicants "no doubt the lands would be disposed of to speculators for small sums of money and would remain uncultivated to the great injury of the neighbouring settlers," yet council could not believe that disabled veterans were "of the description of persons to whom His Majesty's Government could have intended to give grants of land upon conditions of actual settlement." So they came up with a compromise. Discharged soldiers would be allowed their grants and would be allowed to sell them but the requirement for actual settlement would be binding on the purchaser. In the late 1830s the council began regularly approving applications for deeds from all former soldiers who were disabled or infirm and finally rubber-stamped such petitions from all veterans "settlement duties by discharged soldiers being dispensed with."[32]

Despite what has been written already here and elsewhere about the Executive Council's suspicion of people acting as agents for petitioners, it turns out that in a rather surprising minority of cases (some 14 per cent) the use of agents in fact was permitted. Part of the explanation is that most, though by no means all, of the petitions handled by agents were of a cut-and-dried nature where all the necessary documentation was present and in order, so that the *bona fides* of the applicant were clearly established and the rest was just a matter of keeping an eye on the file as it worked its way through the bureaucracy. In looking at cases where agents were used one thing becomes apparent at once. Women were more likely to be represented by someone else than men. In patriarchal Upper Canada many women, whether they were literate or not, evidently were not thought to be able to cope on their own with something as complex as the land system. Of the eighty-seven women petitioners in the N bundles, thirty-one (35.6 per cent) employed agents as opposed to only thirty-eight of the 416 men (9.1 per cent).

Among women petitioners one group stood out – the daughters of United Empire Loyalists, who made up twenty-nine of the thirty-one women using agents. (Only twelve of the thirty-eight men with agents were the sons of Loyalists.) It is fair to say that in the case of daughters, and sons, of Loyalists, the government not only allowed but encouraged the use of agents. As early as 1805 standard land grant applications for the use of the children of Loyalists appeared in printed form which included the phrase "and permit (name of agent) to be (his or her) agent to locate the same and to take out the deed when completed." These were precisely the kind of routine cases which could easily be handled by an agent. If the applicant had a witnessed certificate stating that he or she really was the person requesting the grant and if the father was on the Loyalist List the rest was a mere matter of bookkeeping. Even when petitions from the children of Loyalists were not submitted on printed forms, the identical wording, including the line just quoted, were almost always used, suggesting that it was widely understood that the use of agents was acceptable.

There were actually several kinds of agents. There were family members, usually husbands or fathers, acting for their wives or children, who drew up, signed, and presumably took petitions to the Executive Council. There were public figures, mostly MHAs, who had to make periodic trips to York/Toronto and who undertook to act as agents on behalf of their constituents as part of their jobs as local representatives. In the N bundles a number of these people, Solomon Jones, Isaac Swayze, John Crysler, David McGregor Rogers, James McNabb, and Jonas Jones, turn up quite regularly. There were also professional agents based in York/Toronto itself, who must have worked on some kind of fee basis. No evidence has come to light, at least in the N bundles, of what sort of rates were charged and elsewhere in the land petitions only one instance of payment for an agent's work has been found. In 1809 Thomas Fraser, MHA for Glengarry, brought back a deed for Mary Guernsey, daughter of Joel Adams UE but would not give it to her unless she paid him $6.00 (about £1-1-0). Mrs. Guernsey wrote to the Executive Council to complain about the charge, which could suggest that this was a normal agent's fee, though she thought that as an MHA he should have done it free as part of his duties.[33]

In any case most of the professional York/Toronto agents do not seem to have expected to make a living from the land business alone, because they usually held other jobs and were only supplementing their incomes when working for petitioners. John Detlor Jr., the first of these agents to appear in the N bundles, from 1805 to 1818, had a regular day job as bookkeeper to the merchant Laurent Quetton de St George. Andrew Mercer, holder of the record for most appearances as an agent in the N bundles at twelve and found there as an agent between 1820 and 1833, worked in the Executive Council office from 1803 to 1820, was issuer of marriage licences from 1818 on, and was also a partner in a general store. George Ridout, who handled a couple of N bundle cases in 1815–16, was a lawyer. Thomas Hamilton, active 1810–11, was a store, tavern, and ship owner. The name of John Radenhurst pops up as an agent in 1829 and 1838. In a flagrant conflict of interest which would later get him fired he was also senior clerk in the Surveyor General's Office, where land locations were allocated, from 1829 to 1840.[34]

Only two people seem to have tried to make a living as full-time land agents. Joseph B. Spragge and James Henderson both listed themselves as land agents in the 1837 Toronto *Directory* and are not known to have had any other occupation at the time. They may have been in partnership since they both gave their location as Chewett's Buildings, which, at the southeast corner of King and York streets was an easy stroll to the government offices on Front Street. They appear as agents in the N bundles between 1835 and 1840, with Henderson being second only to Andrew Mercer in number of cases undertaken. In his *Report* of 1839 Lord Durham referred to "the necessity of employing and paying agents acquainted with the labyrinths of the Crown Lands and Surveyor General's departments," so perhaps by that time it was possible to make a living as a full-time land agent.[35]

Two other minority categories among land petitioners deserve very brief mention. Most applicants were plain and even poor people but a few, about 3 per cent, were of higher economic or social status who asked for, and usually got, larger grants. On the other hand almost 15 per cent of the petitioners were unable to sign their names, with women showing a higher illiteracy rate than men (11.1 per cent among the men, 32.3 per cent among women).

The largest identifiable minority among land petitioners in the N bundles, as shown in table 1.3, were women themselves, who made up 17.3 per cent of the total. Most of the explanation for such a high female participation rate is the presence as petitioners, already referred to, of the daughters of Loyalists. They were entitled to the standard 200 acre grant when they came of age or married, though they still had to petition for it. Judging from the N petition record it appears that these women were even more likely to petition for their grants than were the sons of Loyalists, who were more likely to inherit land. Like so many other grantees the daughters of Loyalists were eager for grants but slow to take out patents, forcing the government to periodically threaten to rescind their grants if patents were not applied for.

An intriguing minority of the female minority of petitioners were women who, not being the daughters of Loyalists, were theoretically not entitled to land. The intriguing part is that some of them actually were given land. Here a small opening presents itself for an expanded exploration, in and beyond the confines of the N bundles, of how the land system worked, or for many people did not work, and how for some Upper Canadians it could be worked to advantage.

The system was supposed to work by rules and regulations which were often amended but publicly promulgated. Rules made the Executive Council's task easier because they could be routinely applied. Yet, as in the case of the discharged soldiers, rules could sometimes be bent, changed, or even abolished altogether. So far as women were concerned the rule was "the waste lands of this province are not grantable to any female except the daughters of U. E. Loyalists." This did not stop such women from trying, and indeed petitions for land from women in their own right were often received but were also constantly rejected. As the council noted as early as 1797 while saying no to a woman named Margaret Hainer, "many similar applications have been refused." Nonetheless there were always means by which some women got round the rules, especially early in the Upper Canadian period.[36]

One way was to have connections to people in power. When John White, attorney general of Upper Canada, was killed in a duel in 1800 while deeply in debt, orders came from the imperial government for "such grant in trust for the support of Mr White's widow and children as shall be judged most advisable to be laid out in the most favourable location." Mrs White was not the daughter of a Loyalist and broke another rule, not being a resident of Upper Canada, having left her unhappy marriage to return to England in 1799. Being a widow helped to arouse sympathy in government circles, as shall be seen, but it was not a necessary, and by no means a certain, qualification for a land grant. Like John White, Henry Allcock came from England to be a judge in Upper Canada in 1795. He, his wife Hannah, and his daughter Catharine all petitioned for

land after they arrived in York. All three were granted 1,200 acres in
their own right. Other examples of early grants of land to women
included 400 acres in 1797 to Mary Addison, who was not a
Loyalist's daughter and not even a married woman, which should
have been a double disqualification, but the sister of Rev Robert
Addison, first Anglican rector of Niagara. Grants were also made of
1,200 acres in 1795 and 1798 to each of the three daughters of the
late Captain Andrews, senior officer of the Provincial Marine; of 400
acres in 1798 to Mary Haslip of Kingston, daughter of a hero who
had rescued soldiers of Sir Thomas Ritchie's Horse at Fontenoy "in
the face of the enemy" and a double widow – of a sergeant in Frazer's
Highlanders and of a second lieutenant in the Marine Department.
A town lot in Kingston was given in 1801 to Mary Atkinson, who
wanted to set up "a shoe manufactory" as an adjunct to her husband's tannery.[37]

As time passed it became more difficult for women, no matter how
well connected, who did not conform to the rules to get land. Only
three months after Mary Addison received her grant of land, Mary
and Susannah Hatt, daughters of Richard Hatt, a well-to-do English
immigrant, were told "it is not usual to give land to unmarried
women."[38] Nonetheless, it remained possible for some women to be
successful petitioners. The cases of Jane England, Elizabeth Clench,
and Theresa Nichol demonstrate how women who were persistent,
had some influence, and could arouse sympathy, continued to get
quite generous amounts of land.

Jane England, wife of William England, "trader of Belleville," was
the only child of the late John McIntosh, who had commanded a
flank company of the Hastings Militia from 1812 until his death in
1815. She petitioned the council in 1821 because she had heard,
probably from Andrew Mercer who acted as her agent, that the children of other officers had been given land and that she was entitled
to the 800 acres her father would have been granted had he lived.
The council duly recommended that 800 acres be granted to her,
though she, like so many other grantees, did not soon locate or patent the land. In 1829 she again petitioned the Executive Council with
another angle to pursue. Her father had "been in possession" of a
water lot in Belleville where he had built a distillery which since his
death had been rented out. Jane England now claimed this desirable
commercial space as heiress of John McIntosh and asked for a patent
for it. On investigation it turned out that the lot was in fact reserved

by orders-in-council of 1819 and 1820 as the best potential place in Belleville for ships to dock and her petition was refused. Then "evil disposed persons, enemies to the family," advised the lessee of the distillery to stop paying the rent since the land was government property. Jane England bombarded the council for two years with documents and certificates showing that there were plenty of other water lots in Belleville equally suitable for the accommodation of ships. In 1831 the council gave way and awarded her the patent. Finally, twelve years later, she also got round to reviving her claim to the original 800 acre grant. Again the Executive Council complied.[39]

Elizabeth Clench, who was the wife of Ralfe Clench, lieutenant in Butler's Rangers, assistant deputy quartermaster general between 1812 and 1815, and holder of many offices in the Niagara District, already had land of her own before her husband's death in 1828. She was the granddaughter of Sir William Johnson and Molly Brant and in 1802 had obtained a lease of 900 acres from Joseph Brant "being a descendant of the said nation and wishing to have a part of such land."[40]

When Ralfe Clench died he was deeply in debt. His widow claimed that her public-spirited husband could have made a great deal of money in speculation in Loyalist lands "but he loved his brother soldiers too well to benefit from their hard earned boon." He had however acquired some quantity of land, including the 800 acres awarded for his war services and 600 acres in distant Chatham Township, which in 1831 his widow wished to sell to meet her obligations. The problem was that the land was unpatented and the settlement duties undone. The rules of course said that actual settlement must "be insisted upon" before a patent could issue. But for a woman with such an admirable husband and pedigree, left without means and a large family, "(several of them females)," the executive was prepared to make an exception. Settlement duties were waived and the patent issued.[41]

Theresa Nichol's case can usefully be considered in parallel with that of Agnes Nicholson, who was the daughter of a Loyalist but otherwise without distinction or connections. She was given a 200 acre lot in Huntingdon Township. The settlement duties were duly done on the lot but further clearing revealed that the lot was a dud, "a grate [sic] proportion of it covered with water and what is not covered with water a complete bed of rocks," so she applied to the council to exchange her useless lot for another.[42] Unfortunately she had made a fatal mistake. She had actually taken out the patent on the lot. As a result she ran up against another of the rules – "no change of location allowed after patent." She was stuck with the water and the rocks.[43]

Theresa Nichol's husband, Robert Nichol, played a prominent part in the affairs of Upper Canada before his accidental death in 1824, as a miller and merchant, a politician, and especially as quartermaster-general of militia during the War of 1812. When he, like Ralfe Clench, died in great debt, he left his widow "in a helpless state" with four young children, but also like Clench he left land, quite a lot of it in his case, including 3,600 patented acres in Alnwick Township which he had bought. Sadly this land, like Agnes Nicholson's, was of poor quality and Theresa Nichol applied to the council in 1831 to exchange it, even specifying that she wanted 1,800 acres in Dereham Township and 1,800 acres in Brooke and Iniskillin townships, in a much more fertile and saleable area. The council conveniently ignored its own rule and approved the exchange. In 1835 they added a further grant to Theresa Nichol of 1,000 acres, despite their other rule that forbade grants to any women except the daughters of Loyalists, which Theresa Nichol was not.

Petitions from ordinary non-Loyalist women were on the whole routinely rejected even though they too were very often widows, or orphans, with "no resources." Even the daughter of a Loyalist could sometimes be refused land, as was Mary Hartwell in 1815 because her husband was "reported as being disloyal during the late war by Captain Young, Fifth Lincoln Militia." Nonetheless even for women without political or social leverage there were sometimes ways of getting around the rules. At least two women, Catharine Niding and Catharine Crevey, both the widows of Chelsea Pensioners, got land grants by having the grants issued to dead men – their late husbands. A more common procedure in cases where a dead husband had been entitled to land was to have the grant issued to the widow in trust for her underage male children. A successful example of this approach was the case of Mary Noble, whose oldest child was her nine-year-old son John. Widow Catharine Nugent, whose family consisted only of a thirteen-month-old-daughter, was actually given land in her own name. Elizabeth Callaghan, still another widow of a Chelsea Pensioner, left with three children and "no resources," got land in 1832 through the direct intervention of the lieutenant governor, Sir John Colborne. Her application for a land grant was rejected on

22 May as being contrary to the rules, since her husband had made no attempt to draw land. On 24 May the council's decision was "revised with the sanction of His Excellency." Land was now to be granted to her "for the benefit of her surviving children."[44]

A number of other matters illustrated both in the N bundles and in other land documents merit some discussion. Most petitioners seem not have questioned unfavourable decisions handed down to them from on high, but refusing to take no for an answer, as in Jane England's repeated bothering of the council over Belleville water lots or the collective complaining of the old soldiers, could sometimes get results and, as will be seen in later chapters, not only where land matters were concerned but in a variety of other circumstances as well. Some other examples of petitioner persistence underline this point, for what mattered was that the government did sometimes reverse itself. There is no indication that Agnes Nicholson, who was told that she could not exchange her swamps and rocks for another lot, ever protested a decision that was arguably arbitrary and unfair. On the other hand, Elizabeth Wallace profited by refusing to accept an initial government ruling. Her late husband Robert had been located on a lot in Dalhousie Township in the Bathurst District, then as now largely covered with Precambrian rock. The land had been willed to Elizabeth Wallace in trust for her twelve-year-old daughter but the lot, like Agnes Nicholson's, was unfit for farming, and she applied to the Executive Council in 1840 to be allowed to exchange it. The council's answer was no, on the grounds that there was no evidence that her husband had ever tried to live on the land. Mrs Wallace took immediate counter-action. She produced a certificate from a cooperative magistrate of "settlement and residence" by her husband. Within a month the decision was reversed and a new location ordered.[45]

The story of the Kendrick family's pursuit of land and status illustrates a different approach – if at first you don't succeed, try again, if necessary quite a bit later. Widow Dorcas Kendrick and her sons John, Joseph, Duke William, and Hiram arrived in York in 1794 from New Brunswick. They were all granted the standard 200 acre lots, in the case of the sons in desirable locations on Yonge Street, and Dorcas, John, and Duke William were also given town lots in York. This was not enough for the Kendricks. In 1796 Joseph, Duke William, and Hiram petitioned for an extra 400 acres each on the grounds that they had "been always attached to government." Their petitions were refused as "not judged expedient at present." The following year John Kendrick joined his brothers in petitioning for an additional 1,200 acres each on the basis of their late father's services as a pilot on the St John River during the Revolution and his thirty years service in the British Army, plus their own "merits and pretensions." This petition was deferred "to await His Excellency's return," but also produced no result. John, Duke William, and Joseph were back the next year again asking for more land and this time also asking to be put on the Loyalist list. They were given another 200 acres each "but they have no pretensions to be put on the U. E. List."

The Kendrick brothers' persistence initially brought them only partial success, certainly much less than they thought was their due. There the matter rested until 1829, when the widow of Duke William, Susanna (or Susannah) Kendrick, petitioned to have her late husband put on the Loyalist List. The Executive Council of that time ignored the fact that a previous council had decided that the Kendricks had had "no pretensions" and merely asked for proof of Duke William's service in the Revolution. Satisfactory evidence was evidently provided, for what was denied in 1798 was given in 1829. In that year Susannah received 200 acres in her own right and between 1836 and 1851 her six children all received grants as the sons and daughters of Duke William Kendrick, UE. Persistence could have its rewards, but of course no amount of persistence necessarily guaranteed success.[46]

It has been noted that land regulations were frequently amended but that the government made an effort to keep potential grantees informed. How successful was the information system? What did newcomers appear to know about the land-granting process and where did they actually get their knowledge of it? In a general way it cannot be said that prospective immigrants, especially from the United Kingdom, lacked for sources of information on Upper Canada and the settlement process. Land clearing was only getting nicely underway when the first British author arrived to look on, notebook in hand. In his collection, *Early Travellers in the Canadas*, Gerald Craig compiled a list of no fewer than seventy-five works by British writers concerned in whole or in part with conditions in Upper Canada and published in the United Kingdom between 1793 and 1841. When the Canada Company was formed in 1825 to sell land in western Upper Canada to migrating settlers, its management necessarily became involved in publicity on a wide scale extolling the advantages of settling in Upper Canada. According to one writer of the day "when the Company began selling their own land in the Huron Tract, they filled not only America, but nearly the whole world with papers concerning it." Information came not only from sales pamphlets and from people simply passing through the province, but also from actual settlers with experience. The Reverend Thomas Sockett, chairman of the Petworth Emigration Committee, which sponsored the emigration to Upper Canada of some 1,800 working class settlers between 1832 and 1837, published a unique series of five collections of letters written by these people to friends and families at home.[47]

Overall, these publications, with some few exceptions, painted quite a rosy picture of life in Upper Canada and the experience of establishing a new home in the colony as an independent land owner. Some of them were not just descriptive accounts but purported to be practical guides to help settlers prepare for and cope with emigration and settlement. Such matters as how much capital was needed to achieve subsistence, what to bring, what crops and livestock to raise, local prices and wages, availability of markets and schools, and many more such topics were covered in greater or lesser detail. What nobody prepared newcomers for was the bureaucracy.

Perhaps the prize for understatement regarding the acquisition of Crown land should go to John Howison, whose 1821 book was subtitled "practical details for the information of emigrants of every class." His entry on "the steps that must be taken" to get a land grant merely advised the land seeker to go to "the Land Office" in York, though there was at the time no separate office by that name. As for the "steps" to be taken "it is unnecessary to detail these further than by stating that the chief object of them is to make the applicant prove himself a British subject."[48]

The applicant for land relying on the "practical" advice of people like Howison was in for a rude shock, not to say much frustration and delay, and Howison dealt with the subject in more depth than most. One of the few extensive descriptions of the land bureaucracy was written by an insider, executive councillor John Strachan, whose 1820 book was disguised as a travel account supposedly written by his brother James. Strachan really did include practical details, such as a sample land petition, a table of fees on land, the terms of settlement duties, and an actual three page step-by-step description of the granting process from first petition to the issuing of the patent. Strachan however was not in the business of discouraging emigrants and greatly minimized the complexities of the system. According to Strachan "many" settlers had gone through all the paper work, done their settlement duties ("which are very soon done by active men") and applied for their patents in as little as two months. "Many" disillusioned emigrants could testify that for them this was a gross exaggeration.[49]

When Sir Peregrine Maitland arrived in Upper Canada as lieutenant governor in 1818 the system of the disposal of public lands which he encountered was as much a mystery to him as it was to the average settler. He asked Thomas Ridout, the surveyor general, to prepare a report on "the manner in which the Lands of the Crown in this Province have been granted to individuals." Ridout's 3,700 word attempt to explain a system that was then and now next to inexplicable must have left Sir Peregrine more bemused than ever. If the lieutenant governor needed an explanation of how his own administration worked, what can be said of the ordinary settler?[50]

Yet newcomers do seem to have known something about and generally understood the land regulations and procedures. Whether such knowledge resulted from the availability of government information or from more informal sources cannot be clearly established, though the government did make an effort to communicate. Copies of the regulations and their amendments were circulated in the province via local notables. Printed petition forms were available from the 1790s. The office of the chief emigrant agent opened at Quebec in 1828 to provide guidance to people just off the boats and en route to Upper Canada, and there was a separate chief emigrant office for Upper Canada in York/Toronto from 1832, where there were already several people who had set themselves up as private land agents.[51]

From the beginning, most land applicants appear to have had an idea of what was due to them and how to get it. In the petitions cases of ignorance of the rules such as that of John North, an Irish Quaker, are relatively rare. North arrived in York in 1819 only to discover that a recent order-in-council had been passed "refusing gratuities of grants of land to persons of his denomination," but even he did not suffer from his mistake on the grounds that he had left Ireland before he could have heard of the change in regulations and was given 100 acres.[52] On the other hand it was known that "persons in poor circumstances" who were "unable to apply for land paying fees" were entitled to a grant of fifty acres and that even after the institution of the sales system land "without purchase" could still be had "under the terms of the order-in-council of November 21, 1825." Word spread quickly among qualified old soldiers already on the land that a small gratuity was payable to them under Article 22 of the Regulations of November 24 1829, and in the late 1830s that patents could be had without doing settlement duties. Petitioners largely shunned the restricted mandate of the 1819–25 land boards and the costly land auctions that followed and continued to think their chances better if they directed their appeals to the executive councillors, who were only too pleased to retain a central role in the disposal of public land.

In a general way the most widespread and enduring piece of folk wisdom that new arrivals clung to, or at least wanted to believe in, was that good land in Upper Canada was plentiful and easy to obtain. Of course for ordinary people land was never free and became less so as the imperial and colonial governments invented new means to restrict the amount of land which could be obtained or to try to force people to pay for it. The myth of free land was an extremely hardy one however, even among applicants, particularly women, who had little or no chance of success, partly because loopholes did exist and exceptions were sometimes made. So the petitions continued to roll in, well into the 1850s and 1860s.

Nobody seems to have ever taken on the monumental task of trying to work out just how many people submitted petitions for land in Upper Canada but a rough minimum estimate might be around 75,000 people. The great majority of petitioners as has been seen were successful in getting a grant of land, of 50, 100, 200 or more, acres. So the myth had validity, at least at the initial stage – of land acquisition. For the majority of applicants the system worked. People made the most of a process that was slow, cumbersome, aggravating, and expensive because the possession of land was crucial to their ultimate well-being. To some extent then, to say that the system discriminated against ordinary applicants in favour of the privileged such as Loyalists, military officers, and government officials, while true enough, is somewhat beside the point. People of the "humbler classes" who asked for land were routinely given it. What they made of it was up to them.[53] The daunting tasks of land clearing and pioneer farming which have so often been described still lay ahead, and not all who got land grants made a success of them, but at least they had been given a chance. They had put up with inconvenience and red tape because it was in their interest to do so. In a great many cases they had simply ignored the final step – getting title to their land – because it seemed to promise no immediate benefit. They ignored the extra bureaucratic step, happy to pass that chore to future generations.

2

Working for the Government

The government of Upper Canada could afford to be profligate in its distribution of land; before 1841 there was a seemingly inexhaustible supply of it, and the system supplemented the incomes of the senior public servants and yielded a modest return in taxes for the support of the district governments, from land sales and from the rental of Crown and clergy reserves. But the provincial government also had to spend money on a regular basis and a fair amount of it went into the pockets of Upper Canadians. Although satisfactory early figures do not appear to exist, the government's revenues (derived mainly in fact from a share of the customs revenue at Quebec) and its expenditures were not at first very large. At the time of the American occupation of York in 1813 the entire provincial treasury amounted to £3,109-1-8 3/4. However in the period 1824–40, yearly expenditures of the provincial government rose from about £29,000 to about £140,000, not including money spent on public works.[1]

Most of the areas in which the government of Upper Canada routinely spent money, such as the public service and the judiciary, the legislature, the common and grammar schools, pensions, immigration, the Indian Department, lighthouse-keeping, land surveys, and, late in the period, the penitentiary, always involved some payments to individuals either directly or indirectly. On a smaller scale the district governments, the numerous incorporated towns established in the 1830s, and especially Toronto, incorporated as a city in 1834, all had some employees and spent public money in a number of other ways.

Provincial expenditures on public works varied from year to year but in the decade of the 1830s amounted overall to about £1,000,000.

On the biggest public works projects, the Welland and St Lawrence canals, large labour forces were employed, paid by contractors mostly from funds provided by the government. Smaller numbers of Upper Canadians worked on a variety of other provincially funded construction projects, such as surveys, main roads and bridges, harbours and lighthouses, new parliament buildings and government offices, and the penitentiary. Some categories of normal public spending in Upper Canada, including money spent on the Church of England clergy, on immigration, on the Indian Department, and the Post Office, were actually largely paid for by the imperial government, as was the £822,000 cost of building the Rideau Canal, but the end result was the same. Money in the form of wages and payments for services flowed eventually into Upper Canadian hands. Douglas McCalla reached the somewhat contradictory conclusion that the expenditures of the government were not large enough "to make the provincial state a dominant participant in the provincial economy" but that the financial affairs of the state made it nonetheless "one of the more pervasive and substantial economic institutions in the province." Just how important government expenditures were as a source of income for Upper Canadians as a whole is evidently difficult to calculate. What can be said is that the provincial government was the only agency which regularly put some money into the economy, if in uneven amounts, in every district of Upper Canada: for public works, administration, education, pensions, and many other purposes.[2]

The Upper Canadian public service, consisting of those people directly employed by the government, whose names, positions, and incomes were reported in the annual "Blue Books" of statistics sent home to the imperial government, by no means constituted a bloated bureaucracy. In the year 1827, for instance, when the provincial population was just over 177,000, the total number of "officers of government" listed for the entire province was around 175. By 1840 the provincial population had more than doubled to 432,000 but the public service had increased only marginally in size, to about 250 positions. The chances of getting a government job therefore actually decreased over time and the public service workload presumably increased, obliging the employees to do more with less.[3]

The Upper Canadian bureaucracy was much criticized in its time by many people, ranging from radical provincial politicians to British colonial secretaries, for being secretive, incompetent, inefficient, expensive, arbitrary, over-staffed, and a glaring example of "family compact" exclusiveness and favouritism. Its procedures, especially in the vital matter of the distribution of Crown land to settlers, were held to be much too slow, costly, and inequitable, and involving far too much red tape. Lord Durham's famous *Report* pithily summed up such unfavourable opinions. "From the highest to the lowest offices of the executive government," he wrote, "no important department is so organized as to act vigorously and completely throughout the province and every duty which a government owes to its subjects is imperfectly discharged."[4]

How justified such complaints really were is a question which badly needs to be answered. Unfortunately no comprehensive study of Upper Canada's "Pioneer Public Service" exists, though one is sorely needed. For the time being F.H. Armstrong's indispensable compilation of Upper Canadian government offices and officials at the central and local levels provides a most useful factual guide to the bare bones of the system, and the basis for some brief comment on its general workings and responsibilities[5] (see also figure 2 and table 2.1).

At the pinnacle of the Upper Canadian central bureaucracy in the capital of York/Toronto was the office of the lieutenant governor. The lieutenant governor was the imperial government's representative in the colony and was responsible to the colonial secretary, with whom he was in regular and voluminous correspondence. The lieutenant governor's personal powers were significant, amounting even to matters of life and death, for it was on his authority that pardons were granted to, or withheld from, convicted criminals, including those sentenced to death. The lieutenant governor had wide patronage powers and most provincial appointments of any importance were made on his authorization. Officially all kinds of petitions, such as petitions for land, government jobs, pardons, pensions, compensation, or relief, were addressed to him. The lieutenant governor had a political role, indirectly, in the formation of policy, and directly, as an essential part of the provincial parliamentary system. Acts passed by the House of Assembly and the Legislative Council became law only when given royal assent by the lieutenant governor but he could also refuse assent or reserve provincial legislation for the consideration of the imperial government.

A crucial adjunct to the office of the lieutenant governor was the Executive Council office. The Executive Council normally had five members, though sometimes others were added who were referred

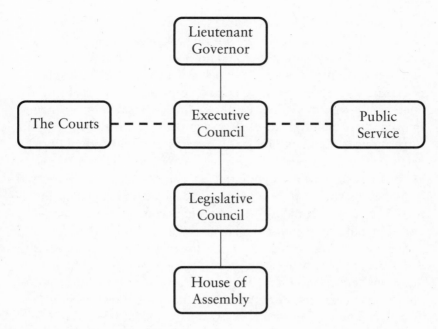

Figure 2 The Upper Canadian state

Table 2.1
Main government offices by function

I.	Administration
	1. Lieutenant Governor's Office
	2. Executive Council Office
	3. Provincial Secretary's Office
	4. Crown Law Office
II.	Revenue and Finance
	1. Receiver General's Office
	2. Inspector General's Office
III.	Defence
	1. Adjutant General's Office
IV.	Crown Land
	1. Surveyor General's Office
	2. Commissioner of Crown Lands
V.	Other
	1. Indian Department
	2. Emigration Office
	3. Provincial Board of Education
	4. King's (or Queen's) Printer

to as "honourary" (that is, unpaid) members of the council. The function of the councillors was officially to advise the lieutenant governor and theoretically they could do nothing without his presence and approval but in fact the council went through a huge amount of business on their own which had been referred to them by the lieutenant governor's office. Until 1826, when Crown land began to be sold, their major single task was to deal with the constant flow of petitions for land, but they also coped separately with matters of "state" delegated to them. This could cover such divergent subjects as requests for pardons, appointments, compensation for losses and licences; educational policy; and the management of the public buildings. The council could also function as a court of appeal and as a board of audit to examine the provincial accounts.

The law officers of the crown, the attorney and solicitor generals, also acted in an advisory way, giving legal opinions on all manner of questions referred to them. They acted as prosecutors on behalf of the Crown in cases at the assizes which they thought were important. They had a hand in drafting legislation and took a further unofficial political part. One or both of them almost always ran for election to the House of Assembly where they usually presented and supported the policies of the executive.

In a predominantly rural agricultural province, the office of the surveyor general had a vital function. The surveyor general supervised the work of the land surveyors who divided the province into townships, and into concessions and lots within the townships. The surveyor general also kept extensive records and maps of "locations," recording who had been granted land, where, and in what amount. After 1826 when the land sale system partly replaced the old method of disposing of crown land, some of the surveyor general's former workload was assumed by the office of the commissioner of Crown lands, who organized the land sales and kept records of them. The chief financial agencies of the government were the offices of the receiver and inspector generals, of which in the Upper Canadian period the receiver general was the more significant. The receiver general was in effect the provincial treasurer, who collected and held the province's growing revenues and paid its also increasing bills. The inspector general's responsibilities were mainly those of an auditor, checking to make sure that the expenditures of the various offices were correctly calculated and had been made on proper authority. His work however could be re-examined if necessary by the Executive

Council. The inspector general also oversaw the customs service and the issuing of licences.

The office of the provincial secretary, who should not be confused with the lieutenant governor's civil, or private, secretary, was primarily concerned with official record keeping. The provincial secretary was also *ex officio* the provincial registrar. This office prepared and recorded all documents requiring the Great Seal of the province, most numerously land grants or "patents," and supplied copies of all such instruments when needed. The office kept records of naturalized aliens and all acts of the provincial legislature were deposited there. After 1832 the provincial secretary's office was given the extra duty of compiling the annual Blue Books of statistics.

Except during rare periods of war or insurrection, when the office assumed a busy administrative role, most of the adjutant general's work was also largely routine record keeping and correspondence. The adjutant general received and kept annual returns of the state of the various militia units, and updated lists of officers and their commissions and copies of general orders. Between 1816 and 1826 the agent for paying militia pensions was part of the staff of the office.[6]

Only a few other notable government offices existed before 1841, not counting the office of the postmaster general, which was in Quebec City. The chief superintendent of Indian Affairs handled relations with the many groups of native peoples in Upper Canada on behalf of the imperial government, including the negotiation of treaties, and oversaw the work of superintendents and agents in the field. A chief emigrant agent was first appointed in 1832 to assist prospective settlers. Some central control was provided for a time in educational matters by a provincial board of education appointed in 1822, but this board was abolished in 1833. The King's (or Queen's) Printer also doubled as the editor of the official government publication, the *Upper Canada Gazette*. From time to time special commissions were appointed to deal with specific problems such as claims for losses arising out of the War of 1812 or the Rebellion. The longest running such body was the Heir and Devisee Commission (see chapter 1) set up in 1797 to sort out the badly tangled questions of claimed or disputed land title.

The people who held the dozen or so major government appointments just briefly described were a kind of equivalent to what would later be called deputy ministers, though there were at the time no actual political ministers for them to be deputies to. They reported, if they reported at all, only to the lieutenant governor. But the work of the various offices was obviously not done by the "heads of department" alone. There was a clerical and ancillary staff of modest size, among which some of the senior appointees held positions of considerable responsibility and influence. The lieutenant governor's private or civil secretary filled an unusually pivotal post, handling and screening the constant stream of letters, petitions, and other documents into the office from within and without the central bureaucracy, and from the Colonial Office, and redirecting the flow of paper as appropriate to other offices. Another sensitive cog in the bureaucracy was the clerk of the Executive Council, who organized the work and the records of that body. The land-granting process outlined in chapter 1 provides an illustration of the fact that most official documents of any consequence inevitably passed through the hands of these two senior officials, often several times. Customarily, each of the other offices had a chief clerk as well (sometimes called a first or senior clerk). Each office might also have up to three less exalted clerks, plus occasional temporary or "extra" clerks. These clerkships made up the bulk of the white-collar jobs that prospective applicants might hope to fill, as infrequent vacancies or slight expansions of staff occurred.

The Upper Canadian public service was not large, but it was fairly costly to run. About half of the province's routine outlay was spent on "the basic administrative, political and judicial apparatus."[7] Did this mean that public servants, compared to other wage earners, were well paid, possibly even overpaid? Making accurate comparisons among occupational groups is always a tricky business, especially because there is in this case a serious lack of evidence to make comparisons possible. We know, since the provincial government was obliged to tell the imperial government, how much Upper Canada's public servants were paid, but figures for other white-collar workers, such as clerks in stores or banks or other major businesses such as the Canada Company, do not appear to exist. Some usable statistics however are available on approximate income levels of unskilled and skilled workers in Upper Canada, and since the excessively high cost of employing such people was a common complaint at the time it is of some interest to compare their wage rates with those of the employees of the central bureaucracy (see table 2.2).[8]

It might seem reasonable to assume that a skilled tradesman ought to have been able to earn at least as much in a year as a clerk in a

Table 2.2
Estimated yearly gross income by occupation in the 1830s

Day Labourers	£40
Carpenters	£84
Blacksmiths	£90
Bricklayers	£90
Masons	£120

Source: Russell, "Wage Labour Rates," 70–6.
Note: Yearly figures are calculated from an average of daily rates. Since income was not only
a factor of the wage rate but also of the number of days of actual employment, the yearly
incomes are based on a generous estimate of ten months of work in the year.

government office. If so it must be concluded that public servants
were on the whole adequately paid, and, it may be added, for less
work. (Labourers were likely to work each day as long as there was
daylight. In one of the busiest government offices, the surveyor general's department, the hours were set in 1802 at ten to three.) The
lowest known yearly clerical salary, recorded in the earliest Blue
Book of 1821, was £112, for a second extra clerk in the surveyor
general's office. This was an amount greater than the likely annual
earnings of any of the unskilled or skilled workers except masons,
but since it was usual for such workers to receive the benefit, while
working away from home, of free board, estimated (in 1819) to cost
the employer 2s 6d a day, the real value of their wages was somewhat
greater. On the other hand there are a number of other factors which
gave public servants an edge in comparison with non-clerical workers. In 1821 a first extra clerk was paid £135 a year and an ordinary
clerk £150, both higher amounts than any tradesman was theoretically likely to earn. Public service salaries moreover were quoted in
sterling values, at a time when £100 sterling was worth an extra
£11-9-0 in colonial currency, so that even the second extra clerk
actually earned in Upper Canada somewhat more than £120. And of
course the lowest clerical salaries were only the tip of the monetary
iceberg. First clerks earned £182-10-0. The scale for the actual heads
of departments in 1821 went up to £365. (The judiciary will be
mostly excluded from discussion here but if it were included then the
top salary, that of the chief justice, was £1,100.) Also many of the
senior officials were allowed to charge fees for various services, a
matter which will be pursued at more length a bit later on. Finally,
while income levels of all the skilled workers have been shown to

Table 2.3
Salaries for selected offices, 1821 and 1840

	1821	*1840*
3rd Clerk, Lt. Governor's Office	£150	£157
2nd Clerk, Lt. Governor's Office	£150	£225
1st Clerk, Lt. Governor's Office	£182-10-01	£282-10-0
Provincial Secretary	£300 (plus fees)	£600 (plus fees)
Inspector General	£365	£565
Chief Justice	£1,100	£1,500

Source: LAC, RG 1, E13, vols 141, 155.

have declined to some degree in the period 1818 to 1840, the public service rates, despite the absence of "even a mild inflationary trend" experienced quite a healthy growth (see table 2.3).[9]

The Upper Canadian public service offered to its professional staff quite decent remuneration, a respectable position in society, and jobs which, while at the lowest level required only a legible copyist's hand and a capacity to endure boredom, were performed indoors and involved no heavy lifting. It is not surprising then that there was a steady and expanding stream of applicants wanting to join the staff at its headquarters in the provincial capital. But government appointments were by no means confined to the little group of pen pushers in York/Toronto. As well as a "headquarters" staff there was a "field" staff of government appointees scattered throughout the province, concentrated mainly, but not entirely, in the district towns, which were the centres of local government. The two main sets of officials in the field who did not fit the district pattern were the collectors of customs and the registrars of deeds. The collectors, for obvious reasons, were based in the officially designated ports of entry, where goods entered Upper Canada from the United States. Registrars were appointed for each county, a division of the province normally much smaller than the districts, though in a few cases the jurisdiction of some registrars included more than one county. They were charged with "the public registering of Deeds, Conveyances, Wills, and other Incumbrances, which shall be made, or may effect any Lands, Tenements or Hereditaments."[10]

The district was always the basic unit of local government in the Upper Canadian period. Initially there were four districts; by 1841 there were twenty. Each district had its core group of appointed office-holders, which have sometimes been described as "oligarchies"

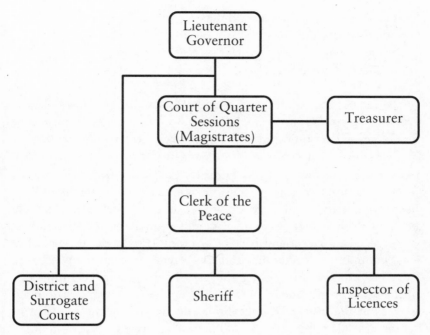

Figure 3   Main district offices

(see figure 3). Central to the system were the justices of the peace, or magistrates. These men had a bewildering number of local responsibilities. Acting as individuals, in pairs, or as a body in the court of quarter sessions, they were the initial level of the justice system, dealing mostly with small debts and petty crimes. They were also deeply involved in local government. It is scarcely an exaggeration to say that they were local government. To quote one partial description of their duties, the magistrates

> controlled the finances of the district, set the rate of local taxation to meet estimated yearly expenditure, appointed and supervised a district treasurer, and supervised the tax assessors and collectors. They arranged to have built and administered the district public buildings, the courthouse and jail, and were responsible for their upkeep and repair. They issued licences and certificates of good character to the many tradesmen, tavern keepers, petitioners and others who needed them. They regulated and set rates for public ferries. They made regulations for the public markets. They supervised the work of all the

township officers such as pathmasters, tax collectors and poundkeepers. All such matters and many more were dealt with at the meetings of quarter sessions, interspersed with the court's judicial activities.[11]

The magistrates were never included among the "officers of government" recorded in the annual Blue Books, perhaps because they worked only part-time and derived relatively little income from their many activities (though they were permitted, under an act of 1827, to charge fees as high as 3s 9d a time for providing various "informations," warrants, discharges, and recognizances). Or they may have been excluded from the reports sent to the Colonial Office simply because all their names would have taken up an enormous amount of space. The government tried to appoint as magistrates men of at least minimum respectability and competence from as many areas of each district as possible. When the last Upper Canadian commissions of the peace were issued in 1834–36 there were, on paper, 169 magistrates in the Home District alone (not including the long list of senior officials appointed as *ex officio* magistrates who could act in any district). In the sprawling district of London there were 121 magistrates, and even the tiny district of Prince Edward was well supplied with forty-two magistrates.[12]

The district treasurer, who received and kept records of the district's funds and made authorized payments from them, was chosen by the magistrates, but the other principal district officials received their appointments directly from the lieutenant governor. The sheriff acted on the orders of the various levels of the courts. He issued writs, made arrests, carried out sentences, and managed the gaol. Sheriffs were also responsible for the sale of land for arrears of taxes. The duties of the inspector of licences, ultimately part of the operations of the inspector general's office, were "to issue shop, tavern, still, steamboat and billiard licences" within the limits of the district.[13]

If the district administration could be said to have had a single centre point, it would have been in the office of the clerk of the peace. While the magistrates' duties were numerous, the clerk of the peace had to keep track of and record and if necessary remind the magistrates of everything they had done. The clerk, who was employed on a full-time basis, gave effect to the decisions and orders of the part-time magistrates and carried out many other functions on his own.

Yet the clerks of the peace never received any salary at all, being entirely dependent on fees for their services. Since by the end of the Upper Canadian period clerks of the peace nonetheless enjoyed yearly incomes in the £200–£300 range, the office is a good starting point for a tentative exploration of how the fee system worked.

It may be helpful to begin with an extract from an act of the provincial parliament of 1807 which regularized the level of fees for the services performed by clerks of the peace at that time. It illustrates the varied and sometimes arcane nature of their duties but also the bits-and-pieces way in which their living was cobbled together.

> For drawing the precept and attending Commissioners to sign the same, and transmitting it to the sheriff, one pound; attending each quarter session, one pound and ten shillings; making up the records of each session, two pounds and ten shillings; notice of every appointment, one shilling; list of jurors, every one hundred names, two shillings and sixpence; making up estreats of each session and transmitting the same to the inspector general, five shillings, to be paid out of the district treasury; every recognizance for the peace or good behaviour, to be paid by the party bound, five shillings; for discharging the same, two shillings and sixpence; subpoena, two shillings and sixpence; bench warrant, five shillings; drawing indictments, ten shillings; allowance of certiorari, to be paid by the person applying for the same, five shillings.[14]

Other provincial acts passed before and after 1807 periodically added to the clerk of the peace's legal chores and to the fees which came with them, such as: five shillings for each barring of dower, five shillings to authorize Presbyterian ministers to perform the marriage ceremony, thirty shillings for providing certified copies of assessment rolls to the collectors, thirty shillings for submitting aggregate assessment returns to the lieutenant governor's office, ten shillings for making out writs for levying assessment on which taxes were in arrears, etc., etc., etc.[15]

These examples of the clerk's duties, besides conveying a picture of an official who performed a multitude of chores, make an additional point about the fee system as a whole. Essentially, payment in fees was a way of saving the provincial government money, but fees were of two types, first, user fees, collected from the public; and

Table 2.4
Salaries and fees of selected officials, 1821

	Salary	Fees
Civil Secretary	£182-10-0	£189-10-6
Clerk, Executive Council	£200	£200
Solicitor General	£100	£267-14-2
Provincial Secretary	£300	£335
Surveyor General	£300	£400
Receiver General	£200	£822-12-5
Attorney General	£300	£1,001-2-10

Source: LAC, RG 1, E 13, vol. 141.

second, fees charged against the treasury for specific duties performed. At the headquarters level, fees charged for public functions,
especially involving the land-granting process, were primarily a way
of augmenting, sometimes by quite a lot, the salaries of a select group
of office holders without raising their salaries. Looking again at the
first Blue Book figures of 1821 yields the following examples.

Almost all the government employees in the capital were paid
some level of salary, whether or not they also received fees, the exception being the government printer, who was paid in fees only, because
he was not considered a full-time employee but a contractor whose
income was "derived from public work performed at regulated
prices." In the field however payment in fees alone was more of a rule
than an exception. The provincial government effectively down-
loaded the expense of land registration, customs collection, and district government and justice either on to the public directly through
user fees, or indirectly via the district treasury. Not only did the provincial government avoid having to pay most of its field staff but
required some officials to pay for any extra help they needed out of
their own pockets. Under legislation of 1806 and 1817, the sheriffs
of the Eastern, Western, London, Niagara. Newcastle, Johnstown,
Gore and Ottawa districts were paid a basic salary of £50 a year in
addition to fees as a supposedly temporary support until their income
from fees alone reached an acceptable level, but they still paid their
deputies and the bailiffs. Customs collectors paid deputies, messengers and, in smuggling cases, informants. Registrars paid deputies,
sometimes as much as one-third of the total income from the office.[16]

So in some cases fees could be used to supplement salaried income.
There was another way in which Upper Canadian public servants

could add to their earnings, which was by holding more than one appointment at a time. Plural office-holding was often permitted by the government for at least two reasons. In the field, in a sparsely populated district, especially early on in the history of the province, a single position might not require full-time attention and therefore was also not likely to generate enough revenue from fees to provide the incumbent with a respectable living, but two or more offices possibly could. As well, assuming that the appointee was a loyal and competent servant of the Crown, the executive could be assured that more than just one public task was in capable hands. Here again the office of the clerk of the peace can be used as a handy entry into the practice of multiple job holding. A glance at the list of government officers in F.H. Armstrong's helpful book produces at least ten cases of men who while clerk of the peace held additional government appointments, the most common being clerk of the district court. Thomas Welsh for example, in the London District, was concurrently clerk of the peace, clerk of the district court, and registrar of the surrogate court. George Rolph was at once clerk of the peace and clerk of the district court in the Gore District. Walter Roe of the Western District was both clerk of the peace and judge of the surrogate court. Because he lived in the provincial capital Thomas Ridout was able to combine positions in both the central and local governments. He was clerk of the peace for the Home District while also serving in the surveyor general's office as first clerk and from time to time as joint acting surveyor general. He also found time to hold the office of registrar of York County. He resigned as clerk of the peace and registrar only after being appointed surveyor general in his own right but was then also immediately commissioned as a Home District magistrate.[17]

Plural appointments eventually became less common in Upper Canada, though they never ceased to exist. Even among the headquarters staff holding more than one office was not uncommon. Executive councillors were paid only a modest honorarium of £100 a year but they almost invariably held other well-paid jobs. During the years 1829–31 John Beverley Robinson earned £1,500 as chief justice of the Court of King's Bench, £100 as an executive councillor, and £360 as speaker of the Legislative Council. At a less exalted level, the position in the adjutant general's office of militia pension agent, while it existed between 1816 and 1826, was held by Edward McMahon, who was at the same time senior clerk in the lieutenant governor's office. The second appointment permitted McMahon to more than double his salary. John Beikie was quite well paid as clerk of the executive council (£400 a year when he died in 1839) but he had doubled since 1805 as clerk of the Heir and Devisee Commission, where, like the clerks of the peace he was authorized to collect fees for a range of services. In the case of the clerks of the peace themselves it would appear that holding other positions at the same time became for many of them both too time consuming and less necessary as their incomes from fees inevitably increased. Another comparative look at some statistics from the Blue Books of 1821 and 1840 illustrates the general trend. In every district except one, where the income of the clerk of the peace was almost identical in both years (Johnstown), increases, some of them quite striking occurred. In the Niagara District the clerk of the peace earned five times as much in 1840 as in 1821; in the Western, Gore, and Newcastle districts the 1840 figures were three times those of 1821, and the incomes of the clerks of the peace in the Home and London districts had more than doubled. Even with this general increase in the value of the office, some pluralism continued. In 1840 in the Newcastle District, Thomas Ward was the clerk of the peace and also the surrogate court judge; in the new district of Talbot, William Mercer Wilson was clerk of the peace and clerk of the district court. When he died on 10 October 1840, Richard P. Hotham still held the offices of clerk of the peace, district court clerk, registrar of the surrogate court, and inspector of licences of the Ottawa District and was as well registrar of Prescott and Russell counties. His total income in 1839 was about £250.[18]

This thumbnail sketch of the Upper Canadian bureaucracy has so far dealt with its professional employees – an elite group distinguished by background and education, and of course by their maleness. It is time to turn to the kinds of government employment that might occasionally be available to Upper Canadians of humbler origins. There was another workaday public service whose personnel and very existence is not always easy to document and whose size and functions are sometimes obscure. In the capital, this was a "downstairs" world of office servants, doorkeepers, housekeepers, cleaners, and messengers. In the districts, mundane and often disagreeable chores were performed by bailiffs, gaolers, court keepers, and criers, and in each township in the districts by clerks, pathmasters, poundkeepers, constables, assessors, and collectors. The penitentiary, when it opened in 1835, added some new blue-collar opportunities for keepers, watchmen, and a matron.

While the early Blue Books recorded the presence of a small group of government office servants in York/Toronto, it is intriguing to find that they largely disappear from that official source by the 1830s and their existence has to be documented in other places. Not only their official but their actual status as employees seems to have been of a somewhat shadowy sort, if the case of Andrew Hawkins, "Messenger and Keeper" in the east wing of the government buildings is at all typical. He applied in 1837 for an increase in pay on the grounds that he was doing work that he was not being paid for. Although his name and position appear in financial accounts for 1836 and 1837 published in an appendix to the *Journals* of the Assembly, his request came as a surprise to the Executive Council because they were under the impression that there was someone else doing his job.[19]

It may be that in deleting some of its employees from the records the Upper Canadian government was attempting to conceal some of its expenses, and a certain modest increase in staff, from the imperial government. The method of concealment, if that is what it was, involved a change in payroll bookkeeping practice for most of the lower echelon of public servants. Rather than receiving their salaries directly from the treasury and being listed among all the others who did, they were after 1832 paid "allowances" out of "contingent" funds assigned in block amounts to several of the government offices. In effect they ceased to be, on the books, actual officeholders, but a form of incidental expense along with such other items as fire insurance and building repairs.

If the government was in fact trying to disguise some of its expenditure on personnel, there really was not all that much to hide. The number of available government jobs of a non-clerical sort that can be identified in the capital added up to only about fifteen positions at the end of the Upper Canadian period and no more than half that number twenty years earlier. Much of what is known about these few individuals can be readily presented in condensed form (see table 2.5).

The government's office servants evidently had three principal functions: housekeeping, security, and inter-office communication. Given what is known about the incessant flow of documents and files from one government office to another it is not surprising that so many of them were designated as messengers, but it is also apparent that most were expected to carry out a combination of duties. For

Table 2.5
Office servants, 1821, 1837–40

A. 1821			
Name	Title	Office	Salary
Isaac Pilkington	Messenger/Keeper	Lt. Governor	£70
John Hunter	Messenger	Assembly	£20
John Hunter	Messenger	Executive Council	£22-4-5
John Hunter	Crier and Usher	King's Bench	£10
William Nixon	Office Servant	Surveyor General	£50-3-9
Hugh Carfrae	Doorkeeper	Executive Council	£22-4-5
Hugh Carfrae	Doorkeeper	Legislative Council	£20
Sarah Lancaster	Housekeeper	Executive Council	£33-6-8
William Knott	Doorkeeper	Assembly	£20
James Bridgeland	Keeper	King's Bench	£10

B. 1837–40			
Name	Title	Office/Location	Salary
Margaret Powell	Housekeeper	West Wing	£75
Andrew Hawkins	Messenger/Keeper	East Wing	£50
William Walker	Messenger	Surveyor General	£50
Hugh Carfrae	Doorkeeper/Messenger	Executive Council	£30
Hugh Carfrae	Doorkeeper	Legislative Council	£20
John McCloskey	Messenger	Crown Lands	£35
J. Powell	Asst. Messenger	East Wing	£25-7-6
J. Smith	Asst. Messenger	West Wing	£25
Æneas Bell	Messenger	Assembly	£20
H. McLennan	Doorkeeper	Assembly	£20
James Bridgeland	Keeper	King's Bench	£20
T. Phipps	Usher	King's Bench	£20
William Cloughley	Messenger/Keeper	Lt. Governor	?
Robert Algeo	Asst. Messenger	Lt. Governor	?
Lewis Bright	Messenger	Legislative Council	?
Julia Bell	Housekeeper	Assembly	?

Sources: LAC, RG 1, E13, vols 141, 155; *HAJ* (1837–38), app., 289–90; Robertson, *Landmarks of Toronto*, 3: 167–9; Nish, *Debates of the Legislative Assembly*, 1841, 219.

example some of the assistant messengers, who seem to have been teenage boys, were expected in the heating season to bring firewood as well as messages into the offices. The long-serving Hugh Carfrae was theoretically responsible for simultaneously guarding two office doors and running messages. In 1821 John Hunter also apparently had to perform more than one function in three places at once.[20]

There was a hierarchy among the servant class, denoted in part by salary levels. It is unfortunate that not all of the servants' salary figures are known in the 1837–40 period, especially that of the office keeper and messenger in the lieutenant governor's office, for that job was at the highest end of the scale in 1821 and probably continued to be, reflecting the prestige, high level of confidentiality, and other attractive salaries associated with the office. It may come as something of a surprise to find that the person in receipt of the highest known salary in 1840 was a woman, Margaret Powell, housekeeper in the west wing of the government buildings. Mrs Powell's story has been told elsewhere, but her career as "the first woman to hold a more than menial position in the public service of the province of Upper Canada" bears brief recapitulation, for it sheds some light on the evolving organization and the working conditions of the bottom rank of public servants.[21]

A housekeeper had been employed by the Executive Council from at least 1803, with the basic duties of "keeping the rooms and furniture in proper order," but the position carried little authority or emolument. When the existing government buildings were largely destroyed by fire in 1824 they were eventually replaced in 1830–32 by a new and larger set of buildings consisting of a central section housing the two chambers of the provincial parliament and two wings for offices. These buildings, which stood on Front Street between York and Simcoe streets, would continue to serve as the provincial parliament buildings until 1892. The majority of the government departments were located after 1830 in the west wing. At that time the Executive Council decided to create a new position, still to be called a housekeeper, but with greater responsibility and authority, to supervise the non-clerical staff in the west wing. They chose Mrs Powell, widow of a British army major, for the post. There may for some time have been concerns about security and about discipline among the staff for the offices had been previously "distributed all over town." At any rate Mrs Powell was put in charge of the affairs of five departments to which she was to keep the keys, because of the importance put on the safeguarding of the records by the Executive Council. She was enjoined to report any "irregularity or negligence" effecting the buildings or the papers in the offices and to make sure that the offices were kept "clean and in good order" by the staff employed for that purpose. Since the messengers and assistant messengers also carried out some of the janitorial functions,

Mrs Powell was given authority over them as well. Some of her male underlings were inclined at first to be quarrelsome under her direction but were advised in 1834 that if they were dissatisfied with the situation "they were at liberty to leave."[22]

In fact before and after Mrs Powell's appointment the servant personnel frequently changed as people left, or were dismissed from, jobs that were often not highly valued by themselves or others, and in which there was no expectation of security of tenure. Between 1803 and 1830 at least seven people (one of them a man) held the job of housekeeper, two of whom were fired. In 1828 the widow Anne Bayley, though originally appointed on the recommendation of Chief Justice Powell, was let go "owing to a misfortune into which she fell and which she seeks not to extenuate." Her successor, Mary Martin (or Martinez), demoted to cleaner on the arrival of Mrs Powell in 1830, lost that job in 1832 along with her husband, who was summarily dismissed after nine years as a messenger "for one inadvertently rude answer he gave Mr. Boulton the then Attorney General." Certainly complaints about the calibre of the servants were not unusual. The fire that destroyed the centre and north wings of the parliament buildings in 1824 was attributed to "a great want of vigilance ... among the servants employed, especially James Bridgeland and John Hunter." As winter set in in November 1831 Attorney General Henry John Boulton made a good deal of fuss about a lack of fire, due in his view to the prevailing laziness of the staff, who had failed to fill any of the wood boxes. Mrs Powell singled out J. Smith, assistant messenger in the west wing, for special condemnation. If Smith had any good points they were a secret to Mrs Powell. In her view he was lazy, slovenly, insolent, and untruthful.[23]

Examples of long service at the bottom of the public service heap were rare. Only two individuals, James Bridgeland and Hugh Carfrae, appear on the two lists of servant employees of 1821 and 1837–40. Aside from his alleged negligence at the time of the fire of 1824 and his apparent willingness to work indefinitely for the least possible wages, little is known of Bridgeland, but Carfrae was something of a special case. His career as a minor public servant actually spanned the period from 1805 to 1839, the year of his death. F.H. Armstrong, who has made a study of the Carfrae family, believes that Hugh Carfrae, who was also a contractor (often on government projects) and eventually a Toronto councilman, probably did not really need the income from government employment but held his positions as "something of an honour granted to a trusted servant," which would suggest that either his duties were very light or were performed by a substitute. Besides being an example of what William Lyon Mackenzie called Family Compact "placemen," Carfrae's career also neatly illustrates the fact that plural office-holding was possible at any level of the public service, for he not only worked for years for the provincial government but at the same time held district offices such as high constable and gaoler.[24]

If Carfrae was in fact being paid for doing little or nothing his case was not unique for a number of the office servants at times enjoyed several varieties of "perks." Mrs Powell was allowed the paid services of a personal "female attendant," Hannah Pike, and also had her own small contingent account. John Hunter, who like Hugh Carfrae held multiple offices, earned in 1821 in one of his capacities, as crier and usher of the Court of King's Bench, an additional £5 in fees. Some of the appointments to minor positions probably constituted "perks" in themselves. The servants of the House of Assembly and the Legislative Council cannot have been overworked since the Parliament rarely met for more than two or three months in the year. A very clear cut instance of being paid for doing nothing was that of Maria Willcocks. Miss Willcocks was the sister-in-law of Dr William Warren Baldwin and daughter of William Willcocks, magistrate, judge of the district court, and frequent business failure. According to the authors of a family history of the Baldwins, Miss Willcocks was an early career woman in Upper Canada who "capably and efficiently carried out the duties of housekeeper for the Executive Council." The minutes of that body for 6 May 1830 tell a different story. Maria Willcocks "who had held the appointment as Housekeeper since the year 1803 but had discharged no duties in consequence, received £10 sterling annually up to the 30th June 1828 when she ceased to receive that allowance."[25]

Though the practice was officially frowned upon, some of the servants reduced their household expenses by keeping livestock on public property behind the government buildings. Margaret Powell herself for a time kept a cow and chickens there. Despite complaints about the mess and the smell, Æneas Bell, the messenger to the House of Assembly, used part of the grounds to keep chickens, cows, pigs, and a horse. Bell's family income was supplemented in still another way: his wife too was able to get a government job, as housekeeper to the Assembly. The choice of Mrs Bell seems to have been part of an unofficial pattern of preferment – the employment of married couples as a kind of package deal. Joseph Martin (José Martinez) and his wife Mary, until they were sacked in 1832, were another man and wife team as messenger and cleaner, as were their successors, John McCloskey and his wife. In a somewhat unusual situation, Bernard Turquand, chief clerk in the receiver general's office, arranged to have his wife Elizabeth installed as an unpaid housekeeper in the (less busy) east wing of the government buildings.[26]

The reason why Mrs Turquand agreed to take a position with no actual pay attached was so that she and her husband might enjoy one of the most significant benefits in the government's gift, available only to a select group of the servants, free rent. The custom, established at quite an early date, was that the housekeepers and "the servants of the Parliament House" were given "apartments" on the premises. This was no trifling consideration. Rents in York/Toronto were said to be "very high indeed." A glimpse of the business affairs of one Upper Canadian landlord helps to provide a small insight into the steep Toronto rental market. Readers of Margaret Atwood's novel *Alias Grace* might recognize the name of Thomas Kinnear, who was murdered in his home near Richmond Hill in 1843. In 1839, in calmer times, he rented one of his properties, an out-of-repair two-bedroom cottage with a badly leaking roof on the western outskirts of Toronto, to three young bachelors. The rent was £30 a year, plus upkeep and taxes. An 1841 publication reported that a two-story house of six rooms cost £50 or £60 to rent. As we know, even £30 was more than most menial servants of the government made in a year, so living rent-free could make a very large difference to people whose wages were modest to begin with. When Mrs Powell was taken on as housekeeper in 1830 her initial salary was £50 a year but in actuality it was worth quite a bit more than that because she and her three children were provided with two large rooms and one smaller one in the west wing. Even though the rooms were in the basement story and according to Mrs Powell were damp and unhealthy, they constituted no drain on an income that she found barely adequate for her other needs, including the cost of sending her two sons to Upper Canada College. For a time Margaret Powell took further advantage of her relatively spacious free quarters and supplemented her income even more by taking in two boarders.[27] To the other servants who had free accommodation, all of whom earned quite a bit less than Mrs Powell, not paying rent meant that for them as well a very handsome bonus went with the job. Nor was that all. Along with free rent went one more very important benefit, a firewood allowance.

Upper Canada had cold winters. Attempting to achieve a minimal level of warmth in draughty uninsulated buildings by burning wood in open fireplaces required staggering amounts of fuel. Of course wood was plentiful in the province and for many rural people available free except for the work involved in cutting it down, chopping it up, and hauling it in, but urban people had to buy their wood. Bought in bulk, firewood could still be had in some places for as little as five shillings a cord in the late 1830s. York/Toronto was not one of those places. Prices in the capital were double or more that figure as early as 1807. By 1830 the forest had retreated from the York area to the point that some firewood was already being imported from the United States and even in summer "brings nearly three silver dollars a cord," in other words, nearly fifteen shillings. The sum given to the servants occupying a modest amount of space in the government buildings was ten shillings a cord in 1824 and 11s 9d five years later, for the "usual allowance" of eighteen cords. (The amount of wood required to heat a two-story house of six rooms was said to be thirty or forty cords.) The saving in heating costs by public servants was thus an additional £9 or £10 a year.[28]

It may be necessary to remind twenty-first-century readers that a genuine cord (not the so called "face cord" now sold to hapless wood burners) consisted of a pile of wood eight feet long by four feet wide by four feet high. Eighteen cords of wood if piled side by side and end to end in two rows would therefore occupy a space sixteen feet wide by four feet high by seventy-two feet long. As Judith Fingard has pointed out, a great many townspeople could not buy their winter's supply of wood in bulk in advance, having neither enough money to pay for it all at once or anywhere to put so bulky a commodity, and were forced to buy small amounts at a time at higher prices.[29] From this added expense as well the fortunate servants were also presumably protected, being able to store at least a cord or two on the space behind their quarters not already occupied by domestic animals.

Outside of the capital of Upper Canada there were few examples of lower-level public servants receiving any special indulgences from government. Some special provision was made for the employees of the Provincial Penitentiary, which opened in 1835. There the messenger was given two free rooms in the institution, the eleven keepers were each allowed £12-10-0 a year for "lodging money," and the matron enjoyed free rent, fuel, and candles. The matron in particular would seem to have deserved some extra compensation since she received only £48 a year, compared to £72 for keepers and £54 for watchmen. (The warden was paid £270 a year and had a free house on the grounds, also with free fuel and candles.) Gaolers in the districts also originally had a "housekeeping room" in the gaols and later separate accommodation.[30]

Gaolers may have enjoyed some perks but have also been said to have received "poor remuneration." No doubt almost any salary would have been inadequate given the dangerous and disagreeable job they did, but compared to other non-clerical government workers they were not always badly off. The problem early on for gaolers, and for other minor district employees, was that the district tax bases did not always produce revenues sufficient to regularly pay even modest salaries and expenses. The Home District supplies an example of the early fluctuating financial fate of district gaolers. Up until 1799 the gaoler, Hugh Cameron, was paid his handsome salary of £91-5-0 by the provincial government, who also paid the bills "for the Maintenance of Prisoners, for the Supplying the Gaol with fuel and with such other incidental necessaries as may from time to time be requisite." In June of that year the government decided that it was time that the expenses of the gaoler's office were paid by the district. Originally the magistrates of the Home District generously undertook to continue to pay the gaoler at his previous rate but they soon had second thoughts, because of the state of "The funds of the District and the incompetency of the Assessments to liquidate the accounts against it." A decision was made in 1801 to combine the offices of gaoler and high constable, at a salary of £50 per year. By this time Cameron was owed £134-10-7 1/2. He was given "a certificate pledging the faith of the District for the payment of the aforementioned Sum," and the treasurer was ordered to pay Cameron a part payment of £50 "out of the first Monies he shall receive from the Collectors of the Assessments." By the autumn of 1803 Cameron, still owed £25-17-6, decided to resign. The magistrates ordered "that the Clerk of the Court be directed to give the Gaoler a Bond as heretofore" and that in future "The Gaoler's Salary be Thirty Pounds p. annum & no more." The new gaoler, Nicholas Klengenbrunner, did not last long at that level. His successor, Thomas R. Johnson, was installed in 1804 at the rate of £40 a year, but when Hugh Carfrae took over in 1807 he was paid only £35, which was the prevailing salary until 1811 when the gaoler was given an extra £10 a year to cover additional duties as "Keeper of the House of Correction." The financial lot of the gaolers eventually improved as the capacity of the districts to pay them for their indispensable services increased. In 1815 the London District gaoler was paid £50 a year. The gaoler of the Eastern District was paid £60 a year in 1825; in 1834 his salary was £125 a year. John Kidd, gaoler of both the Home District and the new City of Toronto, received a salary in 1838 of £62-10-0 in each quarter, plus an extra £29-11-3 per quarter for the maintenance of the insane in the gaol, for a yearly total of £368-5-0.[31]

For most other people however, holding a subordinate position in the districts was more often than not as likely to produce financial loss as profit, as well as imposing on the office-holder a good deal of aggravation and inconvenience. Within the districts the smallest unit of administration was the township. An act of 1793 (George III, C. 12) to "Provide for the Nomination and Appointment of Parish and Town Officers Within this Province," required the "inhabitant house-holders" in each township to meet annually in March (later changed to January) to "choose," by means not specified, a number of "fit and proper" persons to act for the next year in several capacities. These included a township clerk, two tax assessors, a tax collector, as many as six overseers of highways (increased to twelve in 1805), a pound-keeper, and two town wardens. The duties of the wardens were not at first very clearly defined. They were theoretically to be "a corporation" with power to hold property in goods or chattels and to take legal action on behalf of the people but by an act of 1799 they were given a more specific social welfare function, with the power to arrange apprenticeships for orphaned or abandoned children.[32]

The "town meetings" as they came to be called, have been pointed to by historians of municipal government as early manifestations of grassroots control by the common people of their own affairs. "The town meeting was an example of direct democracy," and was "the germ of our democratic system of municipal institutions." The "very fact of their meeting and choosing officers and exercising their meagre powers" created "a keen desire and greater ability for self government." Actually the degree of local authority conferred by law on the residents of the townships was indeed meagre. All that the people at the meetings were supposed to do was to somehow select a slate of minor functionaries and to make rules governing farm fences and domestic animals. In some years, in some townships, town meetings were not held at all, perhaps reflecting their perceived irrelevance. Town meetings occurred only once in each year, affording little scope for the emergence of tribunes among the people. The meetings could only be called on the authority of the district magistrates, one or more of whom seem almost always to have attended the meetings, and often presided, which could suggest that rustic democracy was as likely to be directed as direct. The people chosen to fill the assorted positions, who did not even have to be at the meetings but could be notified after the fact by a constable, were in no way controlled by or answerable to the people but were responsible to and overseen by the magistrates. The townships had almost no financial powers and the taxpayers could not set the rate at which their property was taxed.[33]

Yet in an unplanned and sometimes even perverse way, the meetings did evolve, through local initiative, into institutions which showed signs of local autonomy and a cheerful disregard for the letter of the law and the wishes of higher levels of government. With no authority to do so some townships took on powers and duties to which they had no legal right. In 1800 Sophiasburg Township appointed a treasurer, established levels of various fines and forfeitures, provided for the sale of unclaimed stray animals, appointed "Overseers of the Poor," divided itself, for charitable purposes, into four parishes, each of which was to appoint an "Inspector," and declared that the treasurer, overseers of the poor and the parish inspectors were to form a separate committee to meet as often as they thought fit. At a later meeting, on the recommendation of "the committee appointed who have care of the poor," the township levied its own tax of "one half-penny in the pound on each man's rateable property," All of this was plainly illegal. The Township of Adolphustown also conducted at least some of its own financial affairs by levying fines and dispensing funds to the poundkeeper and to "Apprisers" who assessed damages. Another manifestation of grassroots resistance to the rules was the widespread custom of choosing township constables at the town meetings, though this too was illegal, since "a sufficient number" of constables for each township were supposed by law to be appointed by the magistrates.[34]

William Lyon Mackenzie attended the town meeting in Toronto Township in 1831, where, far from confining their discussion to fences and stray livestock, the "yeomanry" assembled at Cook's tavern "brought under review" such topics as "the militia system, voting by ballot, education, lands granting, road systems, and the application of the sales of wild land and reserves to improve the roads, the navigation of the St. Lawrence, law fees, the revenue, the mode of appointing the magistrates, the judiciary, and the unfairness of allowing 10 or 15 members in parliament for a population scarcely equal to that of this county which sends two." In Etobicoke Township, where Mackenzie also "looked in," a number of proposals brought to the meeting from the lieutenant governor's office by the magistrates "were all negatived, with scarcely a show of support." Mackenzie highly approved of the independent spirit exhibited at the town meetings as an indication that the farmers of Upper Canada were determined to have "equal laws and institutions." He no doubt also approved of the action taken at the meeting in Whitchurch Township in January 1834 when the assembled householders invoked the principle of "no taxation without representation." Mackenzie, who was then the MHA for the area, had been prevented from taking his seat in the House and the meeting therefore refused to choose the assessors and a collector. The clerk recorded that "when they was Nominated and Cried by the Constable the Cry of the people was we want none we have no use for any we are not allowed to have our member to represent us in the house of parliament and we think that we have no use for any such officers." It is pretty plain that in some parts of the province at least, the town meetings did become a focus of local opposition to the provincial establishment, however powerless the meetings were to take any real action. By the end of the 1820s in the Town of York, Reformers were able to control the meetings and chose political radicals like Mackenzie, Joseph Cawthra, John Doel, and Jesse Ketchum to fill the various offices.[35]

Why were some petty and not so petty deviations from the intentions of the government and from lawful practices condoned? At the time that the original Parish and Town Officers Act was passed, the first lieutenant governor, John Graves Simcoe, explained to the British government that a certain amount of local democracy (though he of course did not use that word) was permissible because if the people chose their own township officials, especially "the Collector of the rates," they would be "more willingly obeyed,"[36] and as well if the people's choices proved not to be competent or honest, the

people had only themselves to blame, and could not blame the lieutenant governor's appointees, the magistrates. There may also have
been a further reason why a good deal of leeway within the town
meeting system was tolerated. The annual selection of minor officials
by the residents meant that a number of necessary but thankless and
unpleasant tasks were performed at minimum expense to the province or the districts.

Almost all of the people selected for the various positions at the
town meetings received no regular salaries but were rewarded, if at
all, by fees. Poundkeepers received fees on a sliding scale from the
district treasurer for impounding animals. In the Home District in
1800 these were set at 2s 6d for horses, 2s for oxen, and 1s for pigs
or sheep, but in the Town of York, where there seems to have been
some kind of epidemic of hogs running at large, the fee for impounding them was raised to 5s. So far as can be determined the town
wardens were never paid at all. The overseers of highways (often
referred to as pathmasters) received some compensation for their
time and expenses directing work on the local roads but the district
treasurers' accounts show only relatively small payments to them in
each year, in the range of about £6 to fifteen shillings. Tax collectors
and assessors received fees from the district treasurer for determining
the amount of tax owed by each land occupant and collecting the
relevant amount of tax. These duties, if conscientiously done, were
not likely to make them popular in the community, though the immediate pain of tax-paying could be eased somewhat since collection
often took place in a handy tavern. Their fees were based on the
number of taxpayers in their townships. A township with a good-
sized population meant higher fees, but also more work. The Eastern
District in the 1830s provides a graphic example of such discrepan-
cies in fees, for its front townships on the St Lawrence were by then
well populated, while the back townships remained sparsely settled.
In 1836 J.A. Merkley earned £10-17-8 as assessor in Williamsburg
while Peter Chesley's fees as assessor in backwoods Roxborough
Township came to only £3-2-2 1/2. In 1837 the better-paid position
of collector still earned Duncan McMillan, collector of Finch
Township, only £3-9-3 1/2, while William McDonell, collector of
Charlottenburg, received a handsome £20-8-1 3/4. In the even more
remote townships of North and South Sherbrooke and Goulborn
in the Bathurst District, the collector's fees in 1836 ranged from
£8-14-10 to £1-1-10 and those of the assessor from £6-3-1 1/2 to

11-12-2. The same wide range in fees can be seen in the sprawling London District. Fees earned there in 1837 by the collectors ran from £16-9-1 to £1-2-5 1/2, by the assessors from £9-15-2 to £0-8-9. Not only were the fees small but payment of them could also be slow, in some cases by as much as five or six years.[37]

The township clerks were required by law to keep complete records of all of the business of their townships, which was supposed to include the preparation of an accurate list of the number of male and female inhabitants of the township, to be delivered annually to the magistrates in quarter sessions. No provision was originally made to pay the clerks for their work. Edward Hayward, who was acting as clerk in three townships, York, Scarborough, and Etobicoke, was paid £3 for his services in 1799 and 1800, and in 1802 several of the other clerks in the Home District applied to the magistrates "for a compensation for their trouble," but no such compensation can be found as an expenditure in the succeeding district accounts. A petition from William Bond, a former township clerk for "an allowance" was presented to the Home District quarter sessions in 1809 "to which their Honors were pleased to answer that the Funds of the District were not sufficient to discharge the same." In the London District the magistrates ordered in 1806 that from then on the clerks were to receive five shillings for every hundred names on the population roll of their townships "provided such population roll or rolls be made up carefully, and in due time." The exact population of the district and its townships at that time is unknown, but was certainly small. In 1817 Robert Gourlay estimated the population of the London District at 8,900, with an average of about 500 people per township, which works out to an average of about £1-5-0 for each clerk, not a great incentive to do their work "carefully, and in due time," or, as shall be seen, at all. Eventually, by the end of the Upper Canadian period, all the township clerks received an allowance for their work from the district treasurers in the yearly token sum of £2-10-0.[38]

Of all the township officials, the constables were surely the most blatantly exploited. They were a crucial, though until recently an almost entirely unexamined cog in the Upper Canadian system of local justice and law enforcement, as the important and groundbreaking work by Frances Thompson on the magistrates and constables of the Niagara District between 1828 and 1840 has made clear. Constables were required to intervene to restore order at fights,

assaults, and riots. They had to arrest and deliver accused law breakers to the district gaol. They had the unpopular responsibility for
seizing goods for debt. They risked, and sometimes sustained, physical injury. They served warrants, writs, and summonses. They were
responsible for making sure that litigants and witnesses showed up
in court and they had many other responsibilities for which they
could expect to get "such compensation as the said justices of the
peace ... shall think proper." In the Niagara District study by Frances
Thompson they were found to have travelled an average distance of
twenty-three miles for two or three days to attend the quarterly court
sessions. In pursuit of criminals or in bringing prisoners to gaol, they
often covered much greater distances. Constable Richard McGuire
transported two men to the town of Niagara from the western end
of the district, a distance of seventy-two miles, over a period of six
days. Constable Abraham Chapman logged 225 miles on the trail
of Nelson Petty, accused of having set fire to a barn in Wainfleet
Township. In such cases the constables had to pay the costs of transportation, board, and lodging for themselves and their prisoners,
hoping to be compensated at a later date by the magistrates, but
compensation, if and when it came, was slight and slow. In 1829–30,
when the total expenditure of the Niagara District was £2652-17-7,
the amount paid to all of the township constables as compensation
for their time and expenses came to only £104-16-7. In the same year
the district's clerk of the peace alone received £198-13-4 from the
district, in addition to fees he charged members of the public. Ten
years later the overall district expenditure had risen to £2953-16-0
and the clerk of the peace was paid £370-17-0. The constables shared
£198-13-4. In the specific case of Constable Chapman, who had
travelled so far to get his man, the compensation he ultimately
received covered only about half of his actual expenses. The Niagara
District was by no means alone in expecting that its constables
worked long and hard when necessary for less than adequate reward.
The district treasurer's accounts for the London, Prince Edward, and
Bathurst districts in 1836 and 1837 list payments to constables
mainly in the range of £2 to £4. The highest amount was £6-5-0, the
lowest, fifteen shillings.[39]

A very large number of Upper Canadians spent part of their time
each year working for the government for no compensation whatsoever. All male inhabitants between the ages of twenty-one and fifty
and anyone owning a team of horses, a wagon, or a cart, were

required by law to work a minimum of three days in each year, and all rate-paying landowners, including women who owned property, at least two days a year under the direction of the pathmasters at building, maintaining, or improving the roads in their localities. Above the minimum requirement the system was based on the rates of assessment. Beyond the mandatory two days of labour for rate-payers, additional days were owed by the better-off, the amount of time rising on an increasing scale which matched various levels at which their property was valued for purposes of taxation. People who were assessed for £25 or less owed only the basic two days labour, but the scale, as set by an act of 1819, rose to a possible property assessment of £3,500 (apparently the highest assessment imaginable in Upper Canada) and a requirement of twenty-seven days work. This commendably progressive arrangement was not quite so punitive for the rich as it appeared. Road work was hard work so statute labour could be avoided, by those who could afford it, by paying "composition money" instead. The maximum payment in lieu of labour was five shillings a day so that the very highest amount which could theoretically be owed was £6-15-0, not an impossible sum for a person of means to afford, and at a fairly high (for the time) assessment level of perhaps £500, the payment would have amounted to only £3. Even so there were always some people who failed to either work or pay and were reported by the pathmasters as defaulters. In York in 1804, among others, the lawyer William Weekes was found to owe twelve days labour, Joint Acting Surveyor General William Chewett eleven days, and the former gaoler, Hugh Cameron, four days. Each was ordered to pay the composition money owing, plus a fine of ten shillings. The construction and upkeep of roads by the use of statute labour was long and widely criticized since a constantly changing, temporary, and amateur labour force produced roads which were indifferent at best, but from the government's point of view the essential point was that the labour was free. The legal obligation to perform statute labour continued throughout and long after the Upper Canadian period, until 1927.[40]

At the risk of stating the obvious, it should be kept in mind that people doing statute labour and all of the township officers chosen at the annual meetings or appointed by the magistrates had their own work to do, on farms, in stores or shops, or in many other pursuits. While doing disagreeable chores for the township for little or no financial gain, or sometimes financial loss, they were taking valuable time away from the ways in which they made a living. It is not surprising then to find that some people took on official jobs unwillingly for as short a time as possible, performed their duties inadequately, or tried to avoid local public service altogether. It is not necessary to do more than skim through the minutes of the quarter sessions of the two districts for which records are available in printed form, the Home District in the years between 1800 and 1811 and the London District between 1800 and 1818, to find numerous examples of reluctance or refusal to work on the roads or to take township positions, and of neglect or incompetence in office.

The minutes of quarter Sessions contain no apparent complaints from two sets of township appointees, town wardens and pathmasters. While the wardens seldom had any functions to complain about, the pathmasters, when the weather permitted, were kept quite busy and had serious responsibilities. Pathmasters, though, had some incentives to perform their jobs as efficiently as possible. In improving the roads in their area they were benefitting themselves as well as their neighbours. They also had some real authority to organize and oversee the work of other people, including at times their social and economic superiors who chose to actually do their obligatory statute labour. The positions which consistently gave the supervising magistrates the most grief were those of constable, assessor, collector, and township clerk. Difficulties arose from an early date and persisted, as some entries from the quarter sessions minutes demonstrate. At a meeting of the Home District quarter sessions in April 1800, Thomas Tivey and Hugh McPhie avoided serving as constables by finding substitutes, while Robert Willson and Samuel Marther, also appointed constables, "declined serving," Marther stating "that he would never serve the office of Constable." They were given two days to find substitutes or be fined for neglect of duty. Marther must have succeeded in getting a substitute but Willson was fined £2 at the next sessions. Archibald Cameron, collector, was found not to have completed his collections for the year 1799, and was given six weeks to finish his work. In August of the following year, Abner Miles, a collector in 1800 (who as a ship, store, and tavern owner certainly had business of his own to attend to) claimed that the reason he had collected no taxes was because he had never received any assessment rolls from the assessors, Nicholas Miller and Robert Marsh, who in turn were "directed to shew cause, why they Have not made Return of their Assessment to the Collector." Another collector for 1800, Peter

Vanderberg, had left the area without informing anyone if he had collected any money and if so what he had done with it.[41]

In the Home District, being a constable was clearly the least popular office. Nathan Chapman and William Jackson were excused from serving as constables on the grounds that they were under age, but Joseph Hunt, who refused to serve because "he was upwards of sixty years of age & Infirm and said that he considered it an unreasonable appointment," was fined £2 for neglect of duty. John Vanzantee however was excused as a constable "from ill health." Levy Annis was spared a constable's duties because he "cannot read or write."[42]

The London District's magistrates seem not to have been so much troubled by persons trying to evade township responsibilities but had to deal with sporadic cases of negligence. At the quarter sessions of August 1816 six township clerks were "called forth" for neglect of duty for not having required the collectors in their townships to post bonds. Five of them were fined £2 and 15s 6d court costs. The sixth, Archibald McMillan of Delaware Township, appears not to have accepted his punishment in a sufficiently chastened manner and was fined £10 for neglect of duty and a further £10 for contempt of court. In August 1817 John Rolph, who was later to become famous as a Reform politician, "neglected to serve" as collector of Southwold Township and had to be replaced. No action was taken against Rolph, probably because he was going back to England to study both law and medicine, but all of the other township collectors, including Rolph's replacement, John Barber, were summoned that year to the October quarter sessions for being late in paying the district treasurer half of their twice-yearly collections. The money must have been paid prior to October for they made no appearance there.[43]

The most notorious example of apparent neglect of duty on a broad scale involved the township clerks, and the statutory requirement that they carry out a complete annual census of all the inhabitants in their townships. Some early lists of inhabitants for some areas survive so at least some of the clerks took the task seriously, but the returns from all districts must never have been complete since the system failed to produce province-wide statistics, which only exist from the year 1824. At any rate in that year it was decided to amend the clause in the Parish and Town Officers Act which made the clerks responsible for taking the census since "the laws now in force for that purpose are found not to answer the end." The clerks were relieved of census duties, which were given to the township assessors, who were to count the population as they made their normal rounds. The new system actually worked from the start and historians of Upper Canada can be grateful for the existence of an unbroken run of district population returns from 1824 on, compiled by the clerks of the peace from the assessors' reports.[44]

It would be wrong to leave the impression that Upper Canadians routinely shirked or botched the jobs given them to do in the townships. The office of constable in particular was, understandably, not a popular one, but Frances Thompson's analysis of the services of 539 men who were constables in the Niagara District makes clear that they usually performed their arduous duties competently and conscientiously, if not always enthusiastically, for only 28 per cent of them were willing to serve as a constable for a period of more than one year. (There was though some overlap among officeholders in the Niagara District. About 24 per cent of the constables are known to have at some time held other township offices, and the true figure was probably somewhat higher, for the records for other offices are very incomplete.) If the surviving township records for the Bay of Quinte area are a reliable indication, the office of township clerk, however indifferently performed at times, was evidently seen as a skilled white-collar job not calculated to arouse hostility in the community and carrying, if not a living wage, some local prestige, for it was sometimes held by a single individual for extended periods of time. Bazel (probably a miscopying of Rozel) Ferguson was clerk of Hallowell Township for ten years and Arra Ferguson served as clerk two terms of three years each and a third term of eight years. In Sophiasburg Township John Smith was clerk for five years and John Shorts held the office for four years, as did both Archibald Campbell and Daniel Haight in Adolphustown Township. In Thurlow Township James McDonnell was clerk for seven years, but Roswell Leavens may have established a record there. After serving as clerk in 1803–6 and 1811–12, he "continued uninterruptedly" from 1813 to 1826. It is worth noting that John Shorts of Sophiasburg in 1822 served simultaneously as clerk and as an assessor.[45]

It is evident that government jobs came in many different forms. Some were much sought after, paid reasonably well, and were more-or-less permanent. At the other end of the scale jobs could be unwelcome, hardly paid at all, and fortunately temporary. The way in which government jobs were obtained therefore also varied quite a lot, though it must be said that in many cases the explanation for a particular person getting put into a particular job can be, at this distance in time, something of a mystery. To start again at the bottom of the process, how were the many township officials actually chosen to fill positions that were often more of a nuisance than anything else? The minute books of town meetings for several townships have survived; in some cases covering a period of fifty years or more, and as a result we know the names of quite a few people who filled the township offices. But that is where the mysterious part begins. Why, and how, did the people's choice fall on particular individuals? Despite some early instances of townships failing to hold the annual meetings at all, or being so small that they were held in private homes, town meetings seem usually to have been well attended, occupying the most commodious building available, often an inn or tavern or a school. They were apparently conducted with some formality, often chaired by, or in the presence of, magistrates, and of course the proceedings were recorded as minutes by the township clerk. But minutes of meetings, as anyone accustomed to reading them after the fact soon finds, can be notoriously cryptic, frequently obscuring rather than revealing what actually took place, and township meeting minutes are no exception. They record who was chosen each year for each office, but neither the method nor the rationale behind the appointments is made clear. Only one instance has come to light of an actual contested election, for township clerk in Thurlow Township, in 1836. Ordinarily the minutes merely report that "the following persons were chosen to officiate in their respective offices, the ensuing year" or "the following officers were chosen and elected."[46] Were they really "elected"? Were names proposed and seconded? Was more than one person often nominated for an office and if so was a vote of those present held? On such questions the minutes are almost always frustratingly silent. About all that can be said for certain is that the annual slate of officers must have been approved by most of those among their fellow township residents who turned up for the meeting, and to that extent grassroots democracy really can be said to have been in operation at the township level. But to return to the point, how and why was local approval conferred?

It is apparent that, at least in the Home District and especially in the Town of York, the town meetings became to some degree politicized, as was demonstrated by the yeomen of York and Etobicoke townships who in 1831 opposed executive initiatives and debated a wide range of topics which were strictly speaking none of their business. Reformers, in other words, were in some places eventually numerous enough and organized enough to be able to dominate some of the town meetings and to control the appointment of local officials. As has been seen, Reformers, including William Lyon Mackenzie, Joseph Cawthra, John Doel, and Jesse Ketchum, were chosen to fill offices at the York town meetings beginning in the late 1820s. Such men hardly sought these minor posts for profit or influence. They may have believed they could do the work more competently and more honestly than their political rivals but at bottom they were showing that they had acquired a measure of power and that they could use it to appoint their own, and to thumb their noses at the Tories.[47]

Still, most local officials, most of the time, no doubt came from families and backgrounds which would have been deemed appropriate and safe by the magistrates and other local notables. One suggestive guide to the origins of township officials is provided by Frances Thompson's study of the township constables in the Niagara District in the period from 1815 to 1840. The constables, she found, were from the "middling strata" of Niagara society. They were mostly plain and practical men, farmers and innkeepers predominantly, though a few of them eventually entered the local elite as magistrates and militia officers. By family the majority were connected to the district magistracy and to other leading members of the Loyalist and military oligarchy. They were men who were "respected" by their contemporaries and as part of the legal system formed "a bridge" between the magistrates and the community. In other parts of the province which also began with a Loyalist population base a similar pattern of local office-holding can be detected, at least in the early years. The names of officers for the township of Adolphustown in 1793, and Hallowell Township in 1798, are overwhelmingly those of Loyalists, or sons of Loyalists.[48]

Of course much dilution of Loyalist populations occurred over time and only some sections of the province were settled by Loyalists to begin with, so there was never a question of a permanent and province-wide Loyalist monopoly of local offices. Nor could the local elites always control the appointment of officers. In at least one other part of the province something similar to the capture of local posts by the Reformers of York/Toronto seems to have been happening by the late 1830s. In Hastings County, which was not primarily settled by Loyalists, some township officers are known to have been outspoken Reformers, because Gideon Turner, clerk of Sidney Township, and Anson Hayden, clerk of Thurlow Township, were arrested and thrown into gaol in December 1837 as suspected rebels. Little is known of Turner, but Hayden was a post-Loyalist American immigrant who had studied medicine in the United States and practised near Belleville (though he had been refused a licence by the Upper Canadian medical board). Part of his house in Hayden's Corners (now Corbyville) contained his surgery; another part was used as an inn. Obviously even without his radical political leanings he would have been no member of the Belleville area establishment.[49]

It appears then that men were originally chosen for township office because they were part of a founding group and because they enjoyed some respect in their communities. Eventually politics began to be a factor as rival factions vied for the distinction of holding petty offices. It should also be said that, again especially at first, there was usually a pretty small pool of men who were sufficiently competent, literate, and numerate to carry out the duties of office satisfactorily. When the first Adolphustown township meeting was held in 1793 there were only eighty-three heads of households in the township from whom to select ten officials. Over 12 per cent of an adult male population still struggling to clear the land was working part-time for the township. In 1825 in Montague Township (population 341) Francis Clark was both clerk and assessor, James Edmunds was a pathmaster and a poundkeeper, and Thomas McCrea was collector, and also a pathmaster and a poundkeeper. A different example of the scarcity of suitable material for township office is provided by the Hoover family, a numerous and evidently literate and public-spirited clan living in Rainham Township in the London District. In the years 1803–18, Benjamin Hoover served terms as a constable and as township clerk; John Hoover senior was an assessor and John Hoover junior was a poundkeeper; Daniel Hoover served at times as clerk, constable, and assessor, Henry Hoover as constable and assessor, and David Hoover as collector and constable. On one memorable day in 1807 when Daniel Hoover attended a meeting of the court of quarter sessions as a constable, the jury included five other Hoovers. Frances Thompson also found at least 129 cases of such multiple office-holding among her 539 Niagara District constables.[50]

If the means and criteria used to select people to perform mostly minor and thankless tasks in the townships remains in most cases obscure and could do with further exploration, the ways in which government jobs carrying some status and at least a living wage were obtained have been the subject of quite a bit of investigation. The general conclusion has been that it was a matter of demonstrating a sufficient level of competence and respectability, but mostly of who you knew. If a job candidate had a decent education, was "of good family," was preferably a member of the Church of England, and above all could get the recommendation of influential persons, there was some chance of getting a government job, if a job was available. It could be added that, especially for relatively low-level jobs, being an army or navy veteran was an advantage. It was necessary of course that a veteran had a clean service record and could get the recommendation of his former commanding officer, as ex-Sergeant John McCloskey did when he was appointed a messenger. When it was necessary to replace the York lighthouse keeper, recently died, in 1815, William Allan, then collector of customs, was of the view that the post, which paid only 2d a day, "might be a situation for some old soldier."[51]

Though having the "interest" of a powerful sponsor was undoubtedly a crucial factor in getting an appointment in the Upper Canadian public service, more often than not only the fact of the appointment is known; the shadowy forces which worked behind the scenes to bring it about remain hidden. On the occasions when the names of powerful patrons do surface they are unlikely to cause surprise. When Margaret Powell got the job of housekeeper in the west wing of the government buildings in 1830 her supporters were Archdeacon John Strachan and John Beverley Robinson. John Bostwick became collector of customs at Port Stanley in 1831 on the recommendation of London District oligarch Colonel Mahlon Burwell and Attorney General H.J. Boulton. Charles Rubidge owed his appointment in 1841 as registrar of Peterborough County in part to the fact that John Beverley Robinson's brother, Peter Robinson, legislative councillor and commissioner of Crown Lands, had been Rubidge's patron before Robinson's death in 1838.[52]

No matter how qualified and well-connected an applicant was, a government job was rarely a sure thing, for most jobs of any value attracted a good many candidates and there was always the possibility that someone else, for some reason, had the inside track. When Julia Bell applied to fill the new position of housekeeper to the Assembly in 1836, she faced a rival candidate with apparently superior claims to the job. Sarah Mountjoy came from a distinguished military family. One of her brothers had been lieutenant colonel of the 86th Regiment and another a captain in the 6th Regiment, and she was "near relative" to "the late General Sir Robert Travers." Her husband had been one of those killed in "the fearful casualty" at a meeting in the Toronto market building in 1834 when part of the gallery gave way, impaling spectators on butcher's hooks in the stalls beneath. She was thus a widow and had been left "destitute" with six children. Her petition for employment was supported by Sheriff Jarvis and Archdeacon Strachan and most of the prominent ladies of Toronto, including the wives of Jarvis and Strachan, and of John Beverley Robinson, Christopher Alexander Hagerman, George H. Markland, William Dummer Powell, Grant Powell, Samuel Jarvis, Thomas Mercer Jones, and Dr W.C. Gwynne. But Julia Bell got the job. The Assembly, though then strongly Tory in composition, rejected the establishment candidate in favour of the wife of their messenger, Æneas Bell, and added insult to injury by refusing a subsequent petition from Mrs Mountjoy for financial help to return to Ireland, on the grounds that the use of public funds for such a purpose would set a precedent that would prove "most inconvenient and difficult to resist."[53]

Another lady of military background, Alicia Brenner, attempted to get a government position for her husband Robert on the strength of being the niece of Admiral Sir Ross Donnelly, the sister of Major Francis and Captain John Donnelly, and the fact that "my family are all Tories." Though she described her husband as "a brave active man and a good accountant 5 feet 11 inches high," the Brenners were informed of the lieutenant governor's regret that he had no suitable office to confer upon Robert Brenner. The young Kingston lawyer John A. Macdonald applied in 1841 to be made a judge of Prince Edward County, citing his experience as a barrister "of five years standing," as a director and solicitor for the Commercial Bank of the Midland District, and giving as referees the legal firms of Fairfield and Low of Picton and Cartwright and Kirkpatrick of Kingston. Though Canadian history might have been profoundly altered if Macdonald had been appointed to the bench at the age of twenty-six, the judgeship went to another, and Macdonald had to find alternative ways to make his mark in the world.[54]

Of course Macdonald's disappointing experience was only one among a great many. A not very scientific survey of reasonably plausible petitions for employment submitted to the lieutenant governor's office between 1806 and 1841 (mostly found in the Upper

Canada Sundries Series) yielded a rejection rate of more than two to
one. The lieutenant governor received a steady flow of applications
to fill real or hoped for vacancies and naturally the majority got the
"usual answer," that is they were rejected. This endless stream of
petitions for jobs, and the replies to them by the governor's busy
secretary, which were often delayed quite a bit, can leave the impression of a somewhat *ad hoc* and haphazard process, but there was in
fact a system put in place for keeping track of applicants, the positions they coveted, their referees, and what, if anything, was done for
them. The lieutenant governor's office kept a series of books containing lists of "Candidates for office whose applications are to be taken
into consideration by the Lt. Governor when vacancies occur in any
or in particular situations." These lists varied somewhat in format
but included several classes of applicants from "an old soldier" or
"an old labourer" wanting menial jobs as porters or messengers
or "any situation available," to professional gentlemen seeking such
senior positions as judges, county registrars, clerks of the peace, or
collectors of customs. As might be expected there were inevitably a
good number of names listed as applicants for the various offices
even when the position was not vacant and there was no reason to
think it soon would be. In 1831 there were on file the names of eight
men who wanted to be the clerk of the peace for the Gore District
and five seeking the same job in the Johnstown District. No such
vacancy occurred in Gore until 1841, when none of the eight were
appointed. In Johnstown the 1831 incumbent was still in office in
1849. Obviously being on the official list was no guarantee of an
eventual job. On the other hand not being on any list did not mean
that special consideration could not be given to special people "in
particular situations.[55]

Working for the government, even at the largely unpaid local level,
seems to have conveyed a modicum of prestige on the incumbents,
but only in the permanent posts, obtained through the interest of
influential patrons, were there opportunities to take advantage of the
system. Throughout the Upper Canadian period public servants in
York/Toronto and in the districts regularly sought to improve their
lot by a number of stratagems, by expanding the perquisites of office,
by holding more than one position at a time, by multiplying fees and
in many cases, by staying in office for twenty years or more.

3

Tapping the Public Purse

The number of people directly employed by some level of government was never very large. By contrast, the people employed at one time or another in an arms-length relationship to government, that is, who were employed by private contractors who themselves received funds from the state, could be very numerous indeed. In the 1820s, 30s, and 40s the Rideau and St Lawrence canals were built using imperial and provincial funds. In the same period the Welland Canal was built and then completely rebuilt, at first with government loans to a private company in the amount of £445,000 and then from 1841 as an entirely provincial undertaking. The number of labourers on these projects has been estimated as a maximum of 9,000 on the Rideau and Welland canals combined in the period 1826–32 (5,000 on the Rideau alone) and as 3,000 on the Cornwall section of the St Lawrence Canal in 1834–36. Some 5,000 worked on the second Welland Canal in the early 1840s. If the figures for the 1830s of 3,000 and 9,000 are multiplied by 2s 6d, which seems to have been about the average daily wage for unskilled canal workers at the time, it was costing the imperial or provincial governments at least £375 a day and as much as £1,125 a day during the construction season for canal workers' wages alone, not allowing for the profit margin of contractors and sub-contractors or for the higher wages of skilled workers. Expressed in that way, government levels of employment and expenditure were quite high. For public works the state regularly put large amounts of cash into the provincial economy.[1]

Unfortunately for the labourers on the canals this financial outlay did not translate into a particularly comfortable lifestyle or even full employment of all the prospective workers wanting jobs. The lives of canal workers have been studied in some depth by a number of historians, most thoroughly in William N.T. Wylie's work on the labourers on the Rideau Canal. The title of one of Wylie's articles, "Poverty, Disease and Distress: Labour and the Construction of the Rideau Canal, 1826–32," accurately conveys the gist of his conclusions.

A six day week at the common daily rate of 2s 6d works out to £3-5-0 a month, or, assuming for the moment an unlikely state of year-round full employment, to £39 a year, a sum almost twice the £20 a year which was doled out by the provincial government to military widows and disabled veterans (see chapter 4). It would seem then to have been possible for a worker who was both frugal and lucky to support himself and a family on 2s 6d a day and perhaps even to accumulate some savings. Wylie points out however that the workers had to provide their own shelter and provisions, and when working away from urban centres were dependent on supplies brought in by the contractors and sold at high prices in the company stores. According to surviving contractors' records many men were continually in debt to their employers. Conditions in the camps were primitive and unsanitary and the work itself was back-breaking and dangerous. Men were injured or even killed by blasting accidents or other mishaps. The hours were long; fourteen to sixteen hours a day in good weather. The terrain could be difficult, consisting, as it did on the Rideau, of dense forest, rocks, and swamps. Serious disease, known at the time as ague or swamp fever but actually a form of malaria, periodically broke out on a wide scale, affecting both the workers and their families. Sick workers who could not work did not get paid. They were also not paid when some job sites shut down altogether in winter. Yet despite the conditions faced by the labourers there were usually more men wanting work on the canals than there were jobs. The work may have been far from pleasant and not very well paid, but, especially in a period of high immigration and competition for work, a job was a job.[2]

Before the railway era in Upper Canada, no other projects required such large numbers of workers as did the canals, but there were some other government works carried out by contractors that periodically provided employment for many Upper Canadians. Lighthouses and registry offices had to be built. Gaols and courthouses were built and rebuilt in the district towns, reflecting population growth and increased affluence, as were the parliament buildings themselves after being burnt by the Americans in 1813 and by accident in 1824.

The government spent £10,000, partly for labour, on the new buildings completed in 1832.[3]

A government activity which provided much more consistent employment was surveying. Surveys began in Upper Canada with the arrival of the Loyalists in the early 1780s and went steadily on through the whole Upper Canadian period and far beyond. The deputy surveyors who were in charge of the actual work were required to keep diaries, field notes, and accounts, so there is a fair amount of surviving evidence of their work. Taking a couple of years at random, surveying was going on in twenty-six townships in 1816 and in twenty-eight townships in 1832. In some cases there were as many as five surveyors working in a single township in a single year. A survey crew appears to have been composed of about six to ten men, working as chain bearers, axe men, and flag men, though other men could be hired on a part-time basis as needed. An early account of deputy surveyor Augustus Jones at work in 1791 "surveying the course of the Lake and running the front lines of eleven townships ... from the Mouth of the River Trent to Toronto," names a crew consisting of Stephen Wardell and Henry Johnson, chain bearers; David Beaty, James Everson, Billy (a Delaware), and Henry Heartley, axe men; and Burgoyne Camp, flag man, all of whom had worked for seventy-nine days, plus William Abbott, duties not specified, who had worked for forty-three days.[4]

There were probably about 200 to 300 men working on survey crews in the province at any one time. They were paid somewhat more by the surveyors than ordinary unskilled labourers for work which was only marginally less arduous than that of canal workers: running straight lines through dense bush, often in rough terrain or in swampy areas, in all weathers. The surveyors themselves, who enjoyed some status as professional men, were paid much more handsomely, a salary of four shillings a day, plus up to 8s 9d a day when on "actual service." Beginning in 1818 the government found a way to reduce the survey costs by having the surveys done by survey contractors, who were paid in land rather than in cash, at the rate of 4.5 per cent of the land surveyed. The contractors, who were not necessarily surveyors themselves, still had to hire and pay the survey crews, while their own remuneration was postponed until the land could be developed or sold.[5]

Another long-running government-sponsored activity which also provided chances for employment was the building of major roads.

Projects to construct main roads built by paid labour were undertaken throughout the Upper Canadian period, as were some for toll
roads, in addition to the ongoing work of unpaid statute labourers
on the local roads. In 1799, Peter Russell, administrator of the province
in the absence of the lieutenant governor, told members of the House
of Assembly and Legislative Council that "arrangements have ...
lately been made" to open a road from York "to the eastern settlements," in part so that the provincial parliament could meet in winter, and so that "produce can be carried to market" and "laws for the
due administration of justice enforced." These arrangements had
been made with Asa Danforth, an American entrepreneur of mixed
reputation, who had agreed to build a road "33 feet wide with the
centre 16 1/2 feet wide made smooth and even and with bridges and
causeways 16 1/2 feet wide and high enough to prevent their being
damaged by water," from York to the Trent river, where it would
connect with existing roads. The executive government agreed to pay
Danforth the bargain price of $22.50 for each acre the road should
contain. Danforth employed at least forty men, at unknown wages,
but in order to attract good men and "encourage them to use their
utmost exertions" they were to each get grants of 200 acres from the
province. (Apparently Danforth intended to buy the rights to his
workers' grants for small sums.)[6]

To pay Danforth the Executive Council raised money by selling
the land in Dereham and Norwich townships in blocks of 3,000
acres to speculators at an average price of nine pence an acre. By
1804 the provincial legislature was also convinced of the necessity
of spending public money on main roads on the grounds that some
of them passed through "lands in the occupation of Indians or
aboriginal natives who are not in the habit of performing Statute
Labour on the roads," or where the inhabitants were "so few as not
to be able by their statute labour to keep the said roads in repair."
Commissioners of public highways were appointed, at least two to
a district, responsible for disbursing funds, usually to local contractors. The commissioners were invariably district notables, often
magistrates, and for this work they received no compensation, not
even for out-of-pocket expenses. The initial appropriation voted for
roads by the legislature in 1804 was £1,000. The provincial road
grant thereafter increased steadily, reaching £20,000 by 1815.
Between 1836 and 1840 over £100,000 was granted for roads. In
1838, for labour alone, the sum of £2,184-2-4 was spent on the West

Toronto Road and £9,565-6-2 1/2 on the Queenston and Grimsby Road. When toll roads began to be built in Upper Canada by private boards of trustees or commissioners appointed under provincial legislation, the minimum cost of building a plank road (which wore out quickly and had to be replanked) was found to be £1,050 per mile, and of the superior macadamized roads, £3,710 per mile.[7]

A fairly detailed report on the West Gwillimbury Toll Road, built under a provincial act of 1836 between October 1836 and August 1837, provides a bit of information about some of the people who were hired to work on such projects and the conditions under which they were employed. The size of the road crew fluctuated a great deal from month to month and even from day to day. In the busiest recorded month, June 1837, about fifty people were employed overall, but the numbers in other months went as low as thirty. Labourers seem to have been hired and laid off according to the amount of work to be done, and of course some workers would have left the job for their own reasons. No work was done by anyone in December, January, and February. No one except the superintendent worked full-time. The amount of time worked by individuals varied from two days to twenty-three and a quarter days a month, underlining the point that income often depended as much on how steadily a worker was employed as on the level of the wage. The employment records of Henry Huff and Thomas Declair, who worked more often than some others, illustrate the intermittent nature of the work. Huff worked twenty and a half days in October and November, five and a half days in March, six days in April, and nine and three-quarter days in July, but not at all in May, June, and August. Declair did not begin working on the road until the Spring of 1837 but then worked three days in March, nineteen days in April, ten and a half days in May, twenty days in June, nineteen and a half days in July, and four and three-quarter days in August.

Three different cooks, all women, worked at various times on the site. Two boys were employed part of the time, presumably to carry water, fetch tools, and to do other small tasks. The majority of the work force were adult males of whom all were labourers except for three carpenters, who would have built temporary accommodation for the men who did not live nearby and supervised the construction of wooden bridges and box drains. Wage rates were not consistent. Some of the men for whom room and board was provided were paid 2s 6d a day but others got a lower wage of 2s 3 3/4d. Local men

"who board themselves," making up about a third of an otherwise
transient work force, were paid from 3s 9d to 4s 6d a day. Two of
the three carpenters received 5s a day, the other 3s 9d. One of the
two boys came as a package deal with his father, Nathan Pegg, and
a team of oxen, who altogether worked for 10s a day. Young Master
Pegg's labour must have been thought to have been worth something
for other men with ox teams were paid only 7s 6d a day. The other
boy, Peter Higgins, was paid 9 3/4d a day. Peter Higgins was likely
the son of one of the cooks, Mary Ann Higgins, because they appear
in the records at the same time. Mary Ann Higgins, who was the
cook during most of the course of the work, was paid 1s 5d a day,
but Susannah Higgins (her sister?) who succeeded her in June 1837,
received only 8d a day. "Mrs. Hails," who cooked briefly in the
autumn of 1836 was paid 10d a day.

There is no way of knowing why some members of the work force
were paid more than others. These decisions must have been made
by the superintendent of the works, Richard Titus Willson. Were
married men and women paid more than single workers? The commissioners provided some tools so perhaps men who supplied their
own got a higher wage. Or perhaps Willson simply thought that
some workers, like Jack in the nursery rhyme, "shall have but a
penny a day because he can't work any faster." Willson himself was
paid 7s 9d a day, three times the highest labourer's wage, plus an
extra 5s a day for the use of his team of oxen. Willson even charged
for working on Sundays, thus maximizing his earnings.

The construction of the West Gwillimbury Road did not pump
huge amounts of money into the local economy. The total cost over
eight months in round figures was £1,041, of which £377-5-2, or
roughly £47 per month, was spent on wages. Still, while it lasted, the
project would have put some scarce cash into local pockets, particularly those belonging to workers living close enough to the site to
commute to the job.[8]

The West Gwillimbury Road was one small example of a developing trend at the end of the Upper Canadian period: the shifting of
part of the steadily increasing cost of the roads to provincially char-
tered private road companies. The provincial government had found
another way to save money. The West Gwillimbury road commissioners had been advanced £,1000 from the receiver general to build
the road but by February 1839 they had already paid back £101-16-2
and were now entirely responsible for the upkeep of the road. Like

the trustees of the West Gwillimbury Road, other private road companies promised improved roads for "moderate" tolls. Toll roads however were never popular, for besides not being free they were often poorly maintained by trustees reluctant to increase their costs by spending money on them. Despite this they became common throughout the province and persisted well into the twentieth century. The West Gwillimbury company, besides being one example of the privatization of public works in Upper Canada is also one more example of how the patronage system operated at the local level. The board of trustees was chaired by William Laughton, a well-known area businessman, steamboat owner, magistrate, and Anglican. The man chosen to supervise the work, Richard Willson, was a nephew of David Willson, the founder of the unique religious sect known as the Children of Peace, and briefly belonged to that group, but he had swiftly rejected David Willson's doctrines and his reformist political views. He "went into the public works" and became a "local paragon of Tory patronage."[9]

There were many other ways to make money from government in Upper Canada without picking up a pick and shovel, or even a pen. It has been noted in the case of the West Gwillimbury Road that only about 36 per cent of the expenditure went to wages; the rest was spent on various types of equipment, supplies, and building materials. A contemporary report on the West Toronto Road for the year 1838 gives a breakdown of major costs as:

Labourers' wages   £2,184-12-4
Other costs:
Stone breaking   £1,807-19-7
Carting   £1,798-15-10
Stone bought   £1,626-17-3
Teaming   £95-16-4
Total   £5,329-9-10[10]

The main reason why road building was expensive then was not the allegedly high cost of labour but the actual high cost of buying, crushing, and transporting stone. Michael Cross, looking into the building of the first macadamized York road, found that the contractors originally greatly underestimated the cost of providing the large quantities of crushed stone needed to make a decent road because their projections had been based on British precedents. Canadian stone turned out to be much harder than British stone and therefore much more difficult and expensive to break down. As well, owners of local quarry sites raised their prices well above expected levels leaving the option of expensive local stone or cheaper distant stone which came with very high transportation costs. The general point however is that road building, like many other government activities, involved payment to suppliers and others far beyond the outlay on wages to labourers alone.[11]

The actual number of Upper Canadians who made money by providing goods and services to the government was probably not very high but the ways in which such goods and services were provided were nearly innumerable. Any attempt to list them all, or even categorize them, is well nigh impossible, so that relatively few examples must illustrate the range of opportunities that existed. Farmers and others who provided stone for the construction of roads and public buildings were selling something they had little or no use for, and it came free with the land. The same could be said for trees. In the land-clearing process many trees were simply wasted, but wood had value, as potash, as lumber, and most universally, as fuel. The government periodically needed lumber for construction and sometimes bought finished products such as office furniture. It always needed firewood.

Government buildings and offices in the capital and in the districts, like all living and working spaces in Upper Canada, had an insatiable need for heat during much of the year. The largest government complex which had to be heated was the new parliament and offices completed in 1832. The buildings occupied an entire long block, bounded by the present Front, John, Wellington, and Simcoe streets. The centre block alone, which contained the two legislative chambers, measured 133 by 90 feet. Nineteenth-century photographs show all the rooms having very high ceilings, in the case of the two chambers about 20 feet. By the 1830s the legislature met for about four months of the year, always in the coldest months, and the members in such spacious surroundings would have required an immense amount of firewood to keep them in some degree of comfort. The 1836 "contingent expenses of the public offices," not including the centre block, has an entry of £190-4-8 for firewood. Supposing that the government paid a modest Toronto price of ten shillings a cord, that sum would have bought 380 cords of wood. Unfortunately the account does not identify the dealer who then had the provincial government contract, but the names of some other large and small government suppliers are known. James Robinson, a Kingston for-warder, had a contract in 1815 with the British commissariat in Upper Canada to supply 3,000 cords of firewood, which Robinson must have first bought from a number of local hewers of wood. At a common price of five shillings a cord it would have fetched £750. James Irvine delivered twenty-three cords of firewood and Simeon Washburn sixty cords to heat the Prince Edward County courthouse and gaol in 1838, for five shillings a cord. A man identified only as W. Brown was paid £5-3-9 for firewood delivered to the Eastern District gaol the same year. If he was also paid five shillings a cord, he provided twenty and three quarter cords.[12]

Such bulky raw materials as stone and wood were only the most obvious commodities bought by all levels of government. The "disbursements" of the Provincial Penitentiary in 1837–38 included payment for straw, lath, coal, bread, horsehair (for mortar), hay, candles, leather, lumber, bricks, gunpowder, and milk. On the list of the provincial government's 1836–37 purchases for the public offices in Toronto were, besides firewood, such items as brooms, earthenware, towelling, furniture, and a door lock. Services as well as goods were routinely required. In 1806 the Legislative Council employed, among others, William Smith to make repairs to the council chamber and office, Sarah Hay to "scour" the premises, Philip Clinger to clean the stoves and to make two "holdfasts" to secure the stove pipes, and Elinor Basset to wash and hem the council's towels. At the penitentiary in 1837–38 William Rice dug four graves at five shillings a grave. The penitentiary also opened up a number of other opportunities for local tradespeople and suppliers, including women. Most of the women who submitted some of the 308 vouchers for goods and services supplied in "the year ending October 31, 1837" had made woollen socks for the prisoners, with Ellen McGarvey leading the list with three batches for which she was paid £6-5-8, but Eliza Thomson, widow of Hugh C. Thomson MHA submitted two vouchers totalling £7-17-0 for printing; Mrs A. Macaulay (presumably the widowed mother of Hon. John Macaulay) was paid £18-15-0 for a horse; and a Mrs Hunter supplied lumber at £3-17-0. Some of the "contingent expenses of the public offices" in Toronto for 1836–37 were accounted for by payments to James Barthe, sawyer; John Harper and James Myers, carpenters; William Hutchinson, mason; Thomas Wallis, cabinetmaker; William Musson, tinsmith; Joseph Powell, labourer; and John Craig, painter.[13]

As a recipient of government funds the last name on this list merits a brief digression, for John Craig was a somewhat unlikely further example of official preferment. Craig was not simply a journeyman painter, though he had to take on routine jobs such as painting houses and the not so routine task of putting a coat of paint on the gallows in preparation for a double hanging in 1828. He was also a portrait and heraldic painter and an interior decorator who did marbling and graining of wood and plaster as well as gilding and glass staining. Such exotic skills cannot have been in high demand in the 1820s and 1830s; nonetheless John Craig, a Tory in politics who served as a Toronto councilman, 1834–49, became a sort of official artist to the establishment. In the list of disbursements of 1836–37 just cited Craig was paid only £5-18-8 for unspecified work but some of his commissions were much more lucrative. In 1832 he provided a new depiction of the royal arms to hang above the bench in the Home District courthouse, for which he was paid £120-15-0, and created the stained glass windows for St James church (later cathedral), the locale of the Family Compact at prayer, for a tidy £500.[14]

The district governments were also frequent employers of the skilled and the unskilled. In 1838 the treasurer of the Prince Edward District made payments to J.W. Martin, tinsmith; B. Franklin, blacksmith; and Thomas Gill, a mason. The previous year London District payments went to F.R. Carey for the burial expenses of "Isaac Tuck, found dead," to J.W. Powell for making a coffin for (the same?) "person found dead," to W. Wheeler for lining and cleaning the courthouse stove and stove pipes, to S.H. Park for taking "Thomas Duncan, a cripple to Buffalo," and to John Barclay for the maintenance (presumably for a year, since he was paid £25) of "Janet McBean, insane and destitute." Another local source of supplementary income, for rural people who were reasonably handy with a gun or a trap, was the wolf bounty, under which the district governments paid £1-10-0 per wolf scalp. In 1837 twenty-two wolves were killed in the Eastern District in the month of January alone. A somewhat contentious method of getting a nice little sum from government was as an informant. One common scheme was "telling on" people who sold liquor without a license. The fine was £20, half of which went to "the complainer." Government establishments, at all levels, could be good for business or reward among local suppliers, artisans, and ordinary citizens.[15]

Getting money from the government was not always a matter of payment for the periodic provision of goods and services. Money could be claimed, and eventually paid, in compensation for a wide range of activities of the government itself which inflicted losses on its citizens. Among cases of this kind, claims for losses to property as a result of military action were by far the most numerous, and arose from two main events, the War of 1812, and, to a much lesser extent, the Rebellion of 1837. The settlement of 1812–14 civilian losses claims is a subject which has already received quite a bit of attention from historians and in any case the sheer volume of the claims makes it impossible to discuss them here in any comprehensive way. In fact though, the losses claims contain an extraordinary amount of information which has not been much utilized by scholars and which sheds a good deal of light on the lives and conditions of Upper Canadians of the time. Some claims, like that of Elizabeth Campbell of Niagara, widow of Major William Campbell, for £778-13-0, reflect a pre-war life of some affluence. The Campbell property had been totally destroyed by fire and plundering American soldiers, but Mrs Campbell had impressive powers of recall. She was able to submit a very detailed list of former possessions that had been in the house and outbuildings, ranging from livestock – three horses, a cow, and a calf – to a large number of household items such as ten teaspoons, four salt spoons and a mustard ladle, two silver cups, ten wine glasses, and "a handsome fowling piece." Other claims suggest more modest circumstances and, especially from areas other than the devastated Niagara District, lesser losses. Another widow, Elizabeth Morden of Flamboro East Township, submitted a claim for £71-0-0 for damage inflicted by "friendly" dragoons, who had killed her hogs, raided her bee hives and apple orchard, and used her house and stable very roughly while on her premises. Some claims, such as those of two other widows, Mary Donovan of Malden and Debora Wilson of Niagara Falls, were rejected outright: in Donovan's case because the property, damaged "by our own Indians," was actually in the United States, and in Wilson's case because she was judged to be of a "character disloyal and infamous."

Most other war losses claims eventually were paid, but what all successful claimants had in common was that their claims were routinely discounted, by at least one-third, and they all had to wait a very long time for any compensation at all. Some members of the provincial executive, including Lieutenant Governor Gore, John

Strachan, and John Beverley Robinson, took the view that the majority of claims were greatly exaggerated and that the battlefield areas had actually prospered during the war from British expenditures and were rapidly recovering. As a result even people whose entire livelihood had been wiped out by the war had no choice but to try to rebuild their lives without timely government help. Part of the problem was that an extended wrangle was carried on as to whether compensation was a colonial or an imperial obligation and where the funds were to come from. The bulk of the claims were finally settled only in 1837, just in time for the submission of a second round of claims for rebellion losses. Most of these new claims were dealt with more promptly, though some legitimate claims were still outstanding as late as 1848.[16]

The reluctance of a sceptical government to pay some or any compensation was not restricted to times of war or insurrection. Many Upper Canadians who alleged that they had suffered loss because of something done to them by the state or while acting on behalf of the state faced obfuscation, suspicion, delay, and sometimes financial ruin. One such claimant, prominent enough in his day to now have an entry in the *Dictionary of Canadian Biography*, was James Gordon Strobridge (or Strowbridge). Strobridge, an American engineer, was the contractor hired to build an important public work, the Burlington Bay Canal, which gave the then-struggling town of Hamilton its harbour and an economic shot in the arm. The canal was built as a provincial government project overseen by three appointed commissioners. Strobridge directed the work on the canal from 1824 to 1827 but went badly over budget, he claimed unavoidably, because the severity of the winds, waves, and currents in Lake Ontario created construction difficulties which "could not be certainly foreseen." (His problems were not unusual. At the same time Colonel John By was running up unexpected bills on a much vaster scale in building the Rideau Canal.) Though his work was universally described as having been of first-rate calibre, Strobridge was fired by the commissioners in 1827 and paid nothing for the work he had completed until 1831, when after two acts of the legislature and the intervention of the lieutenant governor he finally received an arbitrator's award of £5,356. Meanwhile Strobridge had been sued by his creditors and put into debtor's prison in 1829. During this period Strobridge developed anti-government sympathies and became closely associated with the radical Irish journalist, Francis

Collins. Be that as it may, the money received from government was not enough to pay all his debts and he was back in debtor's prison in 1833. While in prison he caught fever and two days after his release he died, aged forty-five, leaving a wife and eight children, but before he died he had asked for more. He petitioned the legislature for interest on the payment made to him during the years he had waited for it, amounting, he calculated, to £548-17-11 1/2. His widow, Nancy Strobridge, continued to submit similar petitions annually until 1839. A bill giving her the money passed the House of Assembly in 1837, but the Legislative Council would not agree. No further payment was ever made. Whether Strobridge's troubles really resulted from unpredictable and unavoidable engineering difficulties or from his own mismanagement, the result was the same: penury and prison, and little sympathy for Strobridge or his family.[17]

Widows, especially widows with dependent families, were a particularly vulnerable and all too numerous group in Upper Canada, and Nancy Strobridge was not the only widow to try to help her situation by appealing for some recompense for the past services, or mistakes, of her husband. Not all such compensation cases ended unsatisfactorily. The widow of Hugh C. Thomson MHA based her claim on her late husband's lengthy and meritorious services in the Assembly, particularly for his prominent role in getting the penitentiary established in Kingston and overseeing its construction. Elizabeth Thomson twice petitioned the lieutenant governor, unsuccessfully, and in three successive years, the legislature. In her case her persistence was to a degree actually rewarded: she was voted a lump sum payment of £100. On the other hand, Eliza Powell, who petitioned the lieutenant governor in 1839 for some payment in recognition of the services to the province of her late husband, Grant Powell, who had been clerk in turn of the Assembly and the Legislative Council, and for the services of her late father-in-law, Chief Justice William Dummer Powell, received nothing at all. Neither did Mary Ridout, the widow of Thomas Ridout, who at the time of his death had been a legislative councillor and a public servant, notably as surveyor-general, for thirty-seven years. Her petition to the legislature was read in the Assembly on 6 February 1840, but nothing had been done for her when the Upper Canadian parliament was dissolved, forever, four days later.[18]

The widow of another public servant, Mary Savage, also petitioned the legislature, in 1836, for compensation for "the arduous duties" performed by George Savage as collector of customs for the port of Toronto. Savage had died owing the government £313-2-10, leaving Mrs Savage in serious financial trouble. A select committee of the House reported in favour of a grant of £200 to be applied to the debt, but a motion to advance her case by referring the matter to the committee on supply was defeated by 24 to 18. Maria Garrison, a widow with a family "in great need," petitioned in 1835 for a refund of the £9-10-0 her husband had paid as a first instalment on a Crown lot he had bought fifteen years earlier and from which she had "derived no benefit." Somewhat surprisingly she got the money back. In 1816 Elizabeth Wright was equally successful in claiming payment for militia clothing made during the War by her late husband Charles, a tailor. By a special act of the legislature she received £155-7-3 3/4.[19]

Widow Elizabeth Baker of Kingston was evicted in 1820 from the house her husband, Lieutenant William Baker, had been allowed to build on the military reserve at Point Frederick, the naval establishment having decided it needed the land for other purposes. Though Mrs Baker had no legal title to the property she had lived in it unmolested for twenty-nine years. She was given a town lot in Kingston and apparently some money to build a new house, for Lieutenant Governor Maitland was informed by Governor General Lord Dalhousie's military secretary that she was to have "proper compensation."[20]

Two cases of alleged smuggling in which widows became embroiled with the customs department had somewhat different outcomes. Thomas Turner Orton of Port Hope had merchandise seized and was charged with an "illicit fraud on the revenue." According to his widow Jane's 1837 petition, this accusation, of which of course she believed he was innocent, "made such an impression on a mind of sensibility as to occasion the affliction that terminated in his death." Her plea that she was "alone in the world without a protector and with very slender means of subsistence" got a favourable hearing and the seized goods were eventually restored to her. Eveline Trull was not quite so fortunate. Her husband, Jesse Trull of Whitby, owner of the schooner *Prosperity*, had drowned in 1837 leaving her with four daughters aged twelve and under. She continued to operate the schooner, which was not fully paid for, but the ship and its cargo were seized in 1838 for smuggling while under the command of a C. Trull, probably her brother-in-law. Eveline Trull petitioned the lieutenant governor to have the vessel, her only source of income, restored to her but the Executive Council recommended against her in 1839. They did make a partial concession, the restoration of thirty-six barrels of salt and one barrel of dyestuff "not liable to condemnation."[21]

Elizabeth Derenzy was not a widow, but in petitioning the lieutenant governor in August 1813 she could have cited her recently dead father's distinguished services, for she was the daughter of Prideaux Selby, executive councillor and receiver general of Upper Canada. She could also have mentioned that it was she who had suggested the formation of the Loyal and Patriotic Society of Upper Canada to assist war sufferers. Instead her claim for compensation was based on her own meritorious actions during the American occupation of York in April of that year. Mrs Derenzy was the wife of Captain William Derenzy of the 41st Regiment, then serving in Upper Canada, and at the time was caring for her fatally ill father in his house in York (Selby died two weeks after the Americans arrived). Also at the time, all of the province's funds, then amounting, as noted at the beginning of chapter two, to a little over £3000, were being kept in the receiver general's private home in two iron chests, a large one containing bills and a small one containing public money in coins, plus office papers, warrants, and Selby's private papers and savings. On 26 April while Selby lay "insensible" a meeting was held in the house involving Chief Justice Scott; Judge William Dummer Powell; Stephen Heward, the receiver general's clerk; and Elizabeth Derenzy, who undertook "at personal risk" to have the large chest hidden "in the woods." Powell had the small chest sent to the home of Donald McLean, clerk of the Assembly against the advice of Mrs Derenzy, who believed there was "a person of bad character" living there. In the event the money in the large chest was later surrendered on demand to the Americans and Elizabeth Derenzy was proven right about the safety of McLean's house. The small chest was broken open and the money stolen. Since she had impeccable witnesses to support her claim, it received prompt attention from the Executive Council. She was awarded £150 to replace the personal funds in the chest, £10 for the chest itself and an exceptional, if modest, reward of £12-10-0. As Selby's executrix she later submitted a separate war losses claim of £49-5-0 for damage to fences and crops on the receiver general's property but this time, like most other such claimants, she was allowed much less, about one-quarter of her estimated loss.[22]

Some compensation claims which seem on the face of things to have been entirely legitimate were nonetheless rejected or sidetracked by the bureaucracy. A horse belonging to Isaac Vrooman of Niagara which had been hired by the 6th Regiment during the War of 1812 died in harness while "in the service of government." Though the quartermaster-sergeant of the regiment certified that "the said horse was at the time in good working condition," Vrooman's claim was ruled "inadmissible" and he lost a horse worth about £16 because there was "no proof of the death being occasioned by any casualty of the service." Three residents of the village of Springfield on the Credit River, Ira VanValkenburgh, Eliza Blair, and John Carey, also had an apparently reasonable claim arising out of the building of the West Toronto road past their properties in 1839. Their houses were on a hill which was cut down by the workmen to level the road. When the cut through the hill was finished they found themselves sitting nine to eleven feet above the road, the approach to the road cut off and their location now worthless "for sale, rent or business." They were informed that the government was powerless to help them, and they must hire a lawyer and "seek redress" in court. Whether they eventually got some satisfaction is not known. If they did it would have been at their own expense and no doubt after considerable delay.[23]

It is interesting, if not surprising, to find that the reluctance of the provincial and imperial governments to acknowledge alleged obligations to the citizens of the province was reflected at the civic level. When York became the first town in Upper Canada to be made a city it was given powers of taxation and borrowing well beyond the level allowed to any other municipality, yet the early minutes of the new City of Toronto record the familiar ambivalent response to requests for compensation. A petition of 1837 concerned another horse, this one belonging to George Mumms, which while hauling water to the fire engine during a "calamitous fire in King Street" was "unavoidably" forced by the crowd into the flames and so badly burned that it was afterwards unfit for work. Mumms put its value at £17. A motion to pay Mumms £10 was amended to read £7-10-0. The amendment was defeated, 7 to 6, the original motion by 9 to 3, so Mumms was left with nothing but a useless horse.

Another petition arising out of fire damage was submitted in 1839 by Arthur McMahon and Matthew Sweetman. Their houses, worth they believed £300 and £250 respectively, had been destroyed by "an incendiary" who had been apprehended and had confessed to the crime. McMahon and Sweetman, having "been brought to the brink of ruin," argued that "in all well ordered communities, the losses occasioned by the medium of a wicked incendiary is generally sustained by the public." The council "deeply sympathized with the petitioners" but regretted that "the present state" of the city's finances did not allow them to be of much help. They were given a token £12-10-0 each. James Thomas, an innkeeper, seemed to have a sounder legal case for compensation, but his petition was even less successful. During still another King Street fire in June 1840 the firemen decided it was necessary to pull his building down, resulting in a loss, he said, of £39-3-3. His claim never reached the full council, being rejected, for reasons not stated in the minutes, at the committee level.

Still, at least one petitioner was able to get compensation from the city, even though he had no documentary proof of his claim. During the Rebellion of 1837 William Copeland, a Toronto brewer, had supplied beer which he said was worth £60-19-0 to the militiamen guarding the city, though without the formal approval of the city council. Mayor John Powell was prepared to testify that "the beer allowance was considered necessary at the time as an inducement to persons to enlist in the defence of the city and at a time when the public tumult was such as to render it difficult if not impossible to get a council together." The city's debt of honour was paid in full, by a vote of 11 to 4.[24]

A final indirect method of exploiting the opportunities available from the provincial and local governments for potential profit was by being licensed to perform a particular public function. Licences were issued for several activities, including hawking and peddling, but the main ones were for operating ferries, and for the sale of alcohol. In such cases no benefit to licence holders came directly from government funds; on the contrary licences meant an initial outlay by way of a fee or bond, in the hope of ultimate profit.

Travel in Upper Canada frequently involved water crossings, which meant taking a ferry across rivers or to islands in the lakes where bridges had yet to be, and in some cases would never be, built. The government provided for ferries as required by entering into contracts with individuals to build and maintain docks and "a flat or scow," or by having a ferry built which was then leased to a reliable operator. The fees which the public was charged for using the ferries,

and which governed the operator's earnings, were not set by the
owner or lessee of the ferry but by the magistrates, and in the public
interest, if not in the interest of the operator, were sometimes actually
lowered as traffic increased. Nonetheless the returns from running a
ferry, at least at busy crossings, were high enough to provoke competition for a ferry lease, as was true of the impending expiration of
the Fort Erie ferry lease in 1836, and incumbent lease holders invariably began petitioning for the renewal of the lease well before the
actual expiration date. Like most other dealings with government,
getting a ferry licence had its complications and began with a petition to the Executive Council. The successful applicant was chosen
by the council but should "the magistrates decide otherwise" local
approval was also necessary. The terms of the lease dictated by the
council varied at times and in individual cases. In 1823 the Wolfe
Island ferry lease was renewed for a period of seven years, while in
1837 the renewal of the Fort Erie lease was for only three. The rent
which the ferry operator paid to the government appears to have
been relatively modest. John Davis, the lessee of the Wolfe Island
ferry, died a somewhat ironic death by drowning in the St Lawrence
in 1821. His widow Mary Davis, who had assumed the operation of
the ferry, was allowed to renew the lease in 1827 for an up-front
payment of £1-12-6 plus an annual fee of only 12s 6d.[25]

Getting a tavern licence in Upper Canada also involved two levels
of bureaucracy and, of course, also an initial outlay of funds. Applicants, about 4 per cent of whom were women, had to appear at
quarter sessions to demonstrate that they were of good character and
had suitable accommodation. They had to report on their records, if
any, as previous licence holders and present a recommendation of
fitness signed by a magistrate. Most cases got quite perfunctory treatment. At a single sitting in 1832 the Home District magistrates
approved 140 applications. Successful applicants had to give "certain security," that is they had to post a bond for good behaviour for
a sum decided upon by the magistrates. The magistrates then issued
a certificate entitling the bearer to take out a licence, to be obtained
from the district inspector of licences. For a long time a tavern licence
cost a flat £3 a year but by the late 1830s a sliding scale was introduced, which, depending on location, could cost an innkeeper in the
larger urban centres up to £10. In much the same way however that
holders of location tickets for land grants treated them as legitimate
deeds, some tavern keepers simply avoided the additional paperwork

and expense and did not bother to take out the actual licence. In the Home, Midland, and Gore districts in 1838, 554 certificates were issued but only 443 innkeepers took out their licences.[26]

Whether being an innkeeper was a profitable business to be in is a question almost impossible to answer – sometimes it was and sometimes it wasn't, depending on many factors, such as location, extent of competition, the personality of the proprietor, and the state of the premises. Some inns operated for many years and were substantial businesses. Blanche Westlake, who with the help of her brother-in-law John Hoare opened the first and for a long time the only inn in Adelaide Township in 1832, built a small empire which included her Royal Adelaide Inn, stables, a blacksmith shop, and adjacent farms.[27] On the other hand, though the total number of licensed premises in the province steadily increased, their number in proportion to population, after peaking in 1820 began a general decline (see chapter 6, tables 6.4 and 6.5.) As well there was constant fluctuation in the number of licensed inns from year to year in all the districts, so all of them were not consistently successful. One of the principal problems of the trade was unpaid bills. In 1829, "Catharine Campbell and other innkeepers of the Eastern District," petitioned the legislature for a bill to be passed giving them the legal power to collect bills of up to £2 "from individuals calling upon them, who at the time may not have wherewith to discharge their bills." Another hazard innkeepers faced was illegal competition. Selling liquor without a licence was a common crime in Upper Canada, punishable by a fine of £20 (see chapter 6), but the competition came not only from liquor obtained in private or "disorderly" houses but also from legitimate shopkeepers who were themselves licensed to sell "wine, brandy, rum and other spirituous liquors by retail" but only "in quantities of not less than one quart ... to be drank out of his house." According to the innkeepers of the Eastern District shopkeepers were "allowing liquor to be drank in their shops" which was not only illegal and unfair but caused "the intrusion and frequent annoyance" in their inns "of disreputable persons, who get intoxicated in stores and other places of common resort – which often interferes with the quiet and comfort of respectable travellers." No doubt such occurrences happened but it is a bit hard to believe that all the intoxicated guests in inns were already in that condition when they arrived.[28]

As for the shopkeepers themselves, whether honest or dishonest it is even more difficult to judge whether a liquor licence, costing originally £3 and by 1836, £5, was a profitable investment as a side-line to their regular stock of goods. The statistical pattern of shop-keeping closely parallels the situation of the innkeepers: many small fluctuations over time and within districts in the number of shops, an increasing overall number of shops until 1832, followed correspondently by dropping numbers, and a decline in the number of shops in proportion to population. More rigorous vetting of applicants for both inn and shop licences in the 1830s (a rare case of a document which lists successful and unsuccessful applications for tavern licenses in the Johnstown District in 1834 records a failure rate of 26 per cent) and possibly even the appearance of an incipient temperance movement may have exerted a dampening effect on the liquor trade as a whole. When the first Temperance Society in Upper Canada appeared in Bastard Township in 1828 the number of taverns there dropped from eight to three by 1834, though there is no reason to suppose that such dramatic changes occurred on a wide scale.[29]

The ways in which the people of Upper Canada were able to extract sums of money, large and small, from the state were almost literally countless and involved many different types of people, skilled and unskilled, often self-employed. For many of the opportunities provided by the government no great qualifications were required, but even when the state was disbursing what amounted to little more than petty cash, like the sale to the penitentiary of Mrs Macaulay's horse, it was probably an advantage to know someone in authority.

4

Pensions and Pensioners

A select group of Upper Canadians received money from the provincial treasury on a regular basis, not as employees, or for goods or casual labour, or as compensation, but for services rendered in the past. Not many Upper Canadians ever received a pension from the provincial government; at most the number of men or women on the pension list probably never exceeded three or four hundred. Ordinarily pensions were very much a matter of "grace," awarded in extraordinary circumstances, mostly to people who had held high office, or to the dependents of such people after death. Such pensions however could be for very handsome amounts and were both a strain on the provincial treasury and a source of complaint from critics of the administration. Chief justices, who enjoyed the highest income of all Upper Canadian public servants, were also the most favoured pensioners. William Dummer Powell was allowed to retire in 1825 on a pension of £1,000 Sterling "on account of his long and faithful service," and his successor, Sir William Campbell, received £1,200. Sir David William Smith, first surveyor general of Upper Canada, received a pension of £200 at the early age of forty (he lived for another thirty-three years). He left the province for England in 1802, never to return. On the other hand, John McGill, executive councillor, legislative councillor, and receiver general, was permitted to retire only when he reached the age of seventy, but on a pension of £450. Still it was better for a public officer to be alive than dead when pressuring the provincial government for a reward for past services. The widow of Major General Æneas Shaw began petitioning the government five weeks after her husband's death in 1814 for a pension in recognition of his long military and government services – "until within a few days of his death" – and the fact that "he had no private fortune." The family ultimately was given a comparatively modest yearly pension of £100. By the end of the Upper Canadian period pension payments to former senior officials were generally on a more modest scale (and many former recipients such as Powell, Campbell, Smith, and McGill had died) but the government was still supporting six such individuals, including the Roman Catholic Bishop and Colonel Thomas Talbot, at a combined cost of £1,377.[1]

Not all pensions however went to important people. In fact the great majority of government pensions were not given to prominent people or their families at all but to quite ordinary Upper Canadians, because most pensions resulted from the consequences of militia service in two highly unusual events, the War of 1812 and the Rebellion and subsequent border raids of 1837–38.

The role of the Upper Canadian militia, especially in the War of 1812, has been the subject of a good deal of debate. Nineteenth-century writers in the wake of the wartime period tended to rate the contribution of the militia to the British victory very highly. One of the few matters on which two of the giants of Upper Canadian religious history, the Anglican John Strachan and the Methodist Egerton Ryerson, were in complete agreement was the enormous importance of the contribution to the war effort of a small but gallant and impeccably loyal citizen army. Strachan declared during the war that "never, surely, was greater activity shewn in any country, than our militia have exhibited, never greater valour, cooler resolution, and more approved conduct; they have emulated the choicest veterans, and they have twice saved the country." In even more heated prose, Ryerson, looking back on the events of the war in 1880, wrote that "the Spartan bands of Canadian Loyalist volunteers, aided by a few hundred English soldiers and civilized Indians, repelled the Persian thousands of democratic invaders, and maintained the virgin soil of Canada unpolluted by the foot of the plundering invader." Much later studies of the war and the militia's part in it by professional military historians such as C.P. Stacey and G.F.G. Stanley reached quite different conclusions: that the militia played a useful but decidedly secondary and marginal role in the defence of Upper Canada. A more recent scholarly examination of the militia and the civil society of 1812–14 by George Sheppard is even more sceptical, stressing the small numbers of Upper Canadians who actually took part in the fighting, and the eagerness at all times of the vast majority of eligible Upper Canadian men to withdraw from or avoid military service.[2]

However minor the efforts of the militia may have been in the larger military scheme of things, the fact remains that in 1812–14 and again in 1837–38 quite a number of Upper Canadian men were killed or suffered some form of continuing incapacitation, though it is difficult to be definitive about the exact numbers involved. For the War of 1812 alone the most exhaustive attempt which has been made to establish the number of those who died, were wounded, suffered accidents, or contracted disease on duty has produced a list of about 460 names, but this figure is said by its compiler to be "pre-liminary" because the surviving records are incomplete. The actual number of men, or their widows, who received pensions was likely much smaller than that. The number of 1812–14 pensioners appears to have peaked around 1818, when there were 147 men and 130 women receiving war pensions. Of course not every militiaman who was killed, wounded, or contracted disease was pensioned. Some young men who were killed in action did not have dependents to claim a pension; some who were wounded or sick made a complete recovery and therefore did not qualify for support. And it is possible that some few who did theoretically qualify simply never applied, by virtue of oversight, ignorance, or lack of adequate documentation. A war pension was guaranteed to the deserving citizen by legislation, but it still had to be applied for in the usual form of a petition. Governments then as now did not give money to people who did not ask for it, or failed to fill in the required forms or follow the correct procedures.[3]

Nonetheless pensions were earned as a matter of "right" and could not be denied to legitimate claimants, the great majority of whom were, because of their greater numbers, men who had served at the rank of militia private, or their widows and children. Their right was established by a series of specific acts of the provincial legislature, but the extent of that right varied over time as amendments were made to the legislation. To understand the effect of these amendments on actual pensioners, some explanation, however tedious, of the vagaries of the law is necessary.

The first pension act dealing with 1812–14 casualties was passed during the war itself in 1813[4] to provide for the maintenance of disabled persons and widows and orphans of "persons killed on actual service or by any accident or casualty." The pension rate was set at £12-0-0 per year for single disabled veterans and at £20 per year for married men or widows with children. Officially, only children "lawfully begotten" could benefit from the act. The legislation provided that if a married male pensioner died, his wife and children would continue to receive his pension and on the death or remarriage of a pensioner's widow the oldest son or a guardian was to be paid the pension until the youngest child was sixteen years of age. Although English common law of the time assumed that mothers would not be made legal guardians of their children, it is worth noting that in Upper Canada mothers while in receipt of a war pension, whether remarried or not, were almost always designated as the guardian of their minor children. In other words, they, and not some male relative, got the money directly. In fact, again despite contemporary legal precedent and contrary to what later writers have concluded about the guardianship of children in the nineteenth century, women who were the widows of War of 1812 veterans were more often than not made the legal guardians of their children and could be quite assertive in demanding to fill that role. Margaret Lightheart, the remarried widow of Private Simon Earhart (or Aerhart) of the First Addington Regiment of Militia, had moved to Trafalgar Township after the war. The militia board in Kingston had made her former brother-in-law, John Earhart, the guardian of her five children but Mrs Lightheart complained that he was withholding part of her pension and insisted that she be made guardian in his place. Frances Burke of York applied both for a pension due to the death of her husband at the siege of York in April 1813 and to be made guardian of her children "that she may be enabled to rear and have them educated under her own direction." Scattered pension documents attest to the fact that women were commonly made guardians. In 1818 the London District militia board approved two pensions, both to go to female guardians. Records of guardianship in pension lists of 1817, 1825, 1826, and 1828 refer respectively to sixty-one guardians, of whom forty were women; to sixteen guardians, of whom nine were women; to eighteen guardians, of whom eight were women; and to nineteen guardians, of whom ten were women.[5]

Twice during the parliament of 1815–16, important amendments to the 1813 pension law were made. Some form of veteran's or widow's lobby may have been at work in persuading the members of the provincial parliament to relax and expand the provisions under which pensions could be awarded, for an act of 1815 raised the amount of pension to unmarried disabled men to £20 a year. A change with much wider implications was introduced in 1816. About 38 per cent of all deaths among militiamen on active duty did not result from taking part in battles but from disease. A pension of £20 was now to be given to the wives, children, or orphans of any soldier who had died, or might later die, of disease contracted while performing any duty on active service.[6]

Obviously aware that the inclusion of disease as a cause of death, especially after the fact, could significantly increase the number of female pensioners and the cost to the treasury, and that the new regulations could be open to a good deal of interpretation, especially in cases of militiamen dying of disease well after the war, the legislature also introduced some bureaucratic safeguards and procedures. In 1821 a new government position, of general agent for paying pensions, was created to administer the system (at a salary of £150 a year) but the real decision-making as to who did or did not qualify for support was distributed among three groups: district boards of militia officers, who were to enquire into the "merits" of each case; surgeons, who, for a fee of five shillings a time, were to examine existing or new male claimants and issue certificates of disability if warranted; and the commanding officers of militia regiments, who twice a year were independently to submit returns of all persons connected to their regiments who they believed were entitled to pensions. This division of authority required the bureaucratic involvement of quite a few people, some travel, and considerable paper work. For example the boards consisted of senior militia officers in each district, and each district already had in 1812–14 at least two, and as many as five, regiments, in two or more counties.[7]

Certifying that Catharine Fraser, widow of Captain William Fraser, First Grenville Regiment, and Elizabeth Hamblin, widow of Private Silas Hamblin, Second Grenville Regiment, were entitled to pensions because their husbands had both died of illness contracted on active duty, meant that a meeting, or meetings, was held in 1816 for the joint deliberation of Joel Stone, colonel of the Second Leeds Regiment; William Fraser (obviously not the same one), colonel of the Second Grenville Regiment; L.P. Sherwood, lieutenant colonel of the First Leeds Regiment; Stephen Burritt, lieutenant colonel of the Second Grenville Regiment; and John McDonell, captain of the late Incorporated Militia. Stone and Fraser of course had also to provide their own personal certificates for these cases, and all submissions had ultimately to be approved, or rejected, by the lieutenant governor. The claimants themselves had also to reapply for their pensions twice a year by sending in their own sworn certificates of eligibility, along with still another certificate signed by the relevant colonel of militia.[8]

Despite all of these administrative precautions, the terms of the act of 1816 caused quite a few problems, mainly financial. Under this act "about three hundred and thirty persons were admitted as pensioners," for a total cost of around £6,600. In 1821 a later provincial parliament, urged on by Lieutenant Governor Sir Peregrine Maitland, decided to introduce cutbacks. In 1816 the province seemed to be on a sound financial basis but a revenue crisis beginning in 1819, which was brought on by the failure of Upper Canada to obtain its share of customs duties on goods passing through Lower Canada, put the government into a tight squeeze and forced the lieutenant governor to borrow from the Military Chest. In effect the law of 1821 (2 George IV, C. 4) restored the situation of pension claimants to where it had stood under the law of 1813, thereby largely eliminating the "died of disease" category. It allowed a maximum of a year for the submission of new claims of any kind and two years in which appeals could be made. The justification for this reversal of policy was explained in a preamble to the act. Under the act of 1816 "the classes of militia pensioners were greatly increased so that the Public Revenue has been found wholly unable to bear the charge thereby incurred: And whereas the said Act being limited in its duration is about to expire, and it is become necessary to confine the Militia pensions, with the exceptions hereinafter mentioned, to the objects provided for by the laws of this Province passed during the late war, and to provide for such investigation of the claims of the different Pensioners, as may prevent further loss to the Revenue from any misrepresentation or deceit which may have been practised." In short, the law of 1816 had resulted in an allegedly unbearable financial burden and had been abused by unscrupulous Upper Canadians. The government borrowed £25,000 to pay arrears in militia pensions in 1821–22.[9]

Though the 1821 act was aimed at saving the province money, it also created a new level of bureaucracy in the form of inspectors of militia pensioners. These were to be more medical doctors appointed and paid by the government to examine old and new claimants. The examinations were to be held at stated times but only in the district towns, which meant that disabled claimants from elsewhere in the districts had to make special trips to have any chance of qualifying.

Between 1821 and 1835 a further series of acts tinkered with and periodically extended the 1821 legislation but made only minor changes such as the abolition in 1826 of the office of pension agent, which was absorbed into the receiver general's office. Acts of 1837 and 1838 again took a softer approach by allowing new 1812–14 disability claimants to apply and restored pensions to a few who had been removed from the pension list in 1821. The Rebellion of 1837–38 also produced its own new legislation which applied much the same conditions as had been set out in the 1813 act – £20 per year to militiamen disabled on duty and £20 per year to the widows and children of militiamen who as a result of service in the Rebellion period had died in action, by accident, or from disease contracted while on duty or within one year of their militia service.[10]

The pendulum pattern of generosity in the immediate wake of conflict and later second thoughts was repeated in 1840. An act of that year provided for the re-examination and possible removal from the pension rolls of any former militiamen claiming disability in case a recovery had occurred. Widows could be required to resubmit detailed proof of entitlement and cases of death after discharge were to come under special renewed scrutiny, which could result in widows and children being struck off. A second 1840 act made permanent the terms of an earlier act, of 1835, which was itself a renewal and virtual restatement of the restrictive act of 1821.[11]

What did all this mean to the real people involved – disabled former soldiers and war widows and orphans? How much did they even know about the frequent changes of pension policy and regulations? Did they simply find out about new restrictions when their pensions stopped coming? The provincial administration did make some efforts to try to inform the general public about the steady stream of legislation which flowed from the sessions of the provincial parliament. One legal historian, John David Phillips, has concluded that the government was in fact quite conscientious about informing the people of its actions and that Upper Canadians "were consequently expected to be familiar with the laws of the land," and there is some evidence that this was so. In 1802 the provincial parliament voted "a sum not exceeding £300" to print the acts and *Journals*, but responsibility for distributing this material seems to have been left in the hands of the individual members of the House of Assembly, with uneven results. In that year the magistrates of the Home District asked their local MHA, Angus Macdonell, for copies of the acts of the first session of the Third Parliament. Macdonell sent "six Copies of the aforesaid Acts & four Copies of the *Journals*" but denied that he was under any legal obligation to do so. He provided them to the magistrates only "in their Individual Quality as Gentlemen" since he considered himself to be "under the Control of my own direction only in distributing such acts of the Parliament of the Province." More official provision was made for the "promulgation" of the provincial statutes by an Act of 1804. Again £300 was appropriated "for printing all the acts of the province" to that date and a further £80 for the annual printing of the laws. Under this act four copies of the acts were to go to each member of the executive and legislative councils and to each judge of the Court of King's Bench and twenty copies to each MHA "to be by them distributed in such manner as will best tend to promulgate a general knowledge of the laws." MHAs also again required the clerk of the House in 1819 to provide each of the members with twenty copies of the provincial statutes and in 1823 agreed to pay for one thousand copies of the statutes of 1820–22 "for distribution in the province."[12] The pension act of 1821 itself finally made some official provision for public information on pensions. The pension agent was required to advertise "his readiness to pay the pensions" in the *York Gazette* for a period of three months and required the inspectors of militia pensions to give four weeks public notice of their visits to the district towns. But how much knowledge of the actual terms of the various pension acts really reached all the relevant people, if indeed it did, is not clear. Public notices, such as those announcing the impending arrival of the pension inspectors, would have been put up at a central location, perhaps at the district court houses, where they existed. Access to the statutes themselves could theoretically be had via the MHAs but it is unlikely that many people sought access to documents which were in the hands of local notables and were not written in language that was easily grasped.

Newspapers of course were the main way in which the provincial government, through the official *Upper Canada Gazette* and the other papers of the day, disseminated information on parliamentary proceedings and government actions and regulations. The first set of instructions to prospective pensioners, setting out the necessary procedures in order to qualify for and collect a pension, were published in late February 1813. After the war the fact that pensions were available was made clear by printed newspaper lists of people who were receiving pensions, which must certainly have been read with keen interest. At least once, in 1826, the legislature ordered that an official list be published three times in the *Gazette*, giving the names of all the men, women, guardians, and children in each district then receiving pensions. Yet even access to newspapers was far from universal in Upper Canada, especially access to the *Upper Canada Gazette,* printed in York/Toronto, including to that proportion of the population who could not read, estimated to have been about 20 per cent before 1841.[13] The wording of some of the petitions submitted by prospective early pensioners, beginning shortly after the passage of the 1813 act, suggests that awareness among the militia community about pensions more likely came at first by word of mouth. Perhaps it was generally known that there were pensions to be had, and some applicants seem to have known what was expected of them from the beginning, but not all were clear as to who was qualified, or how or where to apply, or the amount of support available. Two years after the passage of the pension act of 1813 for example, and more than a year after the death of her husband, the petition of Anna Forbes, widow of Private Adam Forbes of the Incorporated Militia and the mother of seven children, merely asked the lieutenant governor for "some speedy relief." Lieutenant Colonel J.B. Baby of the 2nd Essex Regiment submitted a certificate on 11 August 1813 confirming that Peter (Pierre) Badichon had been killed in action at the River Raisin in January of that year but Badichon's widow Anne, the mother of five children aged seven to fourteen "born in wedlock," did not herself apply as his "lawful wife" until 24 July 1815. Private Cornelius Marks of the 1st Oxford Regiment died on 1 January 1813, but it was also two years later before his widow, Ruth Marks, began to make enquiries about the possibility of a pension. Even then she did not follow the normal procedure of sending a petition to the lieutenant governor but wrote to the (acting) receiver general, John McGill, asking him how she might go about getting "a widow's allowance." (In fact since her husband had died of disease she was not entitled to a pension under the act then in force but did qualify under the revised 1816 terms.)[14]

Regardless of the degree of sophistication of the applicant, getting a pension was never a completely uncomplicated matter and sometimes became simply a matter of judgement or of interpretation of the rules. What for example was the status of men such as Gunner Ozias Bacchus of the Provincial Artillery who was returned as missing in action at Ft George in May 1813? Of teamster Samuel Allen of the First Oxford Regiment who was stabbed by another militiaman? Of John Holliday, also a gunner in the Provincial Artillery, who was killed "in an affray at Munn's Tavern"? Of Private John Campbell of the Fifth Lincoln Regiment who was "stabbed by an Indian"? Or of the forty-odd militiamen who suffered serious accidental injury by such means as slipping on ice, or falling off a blockhouse, or being hit in the stomach by a rolling cask or in the chest by the pole of a sleigh, or by being frostbitten? There could often be a fine line between legitimate injury in the course of duty and simple carelessness.[15]

The government, understandably, always required some documentary proof that a claim was valid. Though as has been seen the rules frequently changed, some basic military, medical, and personal certificates were always required. At all times a certificate had to be provided by the officer who commanded, or had commanded, the appropriate regiment, testifying to the authenticity of each case of death or disability. Though the 1816 legislation created permanent boards of officers in each district to "enquire into the merits" of applicants, it still required the commanding officer's certificate, which had to be forthcoming twice in each year. After 1816 it was also essential for the disabled to obtain a medical certificate, for which the examination fee of five shillings was charged. (An amendment of 1817 generously waived the need for a doctor's certificate in the case of the loss of an eye.) After 1816 all applicants, male or female, had to reconfirm by certificate twice a year that they were who they said they were and that their claim was genuine, which would have meant an appearance before a magistrate to make a sworn statement and to pay another fee. For the further inconvenience of most pensioners, the pensions were payable only at the government's offices in York/Toronto, where they were to be collected "personally or by agent." No arrears were paid if a pension was not claimed in two successive years. The act of 1816 imposed a double documentary check against possible forgery. The pensioner, along with his or her own certificate, had to enclose a certificate from the regimental commanding officer, a certificate which that officer had also to submit independently. Widows of veterans needed an extra piece of evidence. They were expected also to provide a certificate of marriage, a document not always readily at hand, especially in the not uncommon case of couples who had emigrated to Upper Canada.[16]

This insistence on documentation, and cross documentation, may suggest a provincial government which was a bit on the paranoid, not to say obsessive, side about fraud and expense, but in fact they were really only emulating standard practice long adhered to by imperial authorities, as a number of Upper Canadian applicants for pensions from the British War Office discovered. Jeremiah French of Cornwall, who had served as a Loyalist lieutenant in the King's Royal Regiment of New York during the American Revolution, died in 1820. His widow Elizabeth, like some of the 1812–14 militia widows, may not at first have been aware that she was eligible for a pension as the widow of a former officer in a British regiment, or it may simply have taken her some time to collect the necessary evidence, for it was not until 1824 that she eventually petitioned the British government. Along with her petition she enclosed: a sworn certificate that she was herself; a doctor's certificate confirming the death of her husband; a certificate from a witness to the marriage of Jeremiah and Elizabeth French which had taken place in Dover, New York, in 1762; and Jeremiah French's lieutenant's commission. Her careful attention to detail brought happy results. She was informed in 1825 by Lord Palmerston, then secretary at war, that she had been provisionally awarded a pension of £40 per year, the amount allowed to the widow of a lieutenant, and then in 1826 that the pension would be continued and made retroactive to December 1823, three years after her husband's death.[17]

The practice of making militia pensioners continually reapply on a half-yearly basis also reflected imperial procedure The British military records relating to Canada contain such examples of pension bureaucracy as that of Elizabeth Andrews, widow of James A. Andrews, late captain in the Provincial Marine (died 1780). One of her surviving applications was sent from York on 25 June 1823, requesting the portion of her pension due to her for the period 24 June–24 December of that year. Her own certificate contained the mandatory declaration that she really was the right Widow Andrews and that she had "no other pension, allowance or provision," except that to which she was entitled as the widow of an officer. She enclosed additional supporting certificates testifying to her *bona fides* from

John Strachan, minister, and Thomas Ridout and J.B. Macaulay, church wardens, of St James' Church, as well as from brevet Major J.T.H. Powell, 76th Regiment, then officer commanding at York. To satisfy the British appetite for red tape, in an age which knew nothing of photocopiers or even carbon paper, each of these documents was provided in five handwritten copies.[18]

Were all these bureaucratic safeguards necessary? Were there attempts to defraud the imperial government or the government of Upper Canada with false claims or forged documents? So far as the 1812–14 pensioners were concerned the available evidence reveals very few attempts to pull the wool over the government's eyes. The one or two cases that have turned up, where death from disease was alleged, seem fairly innocuous. A Private Preston of the Prince Edward County militia was so conscientious and patriotic a soldier that he served, and died, during the war, despite the fact that he was already suffering from tuberculosis, then known as consumption. Unless he was an American secret weapon planted in the ranks to infect his fellow militiamen, this would seem to have been an example of selfless devotion to duty, but his widow's petition for a pension was refused, because his death "never originated on behalf of government" and she therefore had no right to public funds. Anne MacMillan, widow of Lieutenant Duncan MacMillan of the Second Glengarry Regiment seemed to have an even better chance of a pension since the Eastern District board of officers, MacMillan's former colleagues, gave her claim their collective approval. Her story was that her husband's death in September 1817 was the result of a cold caught on duty in February 1814, and he "was never well afterwards." Her petition also failed to convince a sceptical government and was ultimately rejected at the provincial level. The petition of Martha Vrooman of Kingston, widow of Hendrick Vrooman, for a pension met a similar fate. Her luckless militiaman husband first broke his leg and then while recuperating on leave suffered a gunshot wound (whether accidental or not is unknown) and subsequently died. In the opinion of John Beverley Robinson, acting attorney general, no pension was appropriate because death was not due to the "hurt in his leg" but to wounds "afterwards received."[19]

Such examples of bureaucratic wariness can also be seen as a reflection of British military precedents, of which another Upper Canadian instance can be found in the experiences of Lieutenant George Ryerson. Ryerson, of the well known Norfolk County family, older brother of the famous Egerton Ryerson, was severely wounded at Fort Erie in November 1812. A graphic description of the nature of his wound has survived. It was "caused by a musket ball that entered at the mouth, carried away part of his tongue, fractured his lower jaw and carried away one side of it, together with all of his front teeth." In due course he was placed on the Upper Canadian militia pension list, and was also later rewarded by the provincial government with appointments as collector of customs at Turkey Point and as a teacher in the London District Grammar School. However, since Ryerson had served not only in one of the flank companies of the Norfolk militia but also as an officer of the Incorporated Militia, his military status was roughly equivalent to that of an officer in a British regular regiment, which he conceived entitled him, under British military regulations, to a year's pay and expenses for the care of his wounds, followed by a lieutenant's pension of £70 a year. To this end he was twice examined by official medical boards made up of British Army surgeons. Though the first board, held "by order of Lt. General Drummond at York, February 8, 1815," found that Ryerson "cannot chew animal food – health is considerably affected" and the second, also held at York on 12 February 1816, "that abscesses occasionally form in that side of his face which materially affects his general health" and that "the said wound is very injurious to his health and renders him incapable of earning a livelihood," in the end the imperial decision was that his claim was not valid since he was "not labouring under any disability." He refused to accept this verdict and eventually in 1827 even took his case directly to the War Office in London armed with a letter from Lieutenant Governor Sir Peregrine Maitland, but to no known effect. (He may have been aware that Titus Geer Simons, who had also served in the Incorporated Militia but with the rank of major, had been ordered a pension of £250 a year by the imperial government as compensation for the loss of an arm and had also been appointed sheriff of the Gore District.) It may be difficult for the modern reader to believe that the loss of some of Ryerson's jaw, tongue, and teeth did not constitute a disability, but in the end the army's decision was, in a perverse way, vindicated. Though Ryerson's wounds "impaired his utterance and spoiled the ease of his elocution," he chose a career which relied on both, briefly in the classroom, then for many years in the pulpit. He lived to be over ninety years of age.[20]

Like Lieutenant George Ryerson, many other Upper Canadians whose initial applications for pensions were unsuccessful took their appeals elsewhere, for if one petition failed another might yet succeed. A body to which petitions were often also sent was the provincial legislature, which had the power, assuming the lieutenant governor gave his royal assent, to pass laws which overturned previous decisions and even the power to make exceptions to its own existing laws. In 1816 the provincial parliament passed an act "granting relief to Charlotte Overholt," because her husband had died "under circumstances of so peculiar a nature as cannot be reached by any law in force granting pensions." Whatever the mysterious manner of her husband's death may have been, Mrs Overholt received the standard pension of £20 per year. Jane Jones, widow of Captain John Jones of the First Lincoln Regiment, submitted a petition to the House of Assembly in 1818. Her initial application to the Niagara District board of officers had been rejected, presumably because the circumstances of her husband's death left some considerable doubt about the actual cause of death. Certainly Captain Jones had served his country, but he had died of disease and his death had occurred outside of Upper Canada, in Burlington, Vermont, where he was a prisoner of war. Since his death could have resulted from his confinement in an American prison, was he then serving his country? Evidently his former brother officers now on the district board decided that he was not. Nonetheless Jane Jones was eventually successful in getting put on the pension list. Exceptions were also made by the provincial legislature in a small number of other instances, including those of Elizabeth Lawe, Peter Miller, John White, and James Carrol, "for the relief of" whom special acts were passed in the 1820's to provide them with pensions of £20 per year for life. Elizabeth Lawe's husband was well known in the legislature for he was "an old and faithful servant of the province," having been sergeant-at-arms in the House of Assembly from 1792 to 1810. For such a familiar and apparently well-liked individual the provincial politicians were able to find a formula to justify a pension for his widow. Her husband's death had not been caused but had been "accelerated" by wounds received while serving as captain of the First Lincoln Regiment at Fort George in 1813. As well, her son, Private George William Lawe had been killed in action. Private Peter Miller's wartime service left him crippled and "incapable of earning his livelihood" but the Home District pension board reached the conclusion in 1816 that the "fever" which was said to have caused his condition was not a legitimate source of disability and his application "not being provided for by law is not therefore approved." Nevertheless in 1822 the legislature decided for reasons not stated that it was "desirable and proper under such circumstances to make provision for the said Peter Miller." John White was in an even more specialized category for he had not been a member of any militia unit during the war but an artificer in the naval yard at Amherstburg. In a purely volunteer capacity he bore arms during Procter's retreat in 1813, was "grievously wounded" and became "entirely disabled," making him "a proper object of provincial support." James Carrol did serve in the militia, as a private in the Provincial Artillery. He contracted measles while on duty after which he gradually lost his sight, eventually becoming totally blind, and partially deaf. He too fell foul of the regulations of 1821 since his incapacity was declared to be the result of disease. An act of 1824 placed him on the pension list.[21]

Needless to say such special acts passed for the benefit of particular individuals were relatively rare. Many petitions, most also based on apparently plausible grounds for "relief," were received and considered by the House of Assembly but the great majority were unsuccessful. Margaret Rousseau, like Jane Jones, had been refused a pension at the level of the district board of officers. Her husband, Lieutenant Colonel Jean-Baptiste Rousseau of the Second York Regiment, was another well-known Upper Canadian, a fur trader, entrepreneur, interpreter, and captain in the Indian Department, who had served at Queenston Heights but died of pleurisy in November 1812 at Fort George. Margaret Rousseau's petition was referred by the Assembly to a special committee in March 1816 but no further action was taken. She petitioned again in 1821. This time a bill for her relief, as the widow of an officer who had died on duty, was given first reading but then received the three month's hoist, by a decided margin of seventeen to five, putting an end to her hopes. It is a pity that there seems to be no surviving evidence as to why Margaret Rousseau was refused a pension, first by the Gore District board of officers and then by the Assembly, because besides the matter of whether Colonel Rousseau's death was really due to his militia service there appears also to have been some ambiguity about their married state. Though Jean-Baptiste and Margaret Rousseau went through no fewer than three marriage ceremonies, two of them in the Church of England, it is not clear that his previous marriage was ever legally dissolved.[22]

Ann Hostler (or Hosteler) and Margaret Darby, of Grantham Township, jointly petitioned the legislature in 1818 for pensions as

widows of men who had died of disease while on active service.
There was however a technical hitch. Their petition identified the
men as privates in the First Lincoln Regiment but in fact they too had
served only unofficially as volunteers, being exempt from duty "by
reason of age and infirmity." Their petition was initially read in 1818
and referred to the committee on pensions, from which it did not
return. The petition was again brought up in the House at the end of
the session of 1819 when Lincoln MHAS Ralfe Clench and David
Secord moved and seconded a motion that a bill for their relief be
first·on the order of the day at the next session. No such bill ever
appeared. A third Grantham Township widow, Rebecca Thompson,
widow of Cornelius Thompson, had a similar experience. According
to her petition her husband also had been "too infirm" to fight but
had "assisted his country" and his "exertions" brought on his death
from disease. One of her sons also died during the war and another
was wounded. Her petition, also brought up in both 1818 and 1819,
got as far as the committee stage but no farther. Many more such
petitions were received by the Assembly but routinely got only scant
and cursory attention. In the great majority of cases the members of
the House applied the letter of the law pretty strictly and, in the
words of Sir Peregrine Maitland, showed a "desire to do justice to
the revenue." The interesting, and apparently unanswerable question, is why some few petitions got special treatment. No doubt for
some, having the support of influential people had something to do
with it.[23]

By the time of the Rebellion of 1837 the number of 1812–14 pensioners was considerably reduced, especially among pensioner widows. In 1835 fourteen widows of 1812–14 veterans were still on the
list; in 1839 the number was twelve. Among male pensioners however the reduction in numbers was slower, and the list even showed
some increase at the end of the Upper Canadian period, from thirty-
six in 1835 to forty in 1839. Rebecca McIntee, petitioning in 1840
for a pension because her husband had recently died, she believed,
from the effect of wounds received in the war, got no sympathy, but
a small aging veteran's lobby was able to persuade the government
to have their disability cases reopened and new cases of disability
allegedly stemming from war service examined. An act of 1837,
prompted by petitions from ten 1812–14 veterans, allowed for such
claimants to be put on the pension list on the recommendation of a
panel of three surgeons. One of these petitioners can be identified as

militia colonel Ziba Marcus Phillips of Maitland, who had been badly wounded at the Battle of Ogdensburg in 1813 but not pensioned, because he recovered to fight again in 1814 at Lundy's Lane and at Fort Erie. Evidently twenty-seven years later he found that his old wound was acting up and he too became a militia pensioner. In 1838 a special act was passed on behalf of three old soldiers, John Ryan of Toronto Township, Peter Lampman of Niagara, and Adam Stull of Grantham. They had all been wounded and pensioned after the war but had lost their pensions in the reforms of 1821, presumably because the medical examiners at that time had decided that they were no longer suffering from any disability. The lingering effects of their wounds must also have reappeared, for it was now "expedient that they should be restored to the pension list."[24]

The Rebellion period of 1837–38 was of brief duration and featured very few military engagements of any magnitude but it nonetheless produced a surprising number of militia casualties, perhaps because the militia was more actively involved in what fighting did take place than was true in 1812–14. As well, despite the government's best efforts, under continual human pressure the number of former militiamen and widows who were belatedly given pensions continued to grow. By 1841 the total list of pensioners had reached 184 men, widows, and children, the following year the number was 199. The new pension act of 1838 was passed to provide for Rebellion pensioners, and as has been seen, was fairly generous in its terms, including a category for death by disease contracted not only while on duty but within one year of service. The act also eliminated one level of officialdom, not requiring the involvement of district boards of officers. Instead it centralized procedures in the provincial bureaucracy, particularly in the office of the attorney general. The act was also very precise and rigorous in spelling out the specific documents required with each petition and the exact form in which they were to be submitted, but once again it is obvious that the detailed requirements of the act were not successfully disseminated among the community as a whole, for many petitioners fell foul of the regulations, at least on their initial applications, and Christopher Alexander Hagerman, the attorney general who served through the busiest period of 1837–40, was not inclined to be sympathetic to petitioners who sent in incomplete or irregular dossiers.[25]

Mary Jane Latour of Belleville, widow of Charles Latour, who died of disease while serving with the Queen's Own Regiment of Militia under Colonel William Kingsmill, took the precaution of having her petition submitted by Edmund Murney, who was a Belleville lawyer, the sitting MHA for Hastings, and himself a major of militia. Nonetheless even Murney was apparently not sufficiently familiar with the regulations, for her first petition was rejected by Hagerman on the grounds that she had not sufficiently established her claim and that she had not included the required certificate from Colonel Kingsmill. Hagerman was no more satisfied with her second petition, by which he was still unconvinced, since under the act the certificate from the commanding officer "must be positive in its terms." On her third try her application met the attorney general's standards and she was put on the pension list. Death by disease always provided the most difficult cases to document but the bureaucratic demands of the pension act could also prove intimidating. Frances Dulmage of Prescott had to wait almost a year before receiving a pension, though there was never any actual doubt about the validity of her claim, since her husband, Ensign John O. Dulmage of the Second Regiment of Grenville Militia, had been "killed instantly" in action, in full view of many witnesses, at the Battle of the Windmill on 13 November 1838. When her first petition was deemed incomplete she showered the attorney general with additional documents, including proof of her marriage, her husband's service record, and baptismal certificates for her four young children. She also petitioned the legislature. According to Richard Bullock, the adjutant general of militia, the delay was due to the "inexperience of the parties."[26]

Even when all of the correct procedures had been followed it could still be difficult to get Hagerman's approval. The pathetic case of Ellen Ganley provides an example of the attorney general at his most suspicious and hairsplitting. Thomas Ganley, Ellen Ganley's late husband, was an old soldier, a veteran of Waterloo, who had served for more than eighteen years in the 52nd Regiment. During the Rebellion he had joined the City Guards in Toronto but died in October 1838 of "bowel disease," said to have been contracted while on duty. Thomas Ganley did not leave his widow well provided for. By the fall of 1839 she was four months behind in her rent and facing the prospect of eviction and the sale of her possessions. These misfortunes did not move Christopher Hagerman, who through three applications for a pension continued to hold the opinion that it was not proven that Thomas Ganley's death had been caused by a disease contracted on actual duty. Eventually the lieutenant governor intervened on behalf of a British soldier's widow. He wanted Mrs Ganley to "have every possible chance of proving herself entitled to the boon she solicits." His secretary wrote to Hagerman that "it will give His Excellency pleasure if upon a fair consideration of the documents now before you, the claim of Mrs. Ganley to a pension shall be regarded by you as satisfactorily established." Despite this strong hint the attorney general refused to change his mind and Ellen Ganley only finally got her pension approved, to be paid retroactive to the date of Thomas Ganley's death (6 October 1838) in October 1839, over Hagerman's objections.[27]

Hagerman also recommended against a petition from Ann Brown of Niagara, but for her there was no happy final outcome. John Brown, her husband, had died of disease allegedly stemming from his period of service on the Niagara frontier in 1838 with Captain Thomas Runchey's Coloured Corps. Certificates from Runchey, Major Cortland Secord, and Surgeon T.H. Snow failed to provide sufficient proof to satisfy the attorney general. Ann Brown's petition and documents were also ultimately examined at a higher level, by the Executive Council, but whether she was technically entitled to a pension or not, the name of Ann Brown, widow of a black Upper Canadian militia private, does not appear on any subsequent pension lists.[28]

After the Rebellion, as was true after the War of 1812, there were certainly attempts by petitioners to bend or even break the rules governing the awarding of pensions, despite the careful drafting of the pension act and the vigilance of the administration. Hannah Bennett's husband had been discharged by the Queen's Rangers as physically unfit, thereby relieving the government from any financial burden relating to his later death from consumption. Similarly, Mary Reilly was refused a pension because of the narrow terms of the act, her husband not having died within a year after he left the service. The petition of Julia Dodsworth of Toronto for a pension, submitted 18 November 1839, initially received Attorney General Hagerman's speedy approval, on 26 November. Private Edward Dodsworth had drowned in August 1838 crossing Chippawa Creek while serving with the 3rd Battalion of Incorporated Militia. Something about the case however prompted further enquiries to be made. Provincial Secretary R.A. Tucker wrote to Dodsworth's former commanding officer, Colonel William Kingsmill, to ask whether Dodsworth had really been on duty at the time of his death or "in the pursuit of amusement or any other object not directly connected with the public service." Kingsmill's response confirmed official suspicions. Dodsworth had not been on duty when his accidental drowning occurred. He had gone out in a boat "for his own amusement." Needless to say, the attorney general now reversed his opinion. Dodsworth was no less dead and his widow no less bereft of support, but Mrs Dodsworth was informed that the provincial government regretted that in the circumstances the law did not permit her to receive public funds.[29]

A more serious and deliberate attempt at pension fraud also managed to fool attorney general Hagerman at first. The petition of Rosalie McKinnon, widow of Private John McKinnon of the 6th Provisional Battalion of Militia, met all the requirements of the pension act, including the necessary certificates from the commanding officer, Colonel Connel J. Baldwin, and the surgeon, Thomas Rolph. Hagerman examined the papers and gave his approval. Once again however some other government officer found something odd about the case for an investigation was begun, which ultimately ended in charges of conspiracy being laid against three people named William Mills, Rosalie McStravick, and Euphemia Sutherland. At their trial in Toronto on 2 November 1839, which featured the unusual spectacle of the attorney general of Upper Canada admitting in court that he had been duped, a complicated story emerged. The Rosalie McKinnon who had petitioned for a pension had not been married to John McKinnon, though it appears that they had lived together as man and wife, and in fact Rosalie McKinnon was not Rosalie McKinnon at all, but Rosalie (or Rosalla) McStravick. The certificates of Colonel Baldwin and Dr Rolph had been forged. The forger was at first thought to be a man named Jones "said to live near the market" but this information proved to be false and William Mills was arrested and tried for this part of the plot. Euphemia Sutherland was alleged to have impersonated the original impersonator, Rosalie/Rosalla McStravick/McKinnon, in swearing affidavits to attest to the genuineness of the forged certificates. Needless to say, no pension was ever forthcoming as a result of John McKinnon's death but the results of the trial, which involved the attendance of such high profile Upper Canadians as Hagerman; Colonel Baldwin; Edward McMahon, chief clerk in the lieutenant governor's office; George Gurnett, former mayor of Toronto; George Duggan, magistrate and former alderman; and five other witnesses, hardly resulted in severe punishment for the conspirators. Rosalie McStravick forfeited her recognizance and did not appear when called at the trial. She was "said to have gone to the United States." Euphemia Sutherland was acquitted. Mills was found guilty but was subsequently discharged on technical grounds. The indictment against him had been wrongly drawn, naming the wrong regiment of militia, and, perhaps understandably, confusing the names of the persons said to have hoped to benefit from the fraudulent petition.[30] No other example of successful or unsuccessful outright pension fraud arising from the Rebellion has come to light.

The Rebellion produced its share of special cases which were dealt with by the legislature, but unlike the special laws passed in the wake of the War of 1812, which often made exceptions for quite ordinary citizens caught up in extraordinary circumstances, the pension exceptions following the Rebellion dealt mostly with people, especially widows, who came from families of prominent social and military rank, and often conferred pensions well above the basic £20 per year. The case of Joseph Randal of Chatham does fit the 1812–14 pattern because he received £20 per year for the loss of an arm while not a militiaman but as a volunteer, "in cleaning and proving a piece of cannon taken from the enemy at Fighting Island," but many other equally humble applicants, mostly widows of militia privates seeking relief from the legislature, never made it onto the pension list. On the other hand a retired naval lieutenant, Shepperd McCormick, was treated quite differently. He was seriously wounded and disabled while a member of the raiding party which captured and burned the Patriot steamship *Caroline* on 9 December 1837, but he was "credited with splitting at least one man's skull open." An 1838 act provided him with £100 a year "so long as the disability shall continue." He was also appointed collector of customs at Cobourg.[31]

Another act of the same year was passed for the benefit of the widow and children of Colonel Robert Moodie, the first Loyalist martyr of the Rebellion, "inhumanly murdered" by the rebels at Montgomery's Tavern while trying to reach Toronto with word of the rising. Mrs Moodie and her children also received £100 per year until the youngest child reached the age of twenty-one. (The usual cut-off age was sixteen.) In a third 1838 act the legislature was a bit less generous to Maria Church and Harriet McNabb, both of Belleville, widows of captains William Church and James McNabb of the Hastings militia. Each widow received £50 a year "during their widowhood." The lesser level of payment to Mrs Church and Mrs McNabb may have had something to do with the somewhat unheroic, not to say bizarre, way in which the two officers died. Church was accidentally shot by a fellow militiaman in a tavern in Shannonville. His companion in taking off his coat let his loaded pistol fall on a stove. The gun went off and shot Church just as he was sitting down at a table, killing him on the spot. McNabb's death also took place in a public house: "An alarm of fire being given, Mr. McNabb was hurrying through the dark passage of an Inn, where a number of armed militia were quartered, when he ran upon the fixed bayonet of one of the men, which pierced his abdomen. He died within twenty-four hours."[32]

Sarah Ussher, also the widow of a militia captain, and her four infant children received better compensation, £100 a year, no doubt because Edgeworth Ussher of Chippawa, a member of the 10th Provisional Battalion of Militia, died a martyr's death like Colonel Moodie's. He too was "inhumanly assassinated," in his case "in the night time, in his own home, by Brigands from the United States of America," because of "the gallantry and activity displayed by him in resisting the invasion of this Province by the inhabitants and citizens of the said United States." Still by 1840 government austerity, affecting the widows of captains as well as those of rank-and-file militiamen, seems to have set in. Though William Kerry, a captain in the Kent Militia, died a hero's death, being killed "in attempting to capture a Brigand who had invaded this province," his widow, Susannah Kerry, and her children were voted only the standard £20 by the provincial parliament.[33]

Of course not all Upper Canadian pensioners, or pension petitioners, received or claimed pensions on military grounds, nor were all non-military pensioners people who, like the chief justices, had held high positions in government and society. An old soldier, Lewis Bright, held a lowly position, as messenger to the Legislative Council, but he held it for a long time and until he reached a great age. If the scant biographical information about him is accurate he cannot have been a very speedy messenger for he is said to have been ninety-three in 1840 when the legislature enabled him to retire on a pension for "long and faithful services." "An act to pension Lewis Bright and his aged wife" provided £62-10-0 a year to them both and to the surviving spouse. The date of Mrs Bright's death is unknown but Lewis Bright enjoyed the pension for only two years, dying in 1842.

Margaret Powell, the widow of a British officer, served for eleven years as housekeeper to the Executive Council but lost her position, which paid £75 a year, when the government of the United Province of Canada was moved to Kingston in 1841. After five years of petitioning and string-pulling she was finally given a pension of £35 a year in 1846. Even at that she and the Brights were better off than the majority of former public servants who got no pension at all.[34]

Heroism and martyrdom in a civilian as opposed to a military capacity could also result in a pension. Timothy Conklin Pomeroy, while acting as a London District constable, was shot and killed in Bayham Township in 1830 by a man he was attempting to arrest on a charge of larceny. A petition from Pomeroy's widow Charlotte on behalf of herself and her infant son moved Lieutenant Governor Sir John Colborne to send a message to the legislature recommending that provision be made for the wife and son of a fearless law officer "murdered on duty at Big Otter Creek." The two houses of parliament quickly complied, voting the usual £20 per year until the child reached the age of sixteen. A final type of non-military pensioner in Upper Canada was retired clergymen and the widows of clergymen of the Church of England. At the end of the Upper Canadian period seven widows and three retired Anglican ministers were in receipt of pensions, all the widows at £50 a year, two retired ministers at £100 a year, and one at £30 a year. Although these amounts appear in the provincial accounts, the actual funds would not have come from the beleaguered provincial treasury, since most of the support of the Church of England clergy in Upper Canada came from the mother country, via the Society for the Propagation of the Gospel in Foreign Parts.[35]

Though the awarding of pensions in Upper Canada reflected the hierarchical nature of the society of the day and contributed to the support of some people at a much handsomer rate than for others, the great majority of pensioners received the same basic rate of £20 per year. How this particular amount, which dates from the legislation of 1813, was arrived at is unclear. It must be assumed that the parliamentarians of the time considered that £20 was enough on its own to provide an individual, and even a family, with at least a basic level of subsistence, since for wounded veterans the criteria for receiving the money was that they were physically incapable of earning a living, and it would have been assumed that most widows, especially those with children, would not work outside the home.

Table 4.1
Occupation, income, and status

Level	Occupation	Income Range
"Respectable" (3 or more servants)	Manufacturer, merchant, wealthy farmer, clergy, barrister, government department head	£200–£300
"Marginal Respectable" (1 or 2 servants)	Attorney, mechanic, shopkeeper, miller, innkeeper, doctor, grammar school teacher, well-to-do farmer	£100–£150
"Independent" (no or 1 female servant)	Tavernkeeper, peddler, preacher, small-scale farmer, settled skilled journeyman	£40–£70
"Quasi-dependent" (no servants)	Common school teacher, pioneer farmer, labourer, "broken down" mechanic	£25–£35
"Dependent"	Squatter, servant, pauper	£18–£22

Source: Russell, Attitudes to Social Structure, 9.

But, in early nineteenth-century Upper Canada, how much was £20? Where was the "poverty line" in Upper Canada? Such a question is never easy to answer because Upper Canadian economic conditions were subject to a great many fluctuations, but some comparative statistics can be of help. Fortunately, Dr Peter A. Russell, after studying a wide variety of sources on wage and income levels in Upper Canada in the period 1815–40, has compiled a highly useful table, divided into five "status" levels (see table 4.1).

On this scale it is obvious where ordinary pensioners belonged: at the bottom, in the "dependent" class, with an income equivalent to that of squatters, servants, and paupers. £20 a year in other words was by no means a generous level of compensation for risking, or losing, life or limb in defence of the province. It is not an exaggeration to call it a truly niggardly sum, which condemned the recipient, assuming he or she had no other source of income, to the level of barest subsistence. As well the pension system actually penalized some widows and orphans, for the law made no financial distinction between a widow with no children and a widow with ten, or between a single orphaned child and a large family of orphans. In that respect the pension payment was more of a token gesture than a way of helping, in an equitable way, all those whom war or rebellion had left in need.[36]

Though the basic pension may have been paltry, it was a great deal better than nothing at all. It is abundantly clear that for those who qualified, getting and keeping the pension was seen as a highly desirable object, even as being vital to survival. £20 provided at least a small measure of security in a highly insecure, pre–welfare state world. The money was wanted, and needed, in some cases desperately so. Pensioners were willing to put up with a considerable amount of twice-yearly red tape to ensure that their payments continued. People who lost their pensions petitioned to try to get them back. Others petitioned for pensions many years after their militia service in the hope of getting on the list. Some petitioners were prepared to use dubious and even fraudulent means to get their hands on £20 a year. A glimpse of how essential a small pension could be can be found in surviving petitions from Susanna Kendrick, who appeared earlier (in chapter 1) as a land petitioner. Her husband, Duke William Kendrick, one of a numerous family of York County Kendricks, died of disease in 1813 after having served as a lieutenant in the Third Regiment of York Militia. Susanna Kendrick began receiving a pension shortly after her husband's death, but in January 1819 she appealed to the lieutenant governor for help because she was not due to receive another pension payment until March and she had overdue debts which she could not pay. She petitioned again in August 1820, at which time she claimed that she had not been paid on time the pension money owed to her. Though she maintained that she was attempting to support her "helpless family" by "her hard earnings," she was again without funds and asked for at least a temporary advance to pay her rent. Her problems were compounded, to say the least, in 1821, for under the new legislation of that year she was removed from the pension list altogether. She now appealed to the Upper Canadian legislature to make an exception in her case and to continue the payments under special legislation, but this time her petition was rejected, along with three others of a similar nature, by a committee of the House. The chairman of the committee, William Warren Baldwin, acknowledged that the loss of a pension could cause some distress, "but it does not appear to be all of that nature that can be considered as affording them a claim upon the Public Revenue of the Province." Ellen Ganley, encountered earlier as an ultimately successful pension petitioner in 1839, provides another example of the difficulties of living on £20 a year. In January 1840

she and her six children were listed as charitably supported out-
pensioners of the House of Industry in Toronto.[37]

The petitions of a group of old soldiers written in the 1830s, demonstrate that some who were in need were eager to accept a form
of pension which was worth much less than £20, and was highly
temporary in nature. Under the regulations of a Royal Warrant of
14 November 1829, a very specific body of discharged infantrymen
in Upper Canada became eligible for a special "gratuity." If they had
served for at least fifteen years, received a free discharge, received a
grant of land, settled on it and were in the process of improving it,
they could apply for a quarter-year's pension of 6d a day, which
could be renewed quarter by quarter, "for a period not exceeding in
the whole, one year." The total individual sum therefore available
under the warrant came to a little over £9. Judging by the applications for this bounty, including some from men (and one widow)
who came nowhere close to meeting all the criteria, for more than
thirty veterans, £9 too was much better than nothing.[38]

The government of Upper Canada did acknowledge, at least in a
minimum way, that a debt was owed to those who had suffered some
kind of loss as the result of service in the militia or in a civilian capacity, but the government, particularly during the lieutenant governor-
ship of Sir Peregrine Maitland, worried constantly about the high
cost of even such a low level of compensation to the pensioners and
tried from time to time to trim the list by tighter laws and more vigilant administration. Yet a lot of real people had suffered real hardship, many in defence of the province and government which
afterwards treated them more like inconvenient statistics than individuals in need. Inconvenient or not, they were still made of flesh and
blood and often enough their lives had been permanently and tragi-
cally altered. Private Joseph Wheaton of the First Lincoln Regiment
was shot through the left eye at St David's on 22 July 1814 "which
has deprived him of the use of it, and so injured his head, as to at
times cause him very violent pain." Three days later at the battle of
Lundy's Lane (which saw the highest militia casualties) Private Jacob
Snyder of the Incorporated Militia was shot five times, through the
body, the left hand, the left side, the right shoulder, "and a fifth ball
lodged in the cranium behind the right ear, which last wound impairs
his understanding, especially at the change of weather." John Bennet,
whose rank and regiment are unknown, was wounded in the leg at
Fort Erie in November 1812. A year later at Long Point he was shot

in the other leg which this time required amputation. For these men and the many others like them, and for the widows of militiamen, £20 was, to say the least, scant and inadequate compensation.[39]

It was true that the government was short of revenue. Money to pay pensions had to be borrowed in 1821. The government had other obligations such as the claims for payment for property losses arising from the War of 1812. Nonetheless there was some measure of hypocrisy in the official rhetoric, for money could always be found for some people and some purposes. Did former chief justice Powell in his dotage really need a pension almost sixty times the value of that of a disabled militiaman or militia widow? Figures on Upper Canadian government expenditures available for the years 1824–40 show that the amount spent on pensions for the relatively few "privileged" pensioners almost always much exceeded the amount spent on the much greater number of militia pensioners. By the 1830s the Province of Upper Canada was borrowing money in large quantities from English sources, mostly to finance public works. Valuable and necessary works they were, but it seems not to have occurred to anyone in government that a little more money could have been used to allow a modest increase to a relatively small and inevitably diminishing group of veterans and their dependents.[40]

Still the government sometimes did make exceptions, if not to the amount of the pensions at least to the number of people it permitted to benefit from public funds. A few men and women whose circumstances did not quite meet all the required criteria, and some like Charlotte Overholt who did not qualify for a pension under "any law in force," were given special consideration, sometimes on the recommendation of the lieutenant governor or through the efforts of MHAs on behalf of their constituents. At such times the laws enacted invariably used the ritual phrase "it is expedient" that an exception be made, not using the word expedient to mean that it was politically advantageous, but in an older sense of the word, meaning "suitable" or "fitting." The government in other words was capable on infrequent occasions of pretending that matters could be other than the strict letter of the law allowed. In 1816 the provincial parliament passed an "Act Granting Relief to Catherine McLeod." She was a widow, too old and infirm to earn a living, and had lost two sons in the war. But she was not the widow of a militiaman and as such did not come within the terms of the pension act. The House of Assembly, the Legislative Council and the lieutenant governor pretended that she was. The act for her benefit gave her a pension "as if she were" the widow of a militiaman killed on duty.[41]

The pension system, like most of the bureaucratic practices of the Upper Canadian government, was complicated and burdened with a variety of narrow rules and regulations, which the pensioner had strictly to follow, not only once but repeatedly, but the people for whom a pension was theirs by right were determined to have their due. After some initial confusion, potential pensioners, with or without official advice, worked out how the system was supposed to work and took advantage of it. Pension petitioners were mostly not very sophisticated people but they knew that a pension was lawfully theirs even if they had to beg for it twice a year. Susanna Kendrick could not sign her name and therefore presumably could not personally read nor write, but that did not stop her from finding means to petition the lieutenant governor or the legislature whenever she thought that the government was not keeping its side of the pension promise. Hannah Mickle took even more positive action to obtain a pension. She went directly to the centre of male military authority and personally "appeared before the board of militia officers appointed to hear the claims of those entitled to be placed on the pension list."[42]

For ordinary Upper Canadians who were disabled veterans and militia widows a pension application was a "petition of right" because pensions were provided for by law and had been earned by service and sacrifice. Because they were viewed by pensioners as rights to which they were entitled, they, like applicants for land, were prepared to repeatedly navigate a complex bureaucracy and resisted and protested any adverse change to their meagre benefits. To the ordinary pensioners of Upper Canada, £20 a year, while no great sum, was well worth making an effort for even in cases which could not normally "be reached by any law in force."

5

Schools, Teachers, and Trustees

The history of education in Upper Canada cannot be said to be a neglected subject. This chapter, though it draws on the work of many educational historians, especially the contributions of such scholars as Donald Wilson, Bruce Curtis, Susan Houston, Alison Prentice, and Robert Gidney (writing on his own or in collaboration with the late Douglas Lawr or with Winnifred Millar), does not attempt to duplicate or much extend their work, but concentrates on a particular part of the Upper Canadian educational system, the early schools which operated in part under the regulation of the provincial state and with the support of the provincial treasury.[1]

Upper Canadians who wished to be teachers or who wanted their children to be taught came into contact with their provincial government at arm's-length, if at all, for there was nothing to stop an individual from setting up as a schoolteacher entirely without official sanction, subsidization, or regulation, and nothing requiring parents to send their children to a state supported school, or to any school at all. Prior to 1807 the government of Upper Canada took no responsibility for any kind for education. In that year an act of the legislature provided for the establishment of a grammar school in each of the districts to provide a classical education for the training of the future lay and clerical leaders of Upper Canada. Only in 1816 was any provision made for the support of education for ordinary Upper Canadians. The 1816 Common School Act created the possibility of state funding and regulation of schools for the general population, that is for schools which taught the basic "3 Rs," but by no means guaranteed universal access to government supported schools. A maximum sum of £6,000 (about the same amount the province

Table 5.1
Government expenditure on education, 1840

District Schools – 14 at £100	£1,400
Common Schools – annual grant	£5,650
Permanent provision for each district	£3,500
Grant for books	£1,500
Total	£12,050

Source: HAJ (1839–40), app. vol. 2, 146–7.

committed itself to spending on militia pensions in the same year) was voted for the funding of common schools in the entire province, distributed to the districts on the basis of their population. This amount was severely reduced in 1820, in the round of government cutbacks which was also to include pension payments the following year, to £2,500. The Upper Canadian educational budget however was eventually again increased. An act of 1833, renewed annually through 1840, set the sum spent on common schools at £5,650 per year, again allocated to the districts according to population.[2] At the end of the 1830s the total annual expenditure on schools had reached the still modest amount of £12,050 (see table 5.1).

To get a share of the always meagre government fund, parents who wished their children to attend state-aided common schools after 1816 had to conform to a number of government requirements. Each locality applying for a grant had to choose three school trustees to be responsible for the administration of the school, including the collection of additional quarterly fees for each child. A school building had to be built and maintained and at least twenty students had to attend it. A teacher had to be hired who was "of good moral character" and was a British subject or had at least taken the oath of allegiance. Needless to say state-aided schools did not spring up rapidly under these conditions, given the low level of financial inducement and the scattered nature of much of the population. "Private venture" schools, set up usually in their own homes by non–state-supported individuals, continued for a long time to be more common than the official common schools.[3]

For the schools which did come into existence as a result of the grammar school and common school acts, a rudimentary bureaucracy required by the legislation came into being. Where there was bureaucracy there was also a paper trail created, some of which survives to permit an impression to be gained of how the system worked.

A board of education was established in 1816 in each district, consisting of five members appointed by the lieutenant governor. To this body the trustees of common schools were required to make semi-annual reports on the state of their schools, and the district boards were required in turn to report for their districts, on both the common and grammar schools, to the provincial government. A broken run of these reports to the central government exists for the years 1818 to 1841. In addition a valuable set of locally kept and nearly complete records on teachers, trustees, and the distribution of government money has survived for the Eastern District alone, for the years 1816 to 1831.[4]

The records reveal that the number of grant-aided common schools in Upper Canada did eventually increase in a general way over time, though the story was by no means simply one of regular annual increase, as some examples from the reports make abundantly clear. The earliest extant return for the London District for instance, in 1828, listed forty operating common schools. After that the sporadic reports show much fluctuation: in 1829, forty-four schools; in 1832, forty-two schools; in 1835, 113 schools; in 1838, eighty-four schools; and in 1839, ninety-eight schools. All of the other districts for which there are significant runs of reports show precisely the same pattern, or lack of pattern. All of the districts had more common schools in 1839 than they had had ten years or so earlier but much backsliding had taken place along the way (see table 5.2).

The Eastern District records permit a unique look at this phenomenon not only in the district as a whole but at the level of the townships, two of which have been selected for special study (see table 5.3). In most cases the number of common schools in each district did not keep pace with the annual increase in population which occurred in every district. The most extreme cases were the Newcastle and Western districts. There was one common school for every 379 people in the Newcastle District in 1828 but in 1838 there was one for every 813 people. In the Western District there was one school for every 333 people in 1828 and in 1838 one for every 664 people. Exactly why such variations in the number of schools occurred is not certain. Very likely money had something to do with it. Table 5.3 shows a sharp drop in the number of common schools in the Eastern District in 1821 after the provincial grant was cut by more than half and there is some evidence of a reverse trend, observable in table 5.2, of an increase in the number of schools in some districts in the early

Table 5.2
Number of common schools by year and district, 1827–41

	1827	1828	1829	1830	1831	1832	1835	1836	1838	1839	1841
Bathurst	39	42	50		47				84	86	
Eastern	48	47	47	49	59				89		
Gore							47				
Home	32	38	42		36		84		92	110	
Johnstown			39	27			57	73	84	82	
London		40	44			42	113		84	98	
Midland									131		
Newcastle	21	22		33	33		57		44	56	
Niagara	37	32		34	28		41	37	48	41	
Ottawa	11								31		
P. Edward									64		
Talbot									28	23	25
Western	23	25	21	22			28		33	29	

Sources: LAC, RG 5, A1, vol. 58, 30387–8; B11, vols. 2–6; MG 24, I3, vol. 3, K12; *HAJ* (1826–27, 1829, 1830, 1836, 1839–40).

Table 5.3
Number of common schools in the Eastern District and in two townships, 1816–31

Year	Eastern District	Cornwall Township	Williamsburg Township
1816	27	3	3
1817	39	7	4
1818	31	11	6
1819	60	13	6
1820	61	12	6
1821	36	7	3
1822	41	8	4
1823	36	6	4
1824	47	11	3
1825	44	9	3
1826	43	10	4
1828	47	11	4
1829	47	7	5
1830	49	8	3
1831	59	14	4

Source: LAC, MG 24, I3, vol. 3, 205–54.

1830s when increased funds were again directed to the common schools. As well the number of potential students in particular rural areas must at times have fallen below the minimum number required for the grant, for, at least in the Eastern District, schools which existed in one year were not necessarily there in the next. (The Eastern District records also often list a suspicious number of schools with exactly twenty students.) Some communities may not have been able to find people willing to act as trustees, or some trustees may simply have failed to make reports to the district board in some years. It is also more than likely that at times teachers could simply not be found, or kept, for more than a short period.

In the townships of Cornwall and Williamsburg in the Eastern District there were a few unusual individuals for whom teaching was apparently a long-term occupation. William Bower and Samuel Zuill both taught without interruption for fifteen years, from 1817 to 1831 (and probably longer, but there is no record of the names of teachers after 1831). Patrick Edward and William Paterson taught every year from 1820 to 1831. These men were very much exceptions to the rule. Of 103 people who taught in the two townships in those years, sixty, or 58 per cent, taught for only one year or less. There are many examples of teachers in the Eastern District who in a six month period taught for only three months, two months, one month, or for as little as two weeks before leaving, usually not to return. Why and where they went can only be guessed at, for most of them have left little if any further evidence of their later careers. No doubt in some cases teaching was a necessary stopgap or a hoped-for launching pad on the way to more congenial or lucrative pursuits, but scanning the lists of those who taught in the Eastern District for people who subsequently appear in some other capacity in contemporary records or later histories produces very few examples of even modest success following an experience in teaching. Most teachers in the common schools were evidently pretty obscure in their time and afterwards. Of all those who were teachers in the Eastern District between 1816 and 1831 only two can be readily identified as having gone on to achieve some greater level of distinction. Job Deacon, who taught for two years in Cornwall Township, later had a long career as a minister of the Church of England. John Rae, teacher of a common school in Williamstown, Charlottenburg Township, in the 1820s and 1830s, is the subject of a four-page entry in the *Dictionary of Canadian Biography* as an author and economic theorist.[5]

Teachers in grammar schools enjoyed quite secure income levels. In addition to the £100 per district allocated annually by the government, grammar school teachers were permitted to charge their students fees, and some also provided board for out-of-town students at a price. Teachers in grammar schools were by and large respected members of Upper Canadian society, especially since many were at the same time (salaried) clergymen of the churches of England or Scotland, among whom John Strachan is the best-known example. Common school teachers were in a much different situation: their status and their income was a good deal more doubtful. The Common School Act of 1816 stipulated that no single common school teacher was to receive more than £25 a year in government funds. This was cut in half in 1820 to £12-10-0. Here also there was some later gradual improvement but the remuneration from government was never substantial. Teachers were paid only every six months for a half year of teaching, and like militia pensioners had to submit twice yearly certificates to the district board, signed by the local trustees, stating that they had satisfactorily taught at least twenty students. In the period between 1816 and 1820 quite a few common school teachers did receive the whole £25 a year, normally paid in two instalments of £12-10-0, but many got widely varying lesser amounts because they did not teach for the full six months, or missed some teaching days, or because the amount of school funds in the hands of the district treasurer were simply not enough to pay the full sum to all the teachers in the district. The teaching trio of John, Philomen, and Samuel Pennock, who taught in the Johnstown District, provide one example among many of this fluctuation in both teaching time and provincial allowance. John Pennock was paid £12-10-0 for the half year 4 November 1816 to 4 May 1817, but then taught a five-month term, 4 May to 4 October 1817, for which he was paid £10-8-4. Philomen Pennock taught for the full six months, 7 October 1818 to 6 April 1819, but only received £11-12-9 3/4, and for the six months between 10 April and 10 October 1819 got only £9-6-3, or three-quarters of the full allowance. Samuel Pennock had a perfect record, being paid £12-1-0-0 three times in each six months period between 1 May 1818 and 1 November 1819.[6]

After the government school funds were cut back in 1820 and even after they were finally increased again, the amount known to have been paid to teachers for six months of teaching varied even more from time to time and from place to place. In the 1830s the records show six-month allowances as low as £4-4-9 3/4, with the highest rate being £10-6-5 1/2, less than the maximum attainable before 1820. But common school teachers, like those in grammar schools, were also allowed to charge fees for each student, and fees presented the greatest potential income. Robert Gourlay in his statistical survey of Upper Canada taken in 1817 reported the average school fees in the province to be 13s 8d per quarter. This figure was obviously based mostly on fees in non–state-aided schools but if it applied at all to teachers in common schools it would have meant, assuming each school had the minimum twenty students, a yearly additional income of £43-13-4. There is a fair amount of evidence which suggests that in many parts of the province, especially in areas where the parents were still struggling to achieve some level of subsistence themselves, common school teachers were likely to be paid much less in fees, and were likely to be paid in produce rather than in money. S.A.H. Lucas, teaching in Chinguacousy Township in August 1837, complained of being in "great distress." He had been paid £7-10-0 in January but only £4 in July. The parents of his students were "very poor" and could not even provide him with flour, having none for themselves until after the harvest. Another teacher, E.C. Bolton, found that teaching a small school barely supported his family and was unable to pay his rent in February 1835, expecting "hourly" to be evicted. George Mackenzie taught for a time in a school in Esquesing Township, but gave it up, having had only eight regular students and having received no actual money at all, only "store goods." William Pitt went to "this remote place," South Gower Township, to teach in 1826, but reported that he was "almost starving" because there turned out to be no trustees for his school so that he could not be paid either fees or his government allowance. The board of education of the well-settled Niagara District in 1830 regretted that teacher's salaries were "so low as not to induce men of sufficient qualifications generally to engage in the humble and ill-requited duties." Legislation of 1833 finally required local communities to pay common school teachers an additional amount twice the value of the government grant, which could have produced an income as high as £60 a year or thereabouts, but for most of the period, Dr Peter A. Russell, a student of social status and mobility in Upper Canada, was probably right to put the common school teacher in the "quasi-dependent" class, with a yearly income in the £25 to £35 range.[7]

Evidently common school teaching was not a very attractive or popular profession, yet as has been seen the number of schools did increase, meaning that more teachers were inevitably needed. So who taught in these schools? The general impression that historians have conveyed of them is that they were an indifferent, incompetent lot, "men who had failed in every other calling," and that they were often Americans who poisoned the minds of Upper Canadian children with foreign political notions. There is certainly some basis for the claim that teaching was often a calling of last resort. Some of the teachers just referred to who found teaching unprofitable fit this description well enough. George Mackenzie had failed in business and felt "a decay of body." E.C. Bolton had hurt his back and could no longer work as a farmer and teamster. William Pitt had failed badly as a pioneer farmer near Perth "owing to various misfortunes and in some measure to his own mismanagement and imprudence, being quite unfitted for the active duties of a farm, in which he threw away a large sum of money." Other teachers or would-be teachers told similar stories. Samuel Davidson applied in 1820 for a job as a school teacher "or anything whatever that will enable me to make a reputable living as my constitution will not bear to earn my bread by hard labour." Another man named Davidson, Gavin Davidson of York, admitted in 1829 that his old age and bad health prevented him "of falling into any situation except teaching." Joseph Hawkins also hoped to become a teacher, having lost his right hand. Gabriel Bradley came to Upper Canada via the United States where his "commercial prospects were blighted by embarrassments," and had been reduced to supporting himself by teaching. All of these men, and many others like them, also had something else, besides previous misfortune, in common. They were all British immigrants in Upper Canada.[8]

In 1838, the government of Upper Canada, concerned about what Lieutenant Governor Sir George Arthur called "the madness of allowing Americans to be the instructors of the Youth of the Country," carried out a primitive survey to try to determine how serious the alleged domination of the teaching profession by Americans actually was. The district boards of education were asked to provide data on the place of birth of the teachers employed in the common schools. The results were, as usual for the time, incomplete. Some of the more populous districts, including Home, London, Midland and Niagara, failed to supply the required information, though the chairman of the London District board, John B. Askin, did admit that while the board was opposed to hiring American teachers it had been impossible to force local trustees "wholly to exclude them." There may have been a number of American-born teachers in the other districts for which there is no data as well, but in the districts which did report, Johnstown, Bathurst, Ottawa, Prince Edward, Newcastle, and Western, the information gathered is clear enough. Out of a total of 304 teachers in these districts, 259, or 85 per cent, had been born in the United Kingdom. Of the other forty-five, all but one had been born somewhere in British North America, of whom twenty-two (only 7 percent) had been born in Upper Canada itself. Two teachers in the Western District had been born in France and the birth place of three teachers was said to be unknown. None of them was listed as having been born in the United States. This does not mean that there were not nor had not been Americans teaching in Upper Canada. The smoke produced by so much anecdotal evidence must have contained some amount of real fire, especially during Upper Canada's early educational history. But there is some fragmentary evidence to suggest that well before the dampening effect of the Rebellion set in American teachers were far from dominant, at least in the common schools. A few school reports for the Newcastle and Johnstown districts in the early 1830s which unusually also record the birth place of the teachers of common schools, put American-born teachers in a very small minority. In the Newcastle District there were two American teachers out of thirty-two in 1830, two of thirty-three in 1832–33 and three of fifty-seven in 1834–35. In the Johnstown District in 1835 none of the fifty-seven teachers was of American birth.[9]

In fact, if any national group may be said to have dominated among teachers in the common schools it was clearly the Irish. In all cases except one where specific place of birth is included in the school reports (in some cases teachers are identified only as being British) the Irish-born greatly outnumbered all others. In the Newcastle District twenty-eight of thirty-two teachers were Irish in 1830, eighteen of thirty-three in 1832–33, and forty-one of fifty-seven in 1834–35. In the Johnstown District in 1835 only twenty-four of fifty-seven teachers were definitely Irish, but a further thirteen teachers, some of whom may have been Irish, were identified only as being British subjects. (Eight were listed as English and five as Scottish.) In

1838 fourteen of thirty-one teachers were Irish (Scottish, seven; English, three) in the Ottawa District, in the Newcastle District there were twenty-seven Irish teachers out of forty-four. Only in the Western District do the reports of the 1830s show a different result. In 1838 there were only seven Irish-born teachers out of a total of thirty-three in the district, but they were still in second place among the British group, behind the Scots at fourteen but ahead of the English at four. Of course it is quite possible that the birthplaces of the teachers in other districts differed from those in the few actual reports that give place of birth. In the Eastern District for example, while there is no birthplace information on the teachers, we do know the names of virtually everyone who taught in the common schools between 1816 and 1831. A few names such as those of Michael Kelly, Michael Kinney, John O'Connor, William Phelan, Patrick Mulhern, James O'Kelly, and Redmond O'Healy attest to the presence of teachers of Irish (and likely Roman Catholic) background, and an unknown number of the other teachers with less obviously Irish names may have been born in Ireland, but they do not appear to have been dominant there. Still it is no surprise to find the Irish generally predominant among common school teachers since the Irish, and among them Irish Protestants, are known to have been much the largest British immigrant group. What mind-warping impact the Irishness of many of their teachers may have had on the children of the common schools of Upper Canada can only be a matter of speculation. Whatever their influence, it was not in the direction of "Americanization."[10]

The preponderance of Irish and other British-born teachers may have reflected a higher level of education among immigrants than among the Upper Canadian-born, but this is likely at best a partial explanation. In fact most Upper Canadians have been shown to have received at least a rudimentary education well before a general state education system was in place in the 1840s. In any case no great scholarly attainments were necessary to qualify as a common school teacher. It is more probable that teaching was deliberately shunned by most Upper Canadian-born men, who had the built-in local advantage of easier access to better opportunities, principally in farming, commerce, or the professions. The survey of 1838 and indeed numerous earlier school reports however, show that some Upper Canadians, Upper Canadian women, were quite well represented among a small but growing female contingent in the teaching profession.[11]

The presence of women teachers in the common schools of Upper Canada has been a rather well-kept secret. In an entire chapter on women teachers in her book, *Wives and Mothers, School Mistresses and Scullery Maids: Working Women in Upper Canada, 1790–1840*, Elizabeth Jane Errington makes no reference whatsoever to women teaching in the common schools. In *Schooling and Scholars in Nineteenth-Century Ontario*, the eminent educational historians Susan F. Houston and Alison Prentice were aware from a small amount of anecdotal evidence that some women had at times taught in the common schools, but regretted that there were "no statistics from which to assess the proportion of teachers who might have been women in the common schools of early Upper Canada." In fact the contemporary school reports provide quite a bit of information on the part played by women as common school teachers in the period.[12]

Officially women were not supposed to be allowed to teach in the government subsidized common schools at all. In January 1840, Simeon Washburn, chairman of the Prince Edward District board of education, wrote to the provincial secretary posing two questions. The first concerned the vexatious problem of American-born common school teachers who had not been naturalized, specifically an American named Ahira H. Blake then teaching in a common school in the district. Were such teachers eligible to be paid from the government allowance? The second question was about women teachers. Were they eligible to be paid from public funds? These questions were referred by the Executive Council to the law officers of the Crown, the attorney and solicitor generals of Upper Canada. Their answer to both questions was no. The employment of Americans "cannot be upheld" under the law (though they conceded that Blake should be paid for work he had already done) and the language used in the common school acts of 1816 and 1820 did not "contemplate the employment of women teachers." The law then was clear. It is also clear that law was not necessarily practice. Some women and some Americans (who were sometimes the same people) had been teaching in the common schools for the previous twenty years or more. The earliest known official record of women teachers in the common schools dates from 1818–19, when Mary Keeler (who may have been the widow of a male teacher, Charles Keeler) was teaching in Williamsburg Township in the Eastern District. Two women teachers, Mary Ann Hill and Julia Beckwith, taught in the common schools of Kingston in the Midland District in 1821, as did Lucinda Parys in Cornwall Township in the Eastern District in 1821 and 1822. The Eastern District common schools seem to have been something of a hotbed of female teachers for fifteen of them are known to have held teaching positions there between 1819 and 1831. The unfortunately incomplete results of the 1838 survey turned up a total of eighty female common school teachers in Upper Canada. Of these at least six had been born in the United States.[13]

Actually the birth place of only thirty-six of the eighty women teachers was provided in the returns. This skimpy evidence however suggests some differences between male and female teachers. Besides the six American-born female teachers, sixteen had been born in Upper Canada and only fourteen in the United Kingdom. Women teachers appear to have been a much more indigenous group, given that sixty-one per cent of those whose place of birth is known had been born in North America. Upper Canadian men may have spurned teaching as an occupation but some Upper Canadian women apparently welcomed the chance to be teachers, since it was one of the few opportunities open to them to work for pay, if open is the right word. The employment of women teachers was in fact highly restricted, and was also a matter of much regional variation. In 1838 women teachers were employed in only six of the eleven districts for which we have reports, distributed very unevenly (see table 5.4).

Judging from the surviving school reports to the provincial government for the years 1818–39, a number of districts likely never hired women teachers at all. There were no reports of female teachers at any time in the Home, Niagara, Western, Gore, or Newcastle districts. In the Johnstown District, one woman, Florence McCarthy, taught in 1829 and 1830 in Elizabethtown Township, but she was the only female school teacher there, even though the district had more than eighty common schools by the end of the 1830s. No obvious explanation presents itself as to why some districts hired women and some did not, though in some places it may well have been a matter of deliberate policy not to hire women, nor is it at all clear why some districts which did hire women hired proportionately more than others. What can be said is that the reason for hiring some number of female teachers in some districts, was not, as would later often be the case, economic. The salary figures that we have give no cause to suppose that women were paid less than men, at least from

Table 5.4
Female teachers by district, 1838

District	Total Teachers	Women	% Women
Bathurst	84	6	7
Home	89	0	0
Johnstown	84	0	0
London	84	8	10
Midland	131	32	24
Newcastle	4	0	0
Niagara	48	0	0
Ottawa	31	9	29
Prince Edward	64	21	33
Talbot	28	4	14
Western	33	0	0
Totals	720	80	11

Source: *HAJ* (1833), app., School Reports.

the government grants, and in fact in some cases they were paid more. Such differences in any case were always slight, since there was so little government money to go round in the first place. It is possible of course that some women were willing to teach for lower fees than men were or even for no fees at all, or in the circumstances of the day some local trustees may just have been glad to hire anyone who was willing to take the jobs.[14]

The presence of female teachers may help explain why some districts, though less populated than others, actually had more common schools. In 1838 the Midland District for example, as has been seen, had one hundred and thirty-one common schools and thirty-two woman teachers, while the Home District had only one hundred and ten common schools and no woman teachers. The population of the Midland District was then 37,382, compared to 69,885 in the Home District. (The situation in the Home District may also been the result of a deliberate decision to limit the number of schools to make the grant go farther.)[15]

That some number of Upper Canadian-born women were able to become teachers demonstrates the fact that no great educational background was necessary in order to teach, since most of them would be unlikely to have had an education any more extensive than the one they in turn relayed to their students. Like their male colleagues they were unlikely to be prominent people, the sole possible exception being Matilda Cozens, who taught in Cornwall in the 1820s and 1830s and was the daughter of Joshua Young Cozens, Cornwall Loyalist, confidante of John Graves Simcoe, Anglican, and militia officer. And women teachers were a minority within a minority, for girls were less likely than boys in the Upper Canadian period to receive any sort of education at all, especially in the common schools. Scattered reports which provide figures on male and female students in the common schools show an invariable preponderance of boys. In 1827 there were 672 boys and only 368 girls in the common schools of the Niagara District; the numbers in the Bathurst District that year were 573 boys and 434 girls. The London District reported 646 boys and 522 girls in the common schools in 1828. Ten years later the overall numbers were considerably larger but so was the male-female discrepancy, 1,359 boys compared to 744 girls. Nonetheless some rare actual breakdowns of male-female numbers of students within each common school, available for the London District for 1828 and 1838–39, provide some intriguing evidence that where female teachers were present, female students were also likely to attend school in equal or greater numbers than boys. In 1828 there were only four female teachers in the district out of a total of forty, and there were 124 more male students than female. In every one of the schools taught by women, girls outnumbered boys.[16]

Sophia Walker, teaching in Woodhouse Township, actually had fewer than the required twenty students – thirteen girls and only four boys (which suggests that this regulation was not always strictly enforced and also that some parents may not have wanted their boys taught by a woman teacher). Out of eighty-four teachers in the district in 1838, nine were women, but again in all nine schools taught by women there were more girl students than boys. The following year there were ninety-eight teachers of whom twelve were women. Eight of the twelve women teachers had more girls in their schools than boys. In Phoebe Moore's school in Bayham Township there were twice as many girls as boys, eighteen girls and nine boys. The discrepancy was even greater in the Yarmouth Township school taught by Betsey Bostwick, which had twenty girls and six boys. Though these figures represent only a couple of momentary snapshots of one corner of the province for brief periods they do provide at least the basis for speculation. Women teachers may have been a kind of role model for younger girls. The level of female literacy in Upper Canada, lower than the literacy level of Upper Canadian males by about 8 per cent, might well have been higher had there been more female teachers, since the number of girls in the common schools might well have been greater. It is true that most female teachers, as would long be the case, taught for only a short time, but there were exceptions. We know that some women, among them Isabella McFarlane and Margaret Cosgrove in the Bathurst District and Betsey Bostwick and Keziah Stinson in the London District, taught in the same schools for five or more years, and in some cases would have been the only teachers that some students, boys or girls, ever had.[17]

It was the generally expressed view of the Upper Canadian political and educational elite, and apparently of most parents, that boys and girls should, if possible, be educated separately. The Honourable Joseph Wells, bursar of King's College, was "a strong advocate for Boys & Girls being instructed in separate Apartments notwithstanding their studies may be precisely alike." An 1839 committee of the provincial legislature chaired by George S. Jarvis of Cornwall, recommended that "a sum of money" (never actually appropriated) be spent to support schools for girls only, "those who are destined by providence to become the wives and mothers of our future rulers, magistrates and legislators, and who may therefore be supposed to be able to exercise a certain degree of influence over them." Money was already being spent on the "liberal education" of boys in the grammar schools, but no provision was being made for "the other sex whose precepts and example must ever have a great weight in exalting the character of any people."[18]

Of course the common schools, the major government agency of general education, never attempted to separate the sexes. Cash-strapped rural parents could not dream of building two schools or even two classrooms or hiring two teachers for their children; indeed if girls had not attended the common schools a good many of them would not have existed, for want of the necessary numbers. The goal of educating male and female children separately in state-aided schools however, was never entirely given up. It was pursued most vigorously in the district grammar schools, many of which simply excluded girls, and in an unusual institution which differed from both the grammar and the common schools, the Upper Canada Central School in York/Toronto.

The Upper Canada Central School was the subject of much controversy in its day, mainly because it replaced a common school in

York with the resultant dismissal of its teacher, a Yorkshire Methodist named Thomas Appleton. The Upper Canada Central School was established by Lieutenant Governor Sir Peregrine Maitland as a method of using public funds to deliver basic education on a large scale to the humbler classes of York society, and also to counteract the "intrusion" of American Methodist influence. It was based on a system devised by a Dr Bell for the teaching of large numbers of students using the "monitorial" method in which older students were supposed to teach lessons to the junior classes. The Bell system, unlike the similar "Lancastrian" model, was avowedly Anglican, and the students, unless their parents made a point of objecting, were taught the church catechism. The school did have considerable success in its mission to reach out to children who might otherwise have had little if any formal education. In the first seven years of its existence the school taught only a total of 437 students, or an average of about sixty-two a year, but in 1828 there were 150 students enrolled, and figures for the 1830s show a further marked increase. In 1832, 338 students, 196 boys and 142 girls, were "in actual attendance" and in 1835 the figures were very similar, 186 boys and 151 girls, for a total of 337. In 1838, 680 students "received instruction" in the school. It has been calculated that during the school's entire existence, from 1820 to 1844, 5,514 pupils attended the school. Actually the attendance figures do not tell the whole story, for many children attended on a highly irregular basis but nonetheless got some schooling: "From the situation in life of the parents, generally, requiring the assistance of their children, sickness and other casualties, the attendance of the school is very variable." It was not unusual for many of the students enrolled to be absent on any one day. An attendance record of December 1828 listed an average number of forty boys out of a total of ninety-four and an average of twenty-five girls out of sixty-one enrolled who were absent daily. Students also came and went at a high rate. In 1838, 167 boys and 149 girls were noted as having left the school. Still Inspector General John Macaulay was no doubt justified in reporting to the lieutenant governor that the school was "most useful in educating, in a limited way, great numbers of the poorer class of children who would otherwise be brought up in the lowest depths of ignorance."[19]

Unlike the common and grammar schools, the Upper Canada Central School's teachers were not supposed to charge the parents fees as an income supplement, so that no one would be deterred from attending due to a lack of funds. The school's trustees and one of the teachers, John T. Wilson, thought this was a mistake and that all students should have to pay some level of fee, for otherwise their parents would not appreciate the service a generous government was providing. As it was the school was said to be seen as a "charity" school for the poor and as such was not patronized by "respectable mechanics and others." In fact it is known that fees were sometimes charged to parents who were thought to be able to pay, but whether the government in fact got value for its money from the Central School is a moot point. The school eventually employed three teachers who were paid more than £300 a year to teach perhaps 300 students, compared to common school teachers who might make no more than £10 a year in government allowance for teaching 30 or more students.[20]

When the Upper Canada Central School was opened in 1820 it would have looked much like a large common school. A single teacher, Joseph Spragge, who had come from England to take the post, taught all the students, boys and girls together, in a single classroom. Spragge was never happy about this situation. Believing that "it appears to be almost or quite as essential for girls to be instructed in the Principals of Education according with the system of the British National Society, as for boys, with regard to the good effect to be produced when they arrive at maturity," he was disappointed that fewer girls than boys attended the school "for the want of a mistress over the Girl's School, to attend to the necessary employment of sewing." Girls were "generally removed from the Central School, to learn needlework at some other, at the time when their minds become most susceptible of Religious and Moral Instruction." Finally in 1828 a second room was opened above the original classroom and the girls were moved upstairs to be taught by a female teacher hired by Spragge "on his own responsibility," who besides the regular subjects – spelling, writing, reading, church catechism, and arithmetic – taught sewing in the afternoon. The male students were taught two additional subjects not available to the girls, English grammar and bookkeeping. Spragge was pleased to be able to report "increased numbers in the school since the separation."[21]

If the Upper Canada Central School began on much the same basis as a common school, it eventually developed pretensions to become in part like a grammar school. A "second department" was added with an additional (male) teacher to provide advanced education to those of "the humbler classes of life" who hoped "to be materially benefitted" from exposure to further instruction in grammar, geography, bookkeeping, and geometry, the latter two "as circumstances may require." The second department was not a great success, for most students left the school without ever getting into the advanced classes. Girls continued to be taught separately in "the female department."[22]

The real centre of advanced education, the grammar schools themselves, which were distinguished by the teaching of Latin and sometimes Greek, were generally wary of admitting girls, "it being inconsistent with the good discipline of boys or that delicate treatment which is best suited to girls." Girls had no need to go to the grammar schools. "The object of public [i.e. grammar] schools as established by law in this province" according to the Reverend Thomas Creen, assistant rector of St Mark's Anglican Church and master of the Niagara District School, "is to teach the Classics and Mathematics and higher branches of education, and prepare young men for College and the learned professions." Like the laws which theoretically barred women from teaching in the common schools, the rule of exclusion of girls from the grammar schools was early and often broken. The attendance of girls at grammar schools also varied from district to district, in a pattern which sometimes overlapped with the presence of women common school teachers. Unfortunately the extant reports on the district grammar schools are even more incomplete than those for the common schools. What can be said is that in the 1820s and 1830s there were often girl students in the grammar schools in the Gore, London, Western, and Ottawa districts. So far as can be determined there were never any girls in the Niagara, Midland, Johnstown, and Newcastle district grammar schools. There were some girls in the Eastern District grammar school before 1828 but not after that date. Girls attended the Home District grammar school when it opened in 1807 but apparently not for very long. They "were subjected to many annoyances and were unwittingly the cause of many battles between jealous boys."[23] The situation in the other districts is unknown (see table 5.5).

In some cases girls attended grammar schools in considerable numbers. In the Western District school in 1828 there were sixteen girls out of a total of forty-eight students and in the Gore District fifteen of forty-nine students were girls. In the Ottawa District school in 1831 girls actually outnumbered boys, twenty-five to fourteen. As

Table 5.5
Girls in grammar schools in five districts in various years, 1823–35

District	Year	Total Students	Girls	% Girls
Eastern	1827	38	8	21
Gore	1823	28	6	21
	1824	32	7	22
	1828	49	15	31
	1829	46	5	11
London	1828	29	7	24
	1834	27	5	18
	1835	35	10	28
Ottawa	1831	39	25	64
Western	1827	31	10	31
	1828	48	16	33
	1830	43	10	23
	1831	43	10	23
	1834	38	6	16
Totals		526	140	27

Sources: LAC, RG 5. A1, vol. 65, 34299–302, B11, vol. 3, no. 54, vol. 4, no. 279, vol. 5, nos 466, 491 (School Reports, 1827–32, 1834).

would be even more true a generation later when an attempt was made to deny access to secondary education to girls, some parents and their daughters were prepared to ignore the rules in order to gain access to a level of schooling beyond the basic curriculum. But where exceptions were made for girls in the Upper Canadian grammar schools, they were made for exceptional people. The girls who went to grammar schools were, like their brothers, the children of the urban commercial or professional elite. The young ladies who excited such jealousy among the boys of the Home District school in 1807 were members of York's founding Jarvis, McNab, and Ridout families. Among the seven girls in the Gore District school in 1823–24 were Catharine and Keziah Beasley and Sally and Jane Mills, daughters of local entrepreneurs Richard Beasley and James Mills. The Western District school in 1830 was also attended by female members of locally prominent families: two Askins, two Wilkinsons, a Baby, and a McKee. Five of the girls attending the London District grammar school in 1834–35 were the daughters of John Harris, the district treasurer.[24]

No matter what form of government-aided school Upper Canadian children attended, there were likely to be some differences between the educational experiences of boys and girls. Girls were overall a minority in the schools and most were never taught by women teachers. There would also be some differences in what was taught, or what parents wanted taught, to male and female children. In the rural common schools the differences if any would be slight since little except the basics – reading, writing, spelling, and simple arithmetic – were taught to anyone. The larger common schools in the growing urban centres could attempt a more ambitious curriculum. By 1832–33 for example the common school in the town of London was divided into junior and senior classes. In the senior class, besides continuing to take lessons in reading and spelling, students could take English grammar, geography, and "ciphering." But of the fourteen girls in the school only two were taking all the available subjects. No girl in the school was being sent to school beyond the age of fifteen, while the boys ranged in age up to eighteen. Parents also seem to have taken the existence of a "junior" class pretty literally. Sarah Hawley, age three, attended, but was taking only spelling.[25]

The segregation of girls at the Upper Canada Central School after 1828 into a "female department" meant that they too received a different education from the boys. They were confined to learning the same subjects offered in the "first department," reading, writing, and the first principles of arithmetic, and even these were restricted because of the time spent by the girls in being taught "plain sewing." The subjects taught in the "second department," English grammar, geography, arithmetic, bookkeeping, and geometry, were not available to girls.[26]

The greatest differences existed within the few grammar schools which accepted female students. Presumably because of their own and their parents' wishes the girls in the grammar schools also by and large merely studied the basic "3 Rs," while the boys, who were often enough their brothers, progressed to the "higher branches of education." No girl is known to have studied geometry or trigonometry. A few took English grammar and geography. Latin also was a largely male preserve but there were some exceptions. In Hamilton at the Gore District school in 1828, Maria Hamilton, Maria Askin, and Catharine Beasley were being taught Latin by the incumbent

schoolmaster, John Law. In London in 1834–35 the remarkable
Harris girls, Sarah, Amelia, and Mary, were taught Latin, first by
George Boyce and then by the Reverend Francis Wright. Sarah
Harris, the oldest of the Harris girls, was also studying Greek. She
was the only student of Greek in the school at the time and was
probably one of very few in the entire province.[27]

The grammar schools, which were run by and patronized by the
Upper Canadian elite, were much criticized for their exclusiveness,
being both geographically and financially out of the reach of most
parents. By contrast educational historians have often seen in the
common schools another early example of grassroots democracy in
action, for the establishment, maintenance, and supervision of these
schools resulted from local initiative and leadership. The common
school trustees, unlike the great majority of officials in Upper Canada,
have been said to have been "popularly" or "fully" elected, and the
public meetings at which they were chosen have been called, like the
township meetings which annually chose other local functionaries,
"one of the few local organs of democratic self-government in the
period where local government was largely in the hands of appointed
justices." The truth though is that we know almost nothing about
how the common school trustees were actually selected. The
Common School Act of 1816 made it lawful for "a competent number of persons" who were the inhabitants of "any town, township,
village or place" to meet annually on eight days notice, not to elect,
but to *appoint*, "three fit and discreet persons" to act as (unpaid)
trustees for each common school, but how this appointment was to
take place was in no way specified in the act. No written account of
what went on at any of the many such meetings which must have
taken place seems to exist. Probably no minutes were ever actually
taken at the meetings, for unlike at the township meetings there was
no provision in the law for anyone to act as clerk. According to
Susan Houston and Alison Prentice there are no surviving minutes of
trustees' meetings before 1850. Both the process of selection of trustees in Upper Canada and their subsequent proceedings then are
shrouded in some degree of mystery. We do not know if there were
in fact ever "elections" with opposing candidates at the annual
school meetings. We do not know if differing educational philoso-
phies were advanced or discussed. We do not know whether the
meetings were well or sparsely attended. We do not know whether
they were always conducted formally, with someone called to the

chair, or whether they were mere *ad hoc* gatherings of neighbours. In the vast majority of cases we have no idea who the trustees themselves actually were. The extent to which they may or may not have been representative across the province of "democratic self-government" is therefore not easy to determine.[28]

The occasional reference to trustees in the reports of the district boards of education were often disparaging in nature. The calibre of the trustees, like that of the teachers, was generally denigrated because of their alleged ignorance and incompetence. In 1838 a senior government official, Robert Baldwin Sullivan, commissioner of Crown lands, deplored the fact that the direction of the common schools was "left to the care of a few illiterate, ignorant and sometimes disloyal local Township trustees." Especially in rural areas the trustees were seen by the district elites as unsophisticated rustics who, because they were representative of their local communities, were prone to errors of judgement and neglect of their duties. Like the schools themselves, the trustees were evidently "common" people. There would be of course nothing surprising about that since the system was, and was intended to be, class based. The common schools were a minimum means of giving some of the ordinary people of Upper Canada a minimum education, and were never meant to be centres of educational excellence like the grammar schools.[29]

There is not much hard evidence which concerns the common school trustees of Upper Canada, but there is some, and a certain amount of information can be gleaned from it. The most complete list of trustees to have been found for the Upper Canadian period is for the Eastern District, in the same list, preserved in the McGilivray papers, which contains the names and records of the Eastern District teachers of common schools of the time. There are formidable problems of identification involved in working with these records, particularly in those sections of Stormont and Glengarry counties where so many people shared a common name (especially Macdonell and Macdonald) but in a general way an examination of this list of trustees bears out the contention that they were by and large common people, whether or not they were in fact "democratically elected." Taking once more the townships of Cornwall and Williamsburg, where the population was somewhat ethnically mixed, as the basis for a manageable case study, there were some 224 men in those townships who served as trustees between 1816 and 1831. When these 224 names are matched against contemporary lists of regional

notables such as magistrates, government office-holders, militia officers, and members of the House of Assembly, the great majority of
trustees, about 82 percent, while no doubt "fit and discreet persons"
who had the approval of their neighbours, were not prominent people, although almost all of them had one thing in common; they were
of United Empire Loyalist stock, in an area heavily settled by
Loyalists. Probably the majority were farmers but most of them are
now hard to identify by occupation – a few turn out to have been
shop or tavern owners – and some, thirty-five, or 16 per cent, are
known to have been on active service during the War of 1812, thirty
at the rank of private and five as non-commissioned officers. In the
main though, they were not "important" people in the district.
Nonetheless the direction of the common schools was never, in the
Eastern District, left entirely in the hands of "illiterate, ignorant"
people. A significant minority, numbering about forty, or 18 per cent
of the total, could claim some level of local distinction.[30]

Cornwall, the district town and largest settlement, had from 1807
a well-established and well-known grammar school, overseen by a
distinguished board of trustees and taught until 1812 by the Reverend
John Strachan, which in his day not only prepared the sons of the
local elite for leadership roles but drew promising young men from
across the province. Despite having this educational advantage close
at hand, some of Cornwall's leading citizens also took a considerable
interest in the Cornwall Common School, which opened in 1816,
and served as the school's trustees. Joshua Young Cozens, already
identified as a prominent Cornwallian and whose daughter Matilda
later became a common school teacher, was one of the first trustees.
Other Cornwall residents of note who were common school trustees
included Guy C. Wood, merchant, magistrate, and militia officer;
Noah Dickinson, militia officer and medical doctor; Reverend Salter
Jehosaphat Mountain, Anglican rector of Cornwall; Archibald
McLean, magistrate, militia officer, MHA, public servant, and judge;
John Van Koughnet and Benjamin French, militia officers from
Loyalist families; Richard Warfe, public servant; George Anderson,
public servant and militia officer, and Donald Macdonell (Greenfield),
sheriff, MHA, and militia officer. Outside of the district town, such
trustees were thinner on the ground but were still represented in the
smaller villages and rural areas by men such as John Crysler, MHA,
militia colonel, lumberman, merchant, mill owner, and magistrate;
Donald Æneas Macdonell, magistrate, militia officer, and MHA;

Ambrose Blacklock, another medical doctor, a magistrate and MHA;
Henry Merkley, MHA and militia officer; Malcolm McMartin, magistrate and militia officer; and Simon Fraser, merchant, magistrate,
former fur trader, and explorer. It will be evident that service in the
Upper Canadian militia at the officer level was a mark of leadership
shared by many of the "elite" school trustees. All but five of them, or
a total of thirty-five, are known to have been officers in the Stormont
or Dundas regiments of militia, twenty-three of whom had served as
officers during the War of 1812.

Most of the common school trustees of course were not part of the
district elite, but prominent trustees were always a factor in the running of the school system. In 1816, their first year of operation, two
of the six original schools in the townships of Cornwall and
Williamsburg were controlled by elite trustees (that is, they held at
least two of the three trustee positions) and in every following year
except one, at least one out of a maximum of eighteen schools was
run by elite trustees. The locally prominent however can never have
been said to have been dominant in the supervision of the schools
and became even less so over time. After 1822, when three of twelve
schools had a majority of elite trustees, the actual number of schools
generally increased but it was rare for more than one school to be
run by elite trustees. In 1830, for the first time, there were no such
schools in either township. Of course the elite could never have
attempted to control all of the district common schools even if they
had wanted to, not being present in any numbers in the rural areas,
but neither did they entirely neglect or disdain the schools of the
ordinary people or the allegedly democratic process by which trustees were chosen.

Whether the trustees were prominent or ordinary people, there
is evidence that many of them took their duties fairly seriously.
While the names of many trustees, like those of the teachers, appear
in the records only once, among the trustees of the townships of
Cornwall and Williamsburg, more than half (54 per cent) held the
office for two years or more, and some for much longer periods.
Thomas Marcellis, Sephranus Casselman, and Bernard Whitaker of
Williamsburg Township formed a local school dynasty, holding the
three trustee positions at the same school for eight years, from 1823
to 1831, and quite possibly beyond. The one blemish on their record
was the fact that the school did not open in 1825. Simon Fraser was
a trustee in Cornwall Township seven times in the years from 1820

to 1831. The common school on Barnhardt Island, also in Cornwall Township, in existence 1819–22 and 1824, was run almost entirely by members of the Barnhardt family. At least two of John, William George, and Jacob Barnhardt were always its trustees. Another Cornwall Township family, the Loyalist Eastmans, were early and conscientious participants in the affairs of the common schools. Nadab and Benjamin Eastman each served six years as trustees and Samuel Eastman served twice. Joel Eastman's name appears as a trustee only in 1831 though he may have continued beyond that date. Daniel Eastman was one of the original Cornwall Township common school teachers in 1816 and 1817 at a school of which Nadab Eastman was a trustee. Daniel also taught in 1822 and 1823. Nadab Eastman Junior was also a teacher from 1820 to 1823.

Sewell Cutler, tavern owner, and George Gallinger, both of Cornwall Township, former militia privates in the First Stormont Regiment during the War of 1812, each served as a trustee for eight years. The record for length of service as a trustee in the period from 1816 to 1831 was held by Daniel Myers of Williamsburg Township, who held the office continually for fourteen years, from 1816 to 1829. Indeed Myers was one part of another school "team" of extraordinary stability at a time when such stability was extremely rare. In 1816 Myers had as his fellow trustees George Merkley, a war veteran as a captain in the Dundas Militia, and John Marcellis, probably a brother of Thomas Marcellis. They hired Robert Dick as the first common school teacher in their neighbourhood. Dick, like so many others, taught for only one year. In 1817, the trustees, now Myers, Merkley, and Michael Empey, hired William Bower as teacher. Bower was rehired in 1818 by trustees Myers, Merkley, and Marcellis. In 1819, John Crysler, Myers's superior officer in the Dundas Militia, joined Marcellis and Myers as the trustees of the school. These three men were then "democratically elected" as trustees, with Bower as teacher, every year for the next ten years, until 1830, when the school closed, probably when all of the Myers, Crysler, and Marcellis children had had sufficient schooling. It is likely that Bower, unlike many teachers, received adequate fees in addition to the government grant to keep him in the same post so long. After 1830 he continued to teach in the district in Mountain Township.

In most cases, schools, teachers, and trustees came and went on a regular basis and any impression of overall permanency would be highly misleading. Nor was the letter of the law always followed in the way in which the schools were locally administered. In Williamsburg Township, two men, Joseph Southworth and Michael Cook, were shown as being trustees of two different schools at the same time, as was Benjamin Eastman in Cornwall Township. More commonly the legal requirement that each school had to have three trustees was regularly ignored. There were no cases of a school ever having only a single trustee, but in fourteen of the sixteen years covered by the Eastern District records at least one school had only two trustees. In 1827 no fewer than six of fourteen schools operated with only two trustees, in 1831, five of eighteen. For five years in the 1820s Sewell Cutler shared trustee duties with a man named Hector Manson and no third trustee. Such situations were clearly irregular but were evidently accepted by the district board of education and the provincial government as necessary expedients when grassroots democracy could not provide a full complement of trustees on the spot.

Another variant on the rules involved the replacement of trustees who for some reason resigned their positions during the course of the school year. Though again there was no provision for "by-elections" of trustees in the common school act, some kind of *ad hoc* process was evolved by the local citizenry. The selection of trustees was supposed to take place once a year, for a year's term. The school reports were compiled twice a year, for the periods of June to December and December to June, and reveal a much less orderly, far more fluid state of affairs among the trustees, as well as the schools themselves and their teachers. What was true of the first school "term" was not necessarily true of the second. The townships of Cornwall and Williamsburg in the year 1822–23 provide one example. During June–December 1822, Cornwall Township had eight schools and Williamsburg had four. In the period of December 1822 to June 1823, each township had one fewer school. Five of the first term teachers were not listed at all as teaching in the second term. Two of these had taught in the two schools which had closed; there were now three brand-new teachers. In Williamsburg the closing of a school meant that its three trustees also disappeared from the records, but there was one newly "elected" replacement trustee for one of the three remaining schools. The situation in Cornwall Township was more complicated, not to say bizarre. Only four of the eight schools listed for the June–December period continued to operate in the December–June term, with the consequent deletion from the list of four teachers and twelve trustees. Three new schools were opened by eight new trustees (one school had only two trustees) who hired three new teachers. Three schools in the township continued into the second term with the same teachers, but two of these schools had one new trustee each.

The actual functioning of the Eastern District common schools at the local level presents an extraordinary picture of constant change and improvisation, and a degree of local initiative and experimentation beyond anything provided for in the provincial legislation. Given the difficulties involved in keeping the common schools afloat at all, it is not surprising that there was a constant turnover among teachers and trustees and that it was often hard to persuade enough people to fill the trustee positions. The democratic nature of the choosing of trustees must often have been somewhat closer to a formality, a matter of finding three, or if need be, two people willing to serve, nor is it surprising to find that some people who were willing, were chosen as trustees over and over again. That most of the time trustees could be persuaded to act at all in the circumstances is remarkable. The provincial government, which had created the system, and their district appointees who were officially charged with overseeing it, were prepared to turn a blind eye to a considerable amount of bending of the rules by people who coped with local school problems at no cost to the state.

The Eastern District common school records are by far the most extensive source of information on school trustees to have survived, but there are some other, more limited documents. Another complete list of trustees, for the London District but only for the school year of 1837–38, in a number of ways mirrors the situation in the Eastern District. Twelve of the district's ninety-eight schools for example had only two trustees. The London District list also in a negative way largely bears out the conventional contemporary view of common school trustees. Among more than two hundred trustees whose names were listed, the majority, though perhaps enjoying some slightly elevated level of prominence among their contemporaries at the time, cannot now readily be identified as having been "important" people. That most trustees were not part of any elite group is illustrated by the presence of one extraordinary name on the list of trustees for Bayham Township, that of Eliza Phelps. It is impossible to say for sure but Eliza Phelps may have been the very first female trustee ever to hold office in Upper Canada. She must certainly also

have been a "fit and proper person" who had the support of the
people of her local area. But she was in no way part of a traditional
Upper Canadian leadership group.[31]

The extent to which the London District trustees can be said to
have been early examples of "people power" is nonetheless also cast
in some doubt by the presence on the list of trustees, as was the case
in the Eastern District, of a similar minority of men who probably
strongly disapproved of democracy in any form. Two of Eliza Phelps's
fellow trustees in Bayham Township were John Burwell, militia colonel, magistrate, postmaster, and violent Tory; and one of his militia
officers, Cornet John Wright. Trustees in Yarmouth Township
included Edward Ermatinger, retired fur trader and magistrate; militia officer and magistrate John Bostwick; and James C. Crysler, magistrate. John Burwell's better known brother, Mahlon Burwell,
magistrate and chairman of quarter sessions, MHA, county registrar,
and colonel of militia, was a trustee in Southwold Township. Two of
Burford Township's trustees were recently appointed militia officers
in the Fourth Oxford regiment, Captain John Moore and Lieutenant
Jacob Smith. Two other Burford trustees were at least quasi-
prominent by virtue of family connection. John Nelles was the
brother of Colonel Robert Nelles, MHA, and of Hon. Abraham
Nelles, member of the Legislative Council. Lot Tisdale was John
Nelles's son-in-law. Oxford Township boasted as a trustee a member
of a truly distinguished family in the person of Henry Vansittart, who
was either Rear Admiral Henry Vansittart, RN (retired) himself or,
more likely, Henry Vansittart junior, captain in the Third Oxford
Regiment of Militia. On the list of trustees for London Township,
which included the town of London, were some local notables: business partners and magistrates Laurence Laurason and George
Goodhue; Thomas Cronyn, magistrate; and John Harris, district
treasurer. Like their counterparts in Cornwall, the group which has
been identified as the "London District Oligarchy," noted for their
Anglicanism and Conservative views, were evidently not prepared to
leave the running of even the common schools entirely in the hands
of any democratic rabble, especially in a time of political unrest.[32]

It is tempting to speculate, particularly in view of Robert Baldwin
Sullivan's opinion that trustees were "sometimes disloyal," that at
least in normal times the public meetings for the selection of trustees
may have provided some opportunities not just for "plain" people
but for people of dissenting political or religious views to take local

leadership roles. If they did, the available evidence is intriguing but far from overwhelming. It is impossible to even guess at the political affiliation, if any, of most of the people who were trustees in the Eastern District, but it can be said that where a definite political label can be attached to some of the prominent trustees, Reformers were in a narrow majority. Between 1816 and 1831 nine men, Alexander Chisholm, Ambrose Blacklock, Peter Shaver, George Brouse, Archibald McLean, Donald Macdonell (Greenfield), Donald Æneas Macdonell, Henry Merkley and John Crysler, all of whom were at one time MHAS, served as trustees in the district. Five of these men, Blacklock, Chisholm, Brouse, Shaver, and Donald Æneas Macdonell, were Reformers, and at least two, Brouse and Shaver, were members of the Methodist Church, a denomination much underrepresented among the prominent.[33]

The first common school in York, built in 1818 and taken over, as has been seen, by the Upper Canada Central School in 1820, also provides a bit of information about the political and religious attachments of the people who were briefly its trustees, because the displacement of its teacher, Thomas Appleton, eventually led to an investigation by a committee of the Assembly, and because one of the trustees, Jesse Ketchum, was later the subject of a biography. Besides Ketchum, the men who are known to have been trustees of the York Common School between 1818 and 1821 were Ezekial Benson, Colin Drummond, Thomas R. Morrison, Ely Playter, and Jordan Post. So who were these men who were chosen by their fellow citizens to run the York Common School? By occupation, Ketchum was a tanner, Benson a merchant, and Drummond a carpenter and builder. Morrison was at the time a government clerk, later a doctor. Playter was an innkeeper and Post a watchmaker. They were therefore primarily tradesmen, most of them in fact already or eventually quite successful, but they were definitely not part of the small York elite. In religion Ketchum and Morrison are known to have been Methodists. Ketchum, Benson, and Post were of American birth. Four of them had later political careers: Playter, Ketchum, and Morrison as MHAS and Drummond as a city councillor. Morrison, Ketchum, and Drummond can be clearly classified as Reformers.[34]

If there are then some signs of an anti-establishment bent in the Eastern District and among the little group of early York trustees, the evidence on the point for the much larger number of 1837–38 London District trustees is far weaker. Though the London District had a reputation as an area of Reform sympathies it is probably not surprising, in the immediate pre- and post-Rebellion period, that few known political mavericks were to be found on the list of trustees and a search for such people among them yields only a few cases of guilt by association. In Yarmouth Township, trustee Elijah Duncombe, an American immigrant and medical doctor, was a brother of the rebel leader Dr Charles Duncombe. His fellow trustee, Benjamin H. Doan, would have been a member of a Yarmouth Township Quaker family which included two active rebels, one of whom was hanged. George Goodhue of London was never very active politically, but his brother Josiah had been "an active reformer" and his father-in-law, Captain John Matthews was Reform MHA for Middlesex from 1824 to 1830. Though a man of wealth and a magistrate, George Goodhue, also an American immigrant and originally a Congregationalist, was himself sufficiently reform-minded to be appointed to the Legislative Council by the Baldwin-Lafontaine government in 1842.[35]

Political orientation aside, it seems probable that most of the common school trustees, whoever they were and however they were chosen, were fairly representative of the communities which patronized the schools. And no doubt also, most of them, like Jesse Ketchum (and unlike John Harris), sent their own children to the common schools. The fact is that while we know who some of the teachers and some of the trustees were, there are almost no records of the names of actual students who went to the common schools. There are some reminiscences by people who attended the non-elite schools of Upper Canada but it is not always clear whether the schools being described were really common schools or some of the many ephemeral private venture schools of the time. Such recollections, where and if they apply to the common schools, invariably provide evidence, especially in the rural districts, of underfunding, ramshackle buildings, lack of books, equipment, heat, ventilation, sanitation, and of course of a mixed bag of teachers, but the research undertaken for this chapter has turned up only a single example of the names of the students who once attended a common school in Upper Canada.[36]

In April 1838 a recently arrived British immigrant named David Walker, then teaching at a school just outside Picton, submitted a petition to the Executive Council asking to be paid the government allowance for the previous quarter, despite the fact that there had not been more than twelve students on average attending the school on a daily basis, because, not to put too fine point on it, he was poor and needed the money. To support his case he appended the names of twenty-one scholars, nine boys and twelve girls, who had come to the school during his tenure, though obviously not all on a regular basis. His petition was endorsed by the trustees of the school, John A. Conger, James B. Wardle, and Nathan B. Conger. Among the students listed were John, Elizabeth, Mary Anne, Angelina, Margaret, David, and Melissa Conger, and Sarah, Horatio, James, and Mary Wardle. There were also six students named Lewis: Sarah, Benjamin, Joseph, John, and Stephen, so the local Conger, Wardle, and Lewis children made up the bulk of the student body. (For the record, the other children listed were: Catharine Yenex, Lucy Anne Worden, Jane or Sabra Clute, and Jane Lazier.) This unique document cannot of course claim to be representative of all the rural common schools of the time but at least it can be said to contain no surprises. The students were drawn from a few families in the neighbourhood, the trustees had a direct interest in the conduct of the school, the school was irregularly attended and did not quite meet the student numbers requirement, and the teacher was underpaid.[37]

Despite its flaws, educational historians have been right to conclude that the common school system of Upper Canada was not a failure. According to Robert Gidney, Upper Canada had "an astonishingly high literacy level" of as much as 90 per cent. For the majority of Upper Canadians who lived outside the urban areas that literacy was very likely gained in the common schools. Upper Canadian parents took useful advantage of the meagre resources that the state allowed them to give their children a basic education. Local trustees, mostly "unimportant" people, did get to exercise some authority and most of the time ran the common schools in a way that met their needs, if not the official regulations, with little interference or supervision. Above all, the regular inspection of schools, teachers, and students which was to be such an important feature of the later school system barely existed in Upper Canada. Parents and trustees were left to get on with the running of the schools.[38]

6

Getting into Trouble

PART I: NUMBERS

Like the history of education in Upper Canada, Upper Canadian
penal history, though for a long time largely neglected by professional historians, has in the last three decades been given a good deal
of attention, thanks largely to the emergence of the Osgoode Society
for Legal History, founded in 1979. Since then the legal history of the
Upper Canadian period has found its place in a number of the society's publications and elsewhere. Some debate has arisen among legal
scholars as to whether Upper Canada was on the whole a "peaceable
kingdom," mostly free from high levels of crime and violence, or was
a society increasingly threatened by "glaring problems" of lawlessness and disrespect for authority. In an early treatment of the question in 1977, J.M. Beattie concluded that "Upper Canada was not
seriously threatened by crime." Most legal historians writing more
recently have come to a similar conclusion,[1] though there have been
some important qualifications. Susan Lewthwaite in particular has
argued that in some rural areas of Upper Canada the laws could not
be fully enforced "without popular support" and that some degree
of criminal activity was often ignored, or undercharged, or arbitrated
at the local level. In a particular incident singled out by Lewthwaite
in "a remote country place," Burford Township, the efforts at law
enforcement by a magistrate and a constable were successfully
resisted, both by violence and by using the law as a means of coun-
terattack, and she has found evidence of a number of similar cases
elsewhere in the province.[2]

It is no doubt true that many crimes, perhaps especially in rural
areas, went undetected or unpunished where the apparatus of justice

was thin on the ground. That does not necessarily mean however that the overall crime rate was at a dangerous level. Though the situations were likely not entirely comparable, Donald Fyson's research on Upper Canada's sister province of Lower Canada is suggestive. While recognizing that there also many offences never wound up in court, Fyson found that the rate of serious crime, particularly murder, was actually lower in the countryside than in urban areas.[3]

That such incidents as the one in Burford Township happened in Upper Canada and at times took an even more serious form, as they did for example during the period of the "Shiner's War" in the Ottawa Valley in the 1830s, cannot be doubted, but whether they are evidence of a more general province-wide increasing and uncontrolled level of violent and criminal behaviour is far less certain, since the evidence is by its nature sporadic and anecdotal. Peter Oliver pointed out that Upper Canada's judges and magistrates more often commented on the relative absence of crime that they encountered than on a perceived rising tide of criminality. Perhaps more significantly, crime in Upper Canada seems never to have been an important political issue. Critics of the provincial administration constantly complained about a long list of conditions and practices which they wished to see changed or improved, but they never demanded that the government "get tough on crime."[4]

It is unlikely that Upper Canada, rural or urban, was ever really peaceable, but whether overall crime rates were, in proportion to population, increasing or decreasing, and whether the province was more or less crime-ridden than other comparable jurisdictions are questions which probably cannot be answered definitively. Part of the problem, as is so often the case with investigations of Upper Canadian society which aspire to a factual basis, is the lack of reliable, consistent, and complete statistical evidence. Such attempts as have been made to measure levels of crime in Upper Canada tend only to illustrate the difficulty of the task. The lack of data from the early years is a particular problem. In two admirable local studies David Murray has compiled tables of offences for the Niagara District from assize and quarter sessions records which date only from 1827, and John Weaver has done a somewhat similar study for a single town, Hamilton, using gaol registers which do not begin until 1832. The compilations by district of criminal indictments at the assizes made by J. David Wood deal with only three selected years, 1838, 1842, and 1846. Peter Oliver, who dug more widely than anyone else into the available Upper Canadian records and reported the findings of two studies beginning in 1824, one of four and one of six districts, concluded in the end that attempts to firmly establish general crime rates for the province must be "highly suspect" and can only be "crude estimates."[5]

The search for statistical certainty about crime rates then, would appear to be something of a mug's game. Still, crude estimates are better than no estimates, and the pursuit of more and better statistical evidence ought not be given up. But perhaps, rather than trying to establish definitive levels of criminality during the Upper Canadian period some less ambitious questions should be asked, and where possible at least crudely answered. Peter Oliver, John Weaver, and David Murray have demonstrated that in the geographical areas they have looked at, the nature of the crimes for which people were punished changed over time. For many years crimes of violence, especially assault and battery, were the most common offences, but by the end of the Upper Canadian period crimes of violence were replaced by crimes against property (which were mostly stealing), as the leading form of criminality. Weaver and Murray's analysis of crime in the Niagara District and in Hamilton included discussions of ethnicity and gender. Can such factors and trends be examined on a province-wide basis? Can other questions about crime in Upper Canada be addressed, such as: where in the province were most crimes committed? What kind of people committed crimes? How extensive was the variety of offences? What happened to you if you got into serious trouble with the law? And most basically, how and why did ordinary people get into trouble with the law in the first place, and how, if they managed to, did they get out of trouble again?

Some sources do exist which deal on a provincial basis with Upper Canadians who for whatever reason were lodged in the district gaols. One such source, which has not been utilized to any extent by historians, is the returns of gaols and prisoners by district to be found in the Blue Books of Upper Canadian government statistics compiled in the provincial secretary's office dating from 1821. These books were prepared on the orders of the imperial government for their information and forced the provincial government for the first time to actually begin to try to keep track of what it was doing. Bruce Curtis, who has closely analyzed the early volumes found that they were woefully incomplete, inaccurate, late, or for some years non-existent, because "the colonial state commanded neither the financial nor the administrative resources to execute Blue Book inquiries."[6] Despite this fact, the books do contain some information of use to historians. Beginning in 1828 the provincial administration annually included prison statistics in the reports which were sent to the imperial government under some basic categories: the total number of prisoners who had been put into each gaol during the year, whether they were male or female, and the reason for their imprisonment, divided into two headings, Felons and Debtors. Theoretically then it should be possible to compile in tabular form an accurate record of how many people were imprisoned in each district in each year (and from 1835 in the Provincial Penitentiary), their gender, and, broadly speaking, why they were in gaol. So much for theory. In fact there are large gaps in the record. No returns at all have survived for the years 1830, 1831, 1840, and 1841. For 1832 returns exist for only four districts out of eleven. For 1837 the only statistics on ordinary criminals are for the penitentiary. The returns in 1838 and 1839 give only gross numbers for each district gaol, not broken down by sex or category of offence. If these were not problems enough some district sheriffs appear to have been very casual or outright negligent in submitting returns. The London District is a particular blank, providing returns for only five years between 1828 and 1839, with no returns at all before 1834. Clearly analysis of such an imperfect source cannot yield entirely satisfactory results, but flawed as they are the records do provide a general profile of imprisonment across the province over an extended period of time.

But before looking at the data in this and other sources two points should be made. First, the fact that someone was a prisoner in a district gaol did not necessarily mean that he or she was a convicted criminal. Many of the prisoners were in gaol awaiting trials at which they might be acquitted. Being in gaol then can only be said to mean that an individual had in some way run afoul of the law. It should be noted also that in the tables and discussion in this chapter, the debtors have not been included, an omission which perhaps needs a word or two of explanation. As Peter Oliver observed, if debtors (and the insane) are lumped in with the other prisoners, "Upper Canadian gaols probably housed more non-criminals than criminals." His analysis of the prison population, using scattered returns published by the legislature from twelve districts for 1832–35, found that 48 per cent of the prisoners at that time were not criminals as such but debtors, confined until they could satisfy their creditors. A similar exercise using the returns in the Blue Books covering a longer period, 1828–36, also produces a significant if lower figure of 41 per cent, so the point is securely made. Debtors routinely made up a large proportion of the people in the gaols. The plight of Upper Canada's debtors however has been dealt with by other writers, including Oliver and Paul Romney,[7] and for that reason and since they cannot be called genuine criminals they are ignored in what follows here. Suffice it to say that whether they are considered criminals or not they were certainly punished, often more harshly than other prisoners, because their confinement was indefinite and they were not necessarily even fed or otherwise maintained by the state.

A second unplumbed source which also covers the entire provincial penal scene and for a slightly longer period than do the Blue Books, from 1824 to 1840, and in even greater detail, are the actual gaol returns submitted to the provincial secretary's office by the district sheriffs, now filed at Library and Archives Canada as RG 5, B27, volumes 1 and 2. In this case the returns for each district were sent in on a quarterly, and from 1838 a monthly, basis, giving the name of each person in the prison at the time, the crime for which they had been committed, their age and their place of birth. Alas in this case as well such a potentially rich source is sadly incomplete, because for whatever reason the majority of the reports have not survived, if they were ever actually submitted, or at least are not where they are supposed to be. For some districts the records are woefully thin. There are returns for the Ottawa District for only two of the eighteen years covered by the records, only three years for the Eastern District, and only four each for the London and Western districts. Within each year almost no district is represented by a full set of quarterly or monthly returns. Ages, birthplaces, and even the reasons for committal were not always recorded. We are again left with another sad patchwork which as a source of provincial data must obviously be treated with considerable caution. Yet there is a lot of valuable information in the gaol reports. We have the actual names, sex, origin, current district, and recent criminal history of a large number of people. Beginning then from these sets of documents and eventually incorporating provincial data from some more familiar additional sources, what can be added to what is already known about the nature of crime in Upper Canada as a whole?

First of all, the merest glance at table 6.1 makes even clearer what an uncertain source the Blue Books are. The missing years do not help (the only gaol statistics for 1837 are the Rebellion treason cases)

Table 6.1
Prisoners by district and in the penitentiary, 1828–39

Year	Ott	Bath	East	John	Mid	Newc	Home	Gore	Nia	Lond	West	PE	Tal	PP	All Districts	Provincial Population
1828	0	6		4	20	1	35		15		13				94	186,488
1829	0	0	1	9	6	2	52	2	6		4				82	197,815
1830						No Returns										
1831						No Returns										
1832				9	194	3		51							257	263,554
1833	18	2	2	5	119	15	16	78	7		2				264	295,863
1834		2	12	8	117	9	253	77	14	9	6				507	321,145
1835	0	18	2	8	106	12	295	170	11	8	1	6		62	699	347,359
1836	9	18	4	5	107	7	70	158	11	10	3	28		81	511	374,099
1837							No Returns									
1838	10	13		107	249	15	700	298	118	156	34	40	21	154	1,915	399,422
1839	20	10	36	88	206	55	435	202	52	74	27	22	10	148	1,385	409,048
Total	57	69	57	243	1,124	119	1,856	1,036	234	257	90	96	31	445	5,714	

Source: LAC, RG 1, E13, vols 144–55; Canada, *Census*, vol. 4, 1871.

Prince Edward District was created in 1834. Talbot district was created in 1837.

and the figures themselves, especially for the Home District, show some year-to-year fluctuations that are hard to accept as accurate reports. The numbers in the last two years, 1838 and 1839, are obviously artificially swollen by the Rebellion prisoners still in the gaols. What can be said in a general way however is that while there were never all that many people in gaol, the number of prisoners did more or less steadily increase, and not just in simple numbers, but in proportion to the provincial population. The prisoners were also mostly to be found in particular areas of the province.

According to J. David Wood, whose case study covered criminal indictments at the Upper Canadian assizes for the years 1832, 1842, and 1846, crime in Upper Canada was "randomly distributed."[8] The data to be found in the Blue Books over a longer period points to a quite different conclusion. Looking in table 6.1 again at the districts in the eight years between 1828 and 1839 simply in terms of gross numbers in the gaols reveals that a select few districts always had the highest prison populations. The Home District, including the district town of York/Toronto, and the Midland and Gore districts, containing their main urban centres of Kingston and Hamilton, were almost always in first, second, or third place in the number of prisoners in their gaols. If this limited evidence means anything it is that crime, as defined as the number of people who were arrested and put into prison, was by no means random, but was habitually concentrated in a relatively small number of areas.

It would be convenient to be able to report that these rankings neatly correspond with the relevant districts in order of population, but, as can be seen, no such simple correlation emerges. The available figures in the Blue Books when set against the district population figures (table 6.2) do not support a straightforward "more population equals more crime" conclusion. Of course the incompleteness of the data may have something to do with it. The London District is a particular problem here. It was the second or third most highly populated district from 1831 on but since there are no returns for the district before 1834 it is impossible to know what the previous situation was there. Even so, the district never made the top three list in the number of prisoners in its gaol. The Midland District presents a different sort of mathematical problem because its population total was twice sharply reduced by the lopping off from its territory of a separate Prince Edward District in 1834 and then the new Victoria District in 1839, by which it lost a total of about 26,000 people.

Table 6.2
District populations by order of size

Year	Ott	Bath	East	John	Mid	Newc	Home	Gore	Nia	Lond	West	PE	Tal	Vic
1828	11	8	5	6	1(2)	9	2(1)	7	3(3)	4	10			
1829	11	8	7	3(2)	1(3)	9	2(1)	5	6(3)	4	10			
1830	11	8	7	3	1	9	2	5	6	4	10			
1831	11	8	7	4	2	9	1	5	6	3	10			
1832[1]	11	9	7	5(3)	2(1)	8	1	4(2)	6	3	10			
1833	11	9	8	5	2(1)	6	1(3)	4(2)	7	3	10			
1834	11	9	8	5	4(2)	7	1(1)	3(3)	6	2	10			
1835	12	9	6	8	4(3)	5	1(1)	3(2)	7	2	10	11		
1836	12	9	8	6	4(2)	5	1(3)	3(1)	7	2	10	11		
1837[2]	12	9	8	7	4	5	1	3	6	2	10	11		
1838	13	9	8	6	4(3)	5	1(1)	2(2)	7	3	10	11	12	
1839	14	9	7	5	8(2)	4	1(1)	2(3)	6	3	10	11	13	12

Source: Canada, *Census*, vol. 4, 1871.

1 Gaol returns for only Johnstown, Midland, Newcastle, and Gore.

2 No gaol returns except for Rebellion prisoners.

Figures in brackets represent the "top three" gaol populations by district in each year.

But sheer population numbers did have some bearing on crime. The evidence in the Blue Books may not justify hard and fast conclusions on the point but they do invite some speculation. The district with the highest population, Midland until 1831 and then Home, always made the top three list among the prison population. But the fact that the London District, though number two or three in population during the years for which we have returns, never came close to matching the prison numbers of the other districts which at the same time regularly led the list suggests that mere numbers were not the whole story. Susan Lewthwaite may be quite right in saying that crime in the London District was seriously under-reported and under-prosecuted because it was largely a "remote" place and perhaps because of its immense size. Maybe there was as much or more actual crime in the London District as there was, say, in the Gore District, which after 1834 also stood second or third in population.

Or maybe not. Lewthwaite also found crime being ignored and unpunished in rural Prince Edward District, a much more compact and settled part of Upper Canada.[9] And while the London District was still primarily rural and underdeveloped, the Home, Gore, and Midland districts, which usually reported the largest prison populations, were seeing increasing urbanization, especially in Toronto, Kingston, and Hamilton (see table 6.3). While London, the principal settlement in the London District, was still a mere village, not easily accessed and far from the centre of things, Toronto, Kingston, and after the opening of the Burlington Canal in 1827, Hamilton, were busy commercial ports on the St Lawrence-Great Lakes waterway and entry points for the large numbers of immigrants who came to Upper Canada from the United Kingdom during the peak immigration years of 1830–34, an inflow which may be reflected to some extent in the gaol populations in the three districts about the same time. This is not to say that immigrants were necessarily criminals, but heavy immigration, especially to the urban centres, was often accompanied by poverty, homelessness, and even sheer desperation (see chapter 7) which could lead to criminal acts.

It is significant to note that the Midland District did not lose its status as a leading centre of committals to gaol after large chunks of its outlying regions were removed. In fact the district probably became more urbanized as a result. By 1841 Kingston made up 19.5 per cent of the Midland District's population, a percentage even higher than that of Toronto within the Home District at 18.5 per cent.[10] There

Table 6.3
Principal urban places over 1,000 population in Upper Canada, 1811–41

	1811	1821	1831	1841
York/Toronto		1,559	3,969	14,249
Kingston	(1,000)	2,336	3,828	6,292
Niagara		(1,000)	1,230	2,109
Hamilton			(1,500)	3,413
Cobourg			(1,500)	(2,700)
St. Catharines			(1,500)	(2,700)
Belleville			(1,200)	(1,700)
Brockville			(1,000)	(1,500)
Bytown			(1,000)	3,122
Port Hope			(1,000)	(1,200)
London				2,078

Sources: Stelter, "Urban Development," table 2; Taylor, *Ottawa: An Illustrated History*, 210, table 1. Figures in brackets are estimates.

may have been no direct correlation between crime and the populations of the various districts, but it seems likely that crime and urban growth did follow a common pattern.

Crime of course could never be exclusively urban in Upper Canada because the province as a whole was overwhelmingly rural. Even at the end of the Upper Canadian period only 11 per cent of the population was urban,[11] which makes the apparent concentration of people in gaols in the areas with the largest urban centres all the more striking. But it is not necessary to rely entirely on the incomplete returns of prisoners in the Blue Books to argue that crime in Upper Canada was usually concentrated in certain areas of the province. The records of the assizes, which have already been used to an extent to try to establish crime rates by Peter Oliver can also be employed to chart the geographical distribution of crime. The assizes, which were the regular sittings of the Court of King's (or Queen's) Bench in each district to deal with relatively serious crimes, required the attendance of the attorney or solicitor general and of the clerk of assize, each of whom usually submitted reports to the legislature, which were subsequently published as appendices to the House of Assembly Journals. Their reports listed the number of cases tried in each district in each year. These records, covering the years 1822–1839, of course have their own gaps, including for the entire year of 1829, but they are more complete than the reports in the Blue Books and they have the signal advantage of being nearly complete for the London District, so sadly missing in the Blue Books. The figures (shown in table 6.4) do indeed present a very similar picture of the distribution of criminal cases. The same narrow range of districts, Home, Midland, Gore, and Niagara, had the most prosecutions in each year, with the Midland District dominating the list until about 1830 when the Home District took over as the leader in number of criminal cases, just at the time when the district outstripped the Midland District in population and York replaced Kingston as the largest urban centre. As for the London District, which as has been seen became the second- or third-most-populous district after 1831, the number of its criminal cases never even rivalled those in Niagara District, which then ranked fourth or fifth in population. The records for the very rural Ottawa District, whose scattered population never amounted to as many as 9,000 people, show only two recorded cases, both in the Rebellion years of 1837 and 1838.

Unlike the gaol records in the Blue Books, the assize records (where more or less complete) do not show any appreciable increase in the proportion of Upper Canadians within the provincial population who were in trouble with the law. It has to be remembered that just being in gaol did not necessarily mean being brought to trial, especially for serious crimes. People who were confined could have been sent to gaol for a petty offence by the lower courts or the district quarter sessions, or even, like the three prostitutes in the Niagara District gaol in 1834, could be "admonished and discharged."[12]

The Assize records reinforce the conclusion that crime in Upper Canada was predominantly urban but whether there may have been more evil-hearted people *per capita* in urban areas than in rural ones is somewhat beside the point. Denser populations presented more opportunities and stimulus for crime, especially for the common crimes of theft and assault and battery but also for the apprehension and prosecution of criminals by resident constables and magistrates who were close at hand. Urban centres also provided readier access to strong drink, a frequent adjunct to and often alleged cause of (or excuse for) criminal acts. And there can be little doubt that alcohol and crime did often go hand in hand.

The first Report of the Inspectors of the Provincial Penitentiary printed by the legislature in 1836 contained a crude survey of the sixty-two prisoners then under sentence, dealing with, among other things, the role alcohol had played in putting them there. Over half

Table 6.4
Number of assize cases (where reported) by district and gender, 1822–39

Year	Ott M	Ott F	Bath M	Bath F	East M	East F	John M	John F	Mid M	Mid F	Newc M	Newc F	Home M	Home F	Gore M	Gore F	Nia M	Nia F	Lond M	Lond F	West M	West F	PE M	PE F	Tal M	Tal F	All Districts	Provincial Population	% of Crime
1822					5	0	12	1	35	2	7	0	10	2	16	0			6	1	6	0							
1823			1	0	4	0	12	1	31	3	7	0	4	3	12	0			7	1	3	0							
1824			10	0	17	0	13	3	19	2	8	0	7	1	11	0	14	1	9	0	9	0					120	150,066	0.08
1825															16	1	36	1	16	0	4	1							
1826			6	0	12	0	8	0	22	3	4	0	15	5	11	2	19	2	15	0	3	2							
1827			3	0	9	0	9	0	14	4	8	0	21	2	36	0	14	1	11	0	5	1							
1828			4	1	12	0	12	0	24	1	7	1	9	1	19	1	15	2	4	0	2	0							
1830			3	0	13	0	12	0	20	3	17	1	25	1	25	1	17	0	9	0	9	0					156	213,156	0.07
1831			10	1	7	1	15	2	23	3	7	2	40	5	13	0	17	2	14	0	9	0							
1832													74	3	30	1			9	0	7	0							
1833			2	0	6	0	15	2	18	1	13	0	31	2			21	0											
1834			3	0	4	0	13	0	18	2	7	2	41	2	24	0	13	1	10	2	8	0	5	0					
1835			13	1	8	1	12	1	43	2	8	0	63	4	30	7	15	2	13	0	8	0	4	0			235	347,359	0.07
1836			4	0	4	1	11	1	15	2	10	1	43	17	37	1			17	0	7	0	5	4					
1837	1		20	1	7	1	12	1	16	3	5	1					34	0	15	0	10	0	2	0					
1838	1	0	3	1	1	0	13	0					18	7	32	1	7	1	18	0	6	0	4	0	1	0			
1839			6	0	4	0	5	0					30	1															
Totals	2	0	98	5	113	4	174	12	298	31	108	8	431	56	312	15	233	13	173	4	92	4	16	4	1	0		Total M: 2,047 (93.1)	
Total M&F	2		103		117		186		329		116		487		327		246		177		96		20		1			Total F: 153 (6.9)	Total M&F: 2,200

Sources: AOR (1914); Canada, *Census*, vol. 4, 1871.

(thirty-five) of them claimed to have been drunk when they had committed the crime for which they had been convicted (which could also help to explain why they were caught). The statistical connection between drink and crime however is a somewhat ambiguous one, which merits some comment. In the case of the penitentiary prisoners at least the use of alcohol may have been partly responsible for unlawful acts but not for acts of violence, for only two of the sixty-two prisoners had in fact been convicted of violent crimes. The great majority of them, including the three female prisoners, were in the penitentiary for various forms of stealing.[13]

Nor can crime, or the concentration of crime in particular areas, be reliably linked to a proliferation of drinking establishments in certain districts or in the province generally. Statistics compiled by Julia Roberts in her fine study of taverns in Upper Canada make clear that while the total number of taverns obviously increased, there was no actual appreciable increase and some periodic decrease in the ratio of drinking places in proportion to population in Upper Canada. In 1820 there was one tavern for every 256 people in Upper Canada, while twenty years later the figure was only one to 303 (see table 6.5).[14] If the districts are listed by rank order of size by year and by ratio of inns to population, it is not Home, Midland, or Gore, the districts where the prison and court records show the greatest concentration of offenders, that had the highest level of drinking places per capita (though their position in the order seems to have been creeping up by 1837), but districts where the prisons and courts were rarely crowded, such as the Ottawa, Bathurst, and Western districts. Curiously, it was the London District, Susan Lewthwaite's alleged hotbed of rural crime, which consistently and by a wide margin had the lowest number of licensed inns per population (see table 6.6). In any case the assize records make it plain that the London District, at least by the measure of the number of cases that reached the Court of King's Bench, never had a serious crime problem.

So although there was undoubtedly a connection between alcohol and crime, that connection was not a simple matter of more licensed establishments in a district causing more crime, or at least producing more arrests and prosecutions. Of course potential criminals were not necessarily doing all their drinking in licensed premises. An unknown, and probably unknowable, factor in this case was the extent of the number of shops and "tippling houses" where liquor

Table 6.5
Taverns in proportion to the provincial population, 1801–40

Year	Number	Population	Ratio
1801	108	34,600	1/320
1820	428	109,740	1/256
1825	476	154,381	1/324
1827	588	177,174	1/301
1832–33	931	295,863	1/317
1837	1,009	400,286	1/397
1839	1,114	409,048	1/367
1840	1,446	437,681	1/303

Source: Roberts, In Mixed Company, 59.

was sold illegally at all hours, places which were generally believed to attract an unsavoury sort of clientele. Unfortunately nobody thought to ask the penitentiary prisoners in 1836 where they had done their drinking.

It appears then that about all that can be safely said about crime and drink is that a drop in the level of violent crime in the late 1830s detected by scholars like Peter Oliver, David Murray, and John Weaver, a view reinforced by the research that follows in this chapter, coincided with a drop in the number of licensed inns per capita in the province and possibly with less alcohol consumption. But the appearance of temperance societies and the precipitate drop in immigration in the post-Rebellion years may also have had something to do with it.[15]

The survey of penitentiary prisoners that has been referred to demonstrated that convicted criminals were likely to have been drinkers but also that the list of drinkers included all the female prisoners. Here another digression, this time on female criminality may be appropriate. How numerous were female offenders in Upper Canada? On this point some loose degree of precision is possible. At the assizes, where the most serious crimes were heard, women accounted for only 7 per cent of those charged. In the Blue Book returns women made up about 12 per cent of the general criminal prison population.

Female prisoners may not have been very numerous but as a group they demonstrate an even greater tendency to be concentrated in urbanized areas. In fact in the Blue Books they can scarcely be found outside the familiar Home, Midland, and Gore districts. Fully 92 per

Table 6.6
Districts by ratio of taverns per capita in rank order

	1825			1827			1832			1837	
Rank	*District*	*Ratio*	*Rank*	*District*	*Ratio*	*Rank*	*District*	*Ratio*	*Rank*	*District*	*Ratio*
1	Ottawa	1/123	1	Ottawa	1/164	1	Bath	1/169	1	West	1/203
2	Johnstown	1/250	2	Bathurst	1/211	2	Ottawa	1/220	2	Niagara	1/248
3	Eastern	1/275	3	Niagara	1/212	3	Johnstown	1/224	3	Midland	1/283
4	Bathurst	1/303	4	Johnstown	1/243	4	Midland	1/277	4	Gore	1/356
5	Niagara	1/321	5	Western	1/284	5	Niagara	1/291	5	Home	1/368
6	Newcastle	1/332	6	Newcastle	1/292	6	Newcastle	1/302	6	Bathurst	1/394
7	Midland	1/337	7	Gore	1/300	7	Eastern	1/306	7	Ottawa	1/417
8	Gore	1/400	8	Midland	1/305	8	Western	1/339	8	Johnstown	1/425
9	Western	1/421	9	Eastern	1/340	9	Home	1/425	9	Eastern	1/429
10	Home	1/434	10	Home	1/402	10	Gore	1/477	10	Prince Edward	1/558
11	London	1/1335	11	London	1/694	11	London	1/1345	11	Newcastle	1/761
									12	London	1/1151

Sources: LAC, RG 1, E13, vol. 151; HAJ, app., 1825, 1827, 1832, 1837.

cent of women were imprisoned in those three districts, 41 per cent in the Home District, 30 per cent in the Midland District and 20 per cent in the Gore District, a higher concentration than their male equivalents, 83 per cent of whom were in the gaols of the three districts, 30 per cent in the Home District, 29 per cent in the Midland District and 24 per cent in the Gore District (see table 6.7).

The manuscript gaol returns housed at Library and Archives Canada, despite their obvious drawbacks as a source, permit some further tentative exploration of the characteristics of the prisoners, male and female, in the district gaols over a longer period and of the variety of alleged offences which got them into put in prison. These statistics need a bit of explanation. The figures do not represent all the prisoners in the gaols in each year but are a yearly sampling of the prisoners in each gaol reported at a particular time, in this case on January 1, or if no return exists for that date, the next available quarterly (after 1838, monthly) return. Here too a look at the data (table 6.8) makes clear the shortcomings of the surviving returns. They do not present a very useful picture of the geographical distribution of prisoners since for so many of the districts and for many years there are so few returns. It is not significant that there are no or hardly any returns for the new districts, Prince Edward, created in 1834, and Victoria, Talbot, and Brock, created only in 1838, 1839, and 1840, but for many of the older districts such as Ottawa, Bathurst, Eastern, Gore, London, and Western, the lack of returns is a serious problem, because it makes it difficult to compare areas which were growing rapidly with those which were not, or largely rural districts with those with increasing urban populations. It would be useful to know for example if the long-settled Eastern District, whose population grew only marginally during the busy immigrant years and positively stagnated between 1835 and 1840, was as consistently crime free as the three returns from there indicate, in accord with Sheriff Donald Æneas Macdonell's comment on his 1830 return that there had been no prisoners at all in the gaol in Cornwall in the past six months. Unfortunately the data permit no such comparisons. All that can be said is that except for the Rebellion years there were never all that many prisoners in any of the gaols at any one time, though there appear to have generally been more prisoners in the 1830s than in the 1820s. So what use are these records of small numbers of prisoners, mostly from gaols in the central part of the province?

Table 6.7
District Blue Book returns by gender of prisoners, 1828–36

Year	Ott		Bath		East		John		Mid		Newc		Home		Gore		Nia		Lond		West		PE		Totals		
	M	F	M	F	M	F	M	F	M	F	M	F	M	F	M	F	M	F	M	F	M	F	M	F	M	F	Both
1828	0	0	4	2			4	0	18		2	1	33	2			14	1			9	4			83	11	94
1829	0	0	0	0	1	0	7	2	5		2	0	50	2	2	0	6	0			4	0			77	5	82
1830											No Returns		No Returns														
1831											No Returns		No Returns														
1832							9	0	194	0	3	0			46	5									252	5	257
1833	18	0	2	0	2	0	5	0	88	31	15	0	16	0	70	8	7	0	2	0	2	0			225	39	264
1834			6	2	12	0	8	0	107	10	9	0	215	28	73	4	14	0	9	0	6	0			459	44	503
1835	6	0	18	0	2	0	8	0	93	13	11	1	258	37	156	14	8	3	8	0	1	0	5	1	574	69	643
1836	8	1	18	0	3	1	5	0	86	21	6	1	33	37	138	20	9	2	10	0	3	0	28	0	347	83	430
Top "3"									(2)	(2)			(1)	(1)	(3)	(3)											
Totals									591	78			605	106	485	51									2,017	256	2,273
									29%	30%			30%	41%	24%	20%											

Source: LAC, RG 1, E 13, vols 144–55.

Table 6.8
District sheriff's gaol returns, 1824–40

Year	Ott M	Ott F	Bath M	Bath F	East M	East F	John M	John F	Mid M	Mid F	Newc M	Newc F	Home M	Home F	Gore M	Gore F	Nia M	Nia F	London M	London F	West M	West F	PE M	PE F	Vic M	Vic F	Tal M	Tal F	Brock M	Brock F
1824	—		5	0	0	0	3	1	8	1	0	0	3	2	3	0	7	0	3	0	1	0								
1825	—		1	0	2	0	3	2	8	3	0	0	7	1	—		4	0	—		4	2								
1826	—		1	0	—		—		7	1	0	0	5	3	—		4	0	—		—									
1827	—		—		—		2	0	6	2	2	0	4	1	—		10	0	—		—									
1828	—		—		—		4	0	4	0	—		9	0	—		3	0	—		—									
1829	—		—		—		—		—		—		—		—		18	1	—		—									
1830	—		2	1	0	0	8	4	8	1	4	1	16	0	12	0	10	0	—		2	0								
1831	—		—		—		10	0	13	2	3	0	13	1	10	1	7	0	—		—									
1832	—		—		—		—		—		4	0	8	2	8	1	—		—		—									
1833	—		—		—		13	1	9	3	3	0	—		—		7	0	—		—									
1834	—		—		—		13	0	13	2	—		—		—		6	0	—		—									
1835	—		—		—		12	0	15	1	12	0	7	2	—		—		—		—		—							
1836	—		—		—		10	0	6	1	—		—		—		—		—		—		—							
1837	—		—		—		8	0	—		—		—		—		—		—		—		—							
1838	1	0	2	0	—		15	0	—		2	0	—		15	5	7	0	12	0	2	0	—		—		9	0		
1839	4	0	4	0	—		8	0	—		—		22	1	—		11	0	25	0	—		—		—		—		—	
1840	—		—		—		2	0	—		6	1	—		—		3	1	19	3	—		—		—		9	0	8	0
Total	5	0	15	1	2	0	111	8	97	17	36	1	94	13	48	7	97	2	59	3	9	2					9	0	8	0
District Totals	5		16		2		119		114		37		107		55		99		62		11						9		8	

Source: LAC, RG 5, B27, vols 1–2.

Small numbers add up to larger numbers, in this case to 869 of them, 810 men and fifty-nine women, but not all of these were ordinary prisoners. A few were soldiers put into the gaols while awaiting courts martial for unspecified offences. Then there were the debtors and the insane, whose combined numbers, only ninety-three in total, suggest that they may not have been always routinely included in these returns by the sheriffs. Finally there were the 1837–38 rebels accused of treason. Since they are extraordinary cases which have been minutely examined by other historians they, like the military, the debtors, and the insane, are again excluded from discussion here. We are left with 645 prisoners, 590 men and 55 women (8.5 per cent). We know who they were, the district where they were arrested, where they were born (in one case the answer is "at sea"), what crime they were alleged to have committed, and for a minority of them, the sentence they had received.

In forty-four cases no record was entered of the crime of which the prisoner was accused or it was listed only as "misdemeanour," which means only that it probably was not a crime involving violence. The other 601 prisoners had been committed on quite a wide variety of charges, including such rarities as "cutting off the mane of a horse" and "cursing the King."

Before attempting any analysis of the varieties of Upper Canadian crime, a methodological problem must be addressed. It is not practical to deal with each crime individually; some division by types of crime needs to be made. How then should offences be categorized? There are obvious problems with any system which puts specific crimes into general boxes, but fortunately other historians have already wrestled with this question and some standard categories have been established. The organization employed here largely follows the classification used by Donald Fyson in his book *Magistrates, Police, and People*, and is as follows: (1) Violent offences, (2) Property offences, (3) Offences against the State, (4) Public order and moral offences, (5) Regulatory offences, (6) Labour offences, (7) Other offences.[16]

Violent offences, or crimes against the person, include such really serious crimes as murder, manslaughter, rape and infanticide, plus wounding, malicious shooting, riot, and the ever popular assault and battery. Property crimes encompass all forms of theft, robbery, and burglary, plus attacks on property such as arson and trespass. Offences against the State are such direct or indirect attacks on state power as treason, insurrection, assaults on state officers, refusal to do militia duty, and counterfeiting and passing counterfeit money. Public order and moral offences include such matters as disturbing the peace, public drunkenness, vagrancy (a frequent euphemism for prostitution when applied to women), gambling, violation of the sabbath, keeping disorderly houses, and blasphemy.

Regulatory offences are violations of local by-laws and regulations for such offences as selling liquor without a licence, refusal to perform statute labour on the roads, peddling goods while not a British subject, and other infractions of the road acts or police regulations. (According to David Murray such offences emerged as a significant category of crime in Upper Canada only after 1834 when magistrates "were empowered to hear and dispose of minor cases summarily in their own communities.")[17] Labour offences are restricted almost entirely to breaches of the master and servant acts, usually for leaving employment. "Other" offences, the catch-all category, covers unusual or infrequent crimes, or crimes which do not fit easily into any of the other categories. Upper Canadian crimes reported in the gaol returns by these categories which resulted in prison sentences, for men and women, 1824–40, appear in table 6.9.

More than half of all the prisoners and more than half of the woman prisoners were in gaol charged with property crimes. Most of this was simple theft, usually recorded as either grand or petty larceny. Theft of animals (thirty-two cases) and robbery (four cases) were relatively rare and were always men's work. As criminals these Upper Canadians were evidently specialists: they were a decidedly light-fingered bunch.

On the other hand crimes of violence, of which the most common single offence was assault and battery, as well as less frequent cases of murder, manslaughter, rape, other felonies, infanticide, malicious shooting and wounding, make up a sizeable but distant second category. These figures do not seem to support a contention that in the 1820s and 30s Upper Canadian men (and seventeen women) were particularly violent people.

Crime, as represented in the gaol returns, appears to have been somewhat ethnically concentrated. Of the prisoners in the gaols by birthplace, 25.6 per cent were Irish, 16.3 per cent were British North American, 16.1 per cent were American, 6.4 per cent were English, and 4 per cent were Scots. "Others" and unknowns add up to 30.6 per cent.[18] However, the situation was probably not as

Table 6.9
Offences by category of gaol prisoners, 1824–40

Category	Number	Percentage	Male	Female	Percentage Female
Violence	181	30.1	164	17	9.4
Property	317	52.7	287	30	9.5
State	68	11.3	66	2	2.9
Public Order	13	2.2	9	4	30.7
Reg.	8	1.3	6	2	25.0
Labour	2	0.3	2	0	0.0
Other	12	2.0	10	2	16.6
Total	601	99.9	544	57	9.5

Source: LAC, RG 5, B27, vols 1–2

Table 6.10
Birthplaces of the Upper Canadian population, 1842

National Origin	Number	Percentage
Canadian-born	261,634	53.7
Ireland	78,255	16.1
England and Wales	40,684	8.4
Scotland	39,781	8.1
United States	32,809	6.7
Europe	6,581	1.4
Unknown	27,309	5.6
Total	487,053	100

Source: Canada, Census, vol. 4, 1871, 136.

straightforward as that. If the birthplace figures in the first Upper Canadian census of 1842 are at all applicable to the figures presented here for the previous eighteen years, some national groups acquire more, or less, prominence (table 6.10). In the criminal justice system the Irish and the Americans were over-achievers. The Irish made up 16.1 per cent of the population in 1842 but 25.6 per cent of the prisoners listed in the gaol returns, the Americans only 6.7 per cent of the 1842 population but 16.1 per cent of the prisoners and in proportion to their census numbers were the groups who received the most attention from officers of the courts. On the other hand, British North Americans, at 16.3 per cent of the prisoners, were very greatly underrepresented, as were, to a lesser degree, the English and the Scots. Among women the only national group to stand out, in three different ways, were the Irish. In total women made up 8.5 per cent of all prisoners. Irish women alone accounted for 3.6 per cent of all prisoners, 13.9 per cent of all Irish prisoners, and 41.8 per cent of all female prisoners.

Assuming that the Irish and the Americans were not simply genetically predisposed to be criminals, two possible broad explanations for these disparities present themselves: prejudice and poverty. It is probably fair to say that in the view of the civil and judicial establishment of Upper Canada the Irish, especially Irish Catholics, and the Americans were the least favoured groups; people who had been and were likely to be troublemakers, whose political principles were probably dangerous, and whose loyalty to Crown and empire was suspect. Neither group was ever welcomed to any extent into the ranks of the powerful and influential in Upper Canada. The Irish constituted a threat to order by their very numbers and alleged shiftlessness and the Americans, though less numerous, had a reputation for dishonesty and sharp practices. It would not be surprising then that a degree of prejudice against them both might exist among those who enforced the law.[19]

As for poverty there is no apparent reason to suppose that the American-born in Upper Canada were collectively economically disadvantaged, but many of the Irish, who were the largest immigrant group throughout the 1820s and 1830s, would as newcomers have had to go through a difficult period of adjustment before they could reach some level of security. Historians of poverty in Upper Canada have dated its emergence as a worrisome social problem to the early 1830s when the immigrant flow, made up largely of the Irish, was about to reach its peak.[20]

To cast the likelihood of some sort of connection between immigrant poverty and alleged criminal behaviour in a different light it is instructive to look at the situation of the Canadian-born, which is one of striking contrast. By 1842 53.7 per cent of Upper Canadians were native-born but they made up only 16.3 per cent of the prisoners listed in the gaol reports. Again it is unlikely that they were on the whole more inherently virtuous than the Irish or the Americans but it is likely that their circumstances were more favourable. Their parents may also have been immigrants who had struggled to find an economic footing in the province, but native Upper Canadians could have had the advantages of family and friends, of education, or of land.

The Upper Canadian elite did not believe that poverty was an excuse for crime but they did see a connection. In commenting on an 1835 petition from a couple convicted of selling liquor without a licence who claimed that they were too poor to pay their fine, R.B. Sullivan, mayor and chief magistrate of Toronto was of the opinion that "those who offend against the law are always poor, for a person of property will not undergo the risk. They are generally unable or unwilling to work and adopt the trade of keeping these infamous houses perhaps because in many cases, because they have no other recourse, but I do not see that the evil to society is less, because the offenders are poor."[21] Of course Sullivan, who had a sizeable drinking problem of his own, did not have to frequent "infamous houses" and of course he exaggerated. Those who offended against the law were not always poor, but as a magistrate who dealt on a regular basis with a constant flow of petty criminals it must often have seemed to him to be the case.

The matter of national origin and criminal behaviour needs to be nudged on a bit further. Were some national groups prone to offend in particular ways? If the "top ten" leading individual criminal offences are analyzed by birthplace and gender (table 6.11), the numbers to work with become smaller especially in the years after 1838. That was the point at which the provincial administration began to demand monthly gaol returns, but perhaps in compensation for the extra work they no longer asked for the places of birth of the prisoners, so for the last three years of the period there are almost no such details to work with. Except for two returns in 1838 when places of birth were written in, birthplace statistics effectively end in 1837, which not only narrows the sample but clearly skews it in some cases. The crimes of aiding or enticing soldiers to desert for example barely appear in the records before 1838 but when a series of British units began arriving in Upper Canada after the Rebellion the number of cases went sharply up. For none of these offences were the places of birth of the accused recorded and much the same can be said about moral offences which were only then becoming somewhat more common. Nevertheless with these caveats in mind, what can be made of the existing figures?

Looking at the numbers in table 6.11 with the birthplace figures in the 1842 census in mind produces few surprises. The Irish in proportion to their actual numbers again stand out in most of the categories, particularly in the serious crimes of murder and manslaughter and in non-deadly violent crime. Americans were actually even more over-represented among the larcenous than the Irish but were

Table 6.11
"Top ten" offences by birthplace and gender, 1824–40

		Ireland	England	Scotland	BNA	US	Other/Unk	Totals
1. Larceny,	Number	70	18	13	51	46	4	202
Robbery, etc.	Percentage	34.6	8.9	6.4	25.2	22.7	1.9	100
	Male	58	17	13	50	44	4	186
	Female	12	1	0	1	2	0	16
2. Assault,	Number	36	5	2	15	12	7	77
Riot, etc.	Percentage	46.7	6.5	2.6	19.5	15.6	9.1	100
	Male	35	5	2	14	12	7	75
	Female	1	0	0	1	0	0	2
3. Murder,	Number	11	1	5	7	0	1	25
Manslaugh-	Percentage	44	4	20	28	0	4	100
ter, etc.	Male	11	1	5	5	0	1	23
	Female	0	0	0	2	0	0	2
4. Forgery,	Number	6	1	2	0	15	0	24
Counter-	Percentage	25	4.2	8.5	0	62.5	0	100
feiting, etc.	Male	6	1	2	0	15	0	24
	Female	0	0	0	0	0	0	0
5. Rape,	Number	4	3	1	3	1	0	12
Attempted	Percentage	33.3	25.0	8.3	25.0	8.3	0	99.9
Rape, etc.	Male	4	3	1	3	1	0	12
	Female	0	0	0	0	0	0	0
6. Public Order,	Number	3	0	0	3	1	4	11
Moral	Percentage	27.3	0	0	27.3	9.1	36.6	100
Offences	Male	2	0	0	3	1	3	9
	Female	1	0	0	0	0	1	2
7. Selling	Number	3	0	0	0	0	6	9
Liquor	Percentage	33.3	0	0	0	0	66.6	99.9
without	Male	2	0	0	0	0	6	8
a License	Female	1	0	0	0	0	0	1
8. Infanticide	Number	3	1	0	2	2	1	9
	Percentage	33.3	11.1	0	22.2	22.2	11.1	99.9
	Male	0	1	0	0	0	1	2
	Female	3	0	0	2	2	0	7
9. Aiding or	Number	4	2	0	0	0	0	6
Enticing	Percentage	66.6	33.3	0	0	0	0	99.9
Soldiers	Male	4	2	0	0	0	0	6
to Desert	Female	0	0	0	0	0	0	0
10. Contempt	Number	0	0	0	1	5	0	6
of Court	Percentage	0	0	0	16.7	83.3	0	100
	Male	0	0	0	1	5	0	6
	Female	0	0	0	0	0	0	0

Source: LAC, RG 5, B27, vols 1–2

somewhat less over-represented in acts of violence and do not appear at all under the headings of murder or manslaughter. Where the Americans really stand out is as forgers and passers of counterfeit money and they account for all but one case of contempt of court. They seem to have been specialists in the counterfeit money business and in thieving, which suggests that as offenders they may have been partly a transient population, popping over the border periodically for a bit of stealing or to defraud the local populace with phoney money. And when they were apprehended they were likely to show little respect for British justice.

The native-born were satisfactorily underrepresented in all categories, though they were not immune to stealing or violent behaviour. The English and the Scots rarely exceeded their due share of criminal acts with one notable exception. Out of twenty-five cases of murder or manslaughter, Scots were involved in five.

Aside from the question of crime and place of birth, the admittedly incomplete figures in table 6.11 invite some other general comments. The crimes that got people into prison were massively in two familiar categories: property crimes and violence, but property crimes easily outstripped all others. Even if all forms of violence listed here are combined they amount to little more than half the number of property crimes. This raises once more the opposing possibilities that either Upper Canadians were not particularly violent people or that crimes of violence were indeed often much ignored or unreported. There is another line of explanation as well, that Upper Canada's governing elite were prepared to tolerate a certain level of violence so long as it only involved people doing harm to one another, and were much more concerned with deterring threats to private property.

Among women prisoners no group makes a significant appearance except the Irish. Women overall amounted to 7.3 per cent of the sample. Irish women, most of whom had been charged with stealing, made up 64.3 per cent of the female prisoners (Irish men were 33.6 per cent of male prisoners). In other words Irish women were charged with offences even more often than Irish men, a situation also noted by John Weaver in his study of the Gore District gaol returns.

Aside from the common crime of theft, did women in general commit different crimes from men? Well yes and no. A tabulation of all the female prisoners to appear in the surviving gaol returns from 1824 to 1840, and not just in a yearly sample, produces a total of 135 women imprisoned for 140 offences (table 6.12), and they show

Table 6.12
Offences by women, 1824–40

	Number	Percentage
1. Larceny or Robbery	53	37.8
2. Public Order and Moral Offences	30	21.4
3. Infanticide, Abortion, or Concealing Birth	14	10.0
4. Assault, Felony, or Shooting	13	9.3
5. Murder or Manslaughter	7	5.0
6. Arson	4	2.8
7. Receiving Stolen Goods	3	2.1
8. Selling Liquor without License	3	2.1
9. Passing Counterfeit Money	2	1.4
10. Unlawful Threats	2	1.4
11. Misdemeanour	2	1.4
12. Nuisance	2	1.4
13. Selling Goods Under False Pretences	1	0.7
14. Failure to Pay Fine	1	0.7
15. Possessing Military Clothing	1	0.7
16. Assisting Soldiers to Desert	1	0.7
17. Trespass	1	0.7
Totals	140	99.6

Source: LAC, RG 5, B27, vols 1–2.

some interesting, if not entirely unexpected, variations. The leading charge among women was as usual larceny, and women were also actively involved in cases of violence and even murder, but where they particularly differ from men is in two categories, infanticide and public order and moral offences. The fact that infanticide was an almost entirely female offence is natural enough since men did not get pregnant. On the other hand the predominance of women in public order and moral offence cases is an illustration of the fact that such charges were relatively new in Upper Canada until the end of the 1830s. Of the thirty occasions when women were imprisoned on charges of this kind, twenty-five were in 1839 and were for vagrancy or for being "disorderly," probable euphemisms for prostitution. Of these, twenty-three were all imprisoned at the same time in the Toronto gaol, where some sort of sweep of the streets seems to have taken place. It is possible that the presence of large numbers of British troops in the province around the same time may have provided an extra stimulus to a female occupation always present but previously mostly ignored as a social evil.[22]

So far we have been dealing with people who had got themselves into fairly serious trouble and had been sent to gaol, but many Upper Canadians who found themselves in court were not tried at the assizes nor were they necessarily sent to prison at all, even if they were found guilty. Where ordinary people who had allegedly committed an offence, especially of a petty nature, encountered the judicial system, was before a magistrate, or several magistrates sitting as a district court of quarter sessions. The workings of this court, whose role in the districts has been said to have been "all pervasive" not only as a court but as an administrative body, have been described in detail elsewhere. For present purposes it was the lowest court in the judicial system, which dealt primarily with minor crimes and local squabbles. There are many surviving quarter sessions minute books for a variety of Upper Canadian periods and districts[22] but their very volume and somewhat casual organization which mixes their two functions more or less arbitrarily has so far inhibited any systematic attempt at analysis of them on a provincial scale. No such ambitious project has been undertaken here. Yet dipping into them in at least a selective way can be highly rewarding. Their immediate value lies in the vivid picture they invariably present of the varieties of law breaking which occurred at a basic local level among otherwise unremarkable people.

Back at the beginning of the twentieth century, the staff of the Ontario Archives, following the already longstanding example of their federal cousins, began publishing Annual Reports which included large numbers of printed copies of original documents, publications for which historians of the early province have ever since been deeply grateful. Before these kinds of publications, and nearly the Archives itself, were wiped out by the Depression, two Reports appeared in 1932 and 1933 containing in printed form the early quarter sessions minutes of the Home and the London districts. Some sixty years later Peter Oliver used these minutes as a means to analyze the early nature of common crime and punishment in the two districts in the years between 1800 and 1818. His study established that at the early quarter sessions the familiar crimes of violence, mostly assault and battery, and larceny were the dominant forms of criminality, with assault charges then outnumbering charges for larceny by 2 to 1. Oliver did not extend his research into a later period for the Home and London districts specifically, but an examination of the manuscript quarter sessions records of the two districts at a couple of subsequent points produces some suggestive results.[24] At the beginning of the 1830s (1830–32) the court records do not point to any dramatic change in the overall picture of grassroots criminal activity, except that the districts at that time may have been even more violent places, with crimes of violence, mostly again assault and battery, outstripping all others by a margin of more than 3 to 1. Using the same Home and London district sources to jump ahead to the end of the period (1840–41), the statistical picture changes somewhat. Larceny had become the most frequently prosecuted crime, leading assault and battery, which was in second place, by a margin of about 1.5 to 1.[25]

Peter Oliver did expand his research to later years in two more ambitious studies, one which analyzed a mix of quarter sessions and assize records to 1849 in six districts, Home, London, Newcastle, Johnstown, Midland, and Western, and a second dealing with four districts, Home, Gore, Newcastle, and Wellington, in the years 1824–38. His conclusions from the six-district analysis, expressed in percentage terms, were that before 1820 assault and battery was still by far the most common crime at 36.1 per cent of all prosecuted offences, followed by larceny (22 per cent), and that all other crimes were "numerically insignificant." In the period 1825–49, however, he found a quite different pattern. "Public order and Moral offences" now predominated (31 per cent), followed by larceny (22 per cent) and assault and battery, now at only 15.9 per cent. The four-district study results, this time expressed in terms of the number of committals to gaol per 100,000 of population, were similar. Crimes against property (presumably mostly larceny) had increased moderately from 42.5 per 100,000 in 1824 to 54.6 per 100,000 in 1838. "Crimes against the person" (presumably mostly assault and battery) had dropped from 136.5 to 31.7 per 100,000 in 1838, but there had been an "astounding increase" in public order and moral offences from 24.7 to 246.2 per 100,000 between 1824 and 1838.[26]

These figures on the growth of public order and moral offences, especially as they relate to the Upper Canadian period alone, are astounding indeed for several reasons. First of all, no other statistical study, including the data collected for this book, has discerned a dramatic general rise by 1838 of prosecutions for such crimes. David Murray's analysis of quarter sessions and assize records in the Niagara District for the years 1827–46 found that public order and moral order offences "made up only a small proportion of prosecuted crime," averaging only "12 or 13 per cent of the crimes for which arrests were made." John Weaver's statistical work on the Gore District gaol records, 1832–51, resulted in almost identical results. He concluded that "before 1843 they (public order and moral offences) constituted only 12 per cent of all committals," though in the 1843–51 period that figure rose to 35 per cent. According to Weaver these types of offences "were endured and accepted as of minor consequence until the early 1840s."[27]

How are we to account for these very different research results? The conclusions reached in Oliver's six-district study are not necessarily out of line with the others since it extends to 1849, so that the increase in public order and moral offences he identified could still have occurred sometime after 1840. It is the four-district study, which claims such a remarkable increase in prosecution for public order and moral offences by 1838, that appears to be so anomalous. But wait a bit. Is it possible that Peter Oliver and his researchers made an error? One of the districts in the study, Wellington, though provided for in legislation of 1838, did not formally exist until 1840. A study including data from Wellington District therefore could not possibly have an end date of 1838. This work, like the six-district study, must have actually extended to some later date, perhaps also 1849.

A further test of the validity of Oliver's results is at hand. Beginning in 1832 a number of municipalities were separated for administrative and judicial purposes from the districts in which they were situated. Instead of being under the control of the district magistrates they were given elected supervisory bodies called boards of police, or in the case of Toronto, the only incorporated city, a city council. These new organizations were responsible for the civil administration of the communities and also composed the lower courts which enforced local bylaws. Peter Oliver speculated that "population growth, municipal incorporation, and a somewhat more intensive commitment to policing" may have produced a radical shift in the pattern of prosecuted crime,[28] that is, that it was likely in the newly incorporated towns and in the City of Toronto with their paid constabularies that an increase in the prosecution of moral offences in the 1830s was taking place. We know from Weaver and Murray's research that no such phenomenon occurred in the Gore District or in the Niagara District. Was it then happening somewhere else? In a word, no, at least not in four Upper Canadian communities whose court records have been more-or-less arbitrarily chosen for detailed analysis – Toronto in 1834 and 1839–40, Brockville in 1832 and 1834, Cobourg in 1837–39, and Port Hope in 1834 and 1838.

Certainly preserving order and suppressing sin were matters of concern for the new urban courts. The charter of the town of Port Hope for example gave the board of police the power to make by-laws "generally to prevent vice and preserve good order." No doubt also improved policing did have an effect. The first constable hired in Brockville in 1832, a man named William Smith, was so zealous in his duties that he charged Ormond Jones, a member of that highly influential Brockville family, with riding too fast in the street. (Smith was summarily dismissed for this impertinence. Ormond Jones, taking no chances, got himself elected to the board of police the following year.)

Be that as it may, a tabulation of the actual type and frequency of offences in the four centres is quite instructive. The breakdown, in percentage terms, amounts to: Crimes against property 32 per cent; Regulatory offences, 29 per cent; Crimes against the person, 23 per cent; Public order and moral offences, 16 per cent.[29]

A preliminary clarification must be made here. Though crimes against property, all of which were cases of larceny, lead the list, this much understates the number of charges of that kind since they reflect only the situation in Toronto; no charges of this nature were laid in the towns. Since it is impossible to believe that no one ever stole anything in Cobourg, Port Hope, and Brockville, and since larceny continued to flourish in the province generally, it appears that larceny cases, except in the city of Toronto, continued to be heard at the district quarter sessions or at the assizes.

Finally, getting to the matter of public order and moral offences, instances of these in the four entirely urban places seem to have been, not surprisingly, a bit more common than in the mainly rural populations of the Gore and Niagara districts at the same time, but they clearly do not point to the "astounding" upsurge in prosecutions for vice and disorderliness alleged by Peter Oliver to have taken place by 1838. In this case what Oliver believed had happened did not happen.

Thieves and batterers then, early and late, were the most frequent offenders, especially at the local level. They were not however necessarily filling the gaols. As Oliver had found in the years from 1810 to 1818 in the Home and London districts, the magistrates did not usually impose harsh sentences for what were apparently considered fairly petty and routine violations. As well many who were charged were simply acquitted, the chances being a little over 50 per cent in their favour. Most convictions when they occurred resulted in only a fine. Imprisonment was rare, occurring in no more than 10 per cent of cases and usually for short periods. Many cases were arbitrated or required the offending party or parties to post a recognizance, normally along with two guarantors, to assure the court of their good behaviour for a stated period.[30]

The dual functions of the magistrates of the court of quarter sessions could sometimes overlap. They imposed fines for a variety of violations of their civic authority, such as failing to serve in an office to which one had been appointed, neglect of duty, failing to do statute labour on the roads, not paying taxes or not declaring rateable property, avoiding jury duty, impeding the public roadway, or operating an unlicensed tavern or still. Since as has been seen the district treasuries were usually dangerously close to empty, every little bit helped. As Oliver pointed out, it cost money to keep someone in gaol. And in the unlikely event that the terms of a recognizance were breached, the money put up by the offender and the "sureties" went straight into the district funds.

In the Home and London districts at the beginning of the 1830s the pattern was still much the same. Cases were still settled "with the consent of the court." Guilty persons were fined "five shillings and costs" and only rarely "£2 and one month in gaol and costs" or more, or were "bound in the sum of £50."

After the Rebellion things began to change. Assault and larceny cases which had previously brought such low fines now more often meant a fine of ten shillings and even as much as £10. More significantly, the chances of acquittal, once so favourable, had dropped. In the district quarter sessions in 1840–41 the statistical odds were close to 2 to 1 against. In the new municipal courts in the towns getting tough on crime was even more pronounced. The chances of acquittal there were about 3 to 1 against for violating a long list of mainly petty regulations against such offences as firing a gun in town, fishing on Sunday, swearing, ringing a ship's bell on Sunday, permitting gambling, riding faster than a moderate trot, bathing too close to town, allowing animals to run loose, keeping "a ball alley" without a licence, and riding a horse with no bridle or halter.[31] The respectable middle-class Upper Canadians who comprised the boards of police were not fighting a rising crime wave but they were certainly clamping down on what they took to be disorder.

PART II: PEOPLE

Upper Canadians who got into trouble with the law did so in many ways and at a wide range of ages. The youngest persons to turn up in the records were William Read and Mary Oliver, both aged eleven and both convicted of stealing. The oldest was Phoebe Ashley, acquitted of stealing at seventy, a good age for the time.[32] As for variety, a brisk scan through the gaol returns and the minutes of the quarter sessions and the assizes produces a list of more than fifty common crimes, ranging from the trivial to the extremely serious. Whatever the offence there was quite a bit of fluctuation in what happened to people who were apprehended, tried, and convicted. Take the common crime of larceny. The charge could be grand or petty larceny, depending on the value of the property involved, though that distinction was not always made in the minutes and was abolished in any case by an act (7 Wm. IV c.4) of 1837 which allowed quarter sessions to try all cases of "simple" larceny up to a value of £20. Larceny was an offence for which at first, as well as a gaol sentence, a whipping was often administered, until "shaming" punishments such as whipping and the pillory were largely phased out during the 1830s. At what date a prisoner was sentenced then could make a difference to what punishment followed. So could gender. In 1824 in the Johnstown District, James Brown, Anthony Gallagher, Catharine Sharpley, Mary Little, and Susannah Barrington were all convicted of grand larceny. Both men were sentenced to two months in gaol and to two public whippings of twenty lashes each time.[33] For the same crime the women were put into gaol for only two weeks, each to have one whipping of ten lashes each, given in private. By the mid-1830s corporal punishment was mostly a thing of the past but the sentences had increased. The penalty given to men for larceny was now usually one or two years in the penitentiary, while women normally received three or six months in gaol or at most a year in the penitentiary. When more than one person was involved it also depended on who the court found most culpable; usually a man, since men were assumed to be in charge. In a serious case in the Gore District in 1835 a gang consisting of Joseph Edwards, John Thompson, Hannah Bagley, and Sarah Smith were charged with both grand and petty larceny and with receiving stolen goods, to wit: four pairs of shoes, several pieces of calico, two shawls valued at ten shillings each, and 14 yards of silk valued at 2/6 a yard. Sarah Smith was acquitted. Thompson was convicted on the lesser charge of petty larceny and given a year in the penitentiary. Bagley was found guilty of grand larceny and was also sent to penitentiary for a year's solitary confinement. Joseph Edwards, who was evidently considered the ringleader, received two years at hard labour in the penitentiary plus an additional year to follow.[34]

Age as well as gender could sometimes also be taken into account. Though being only eleven did not save William Read from being sent to penitentiary for two years for larceny in 1839, Mary Oliver, also age eleven and also convicted of larceny in 1836, received only a six month sentence. Anna Maria Mott, charged jointly with larceny with her mother Elizabeth in the Victoria district in 1840, was even more fortunate. Her mother, under whose guidance Anna Maria was assumed to be acting, was sentenced to two years hard labour in the penitentiary. Anna Maria went to gaol for a week.[35]

Sentences for the common crime of selling liquor without a licence show less variation; a conviction almost always meant a fine of £20, a sizeable sum whether the offender was male or female. Penalties for "keeping a disorderly house," though primarily a female offence, were also applied equally when husband and wife were jointly charged, with the sentence ranging between two and four months in prison.

In some cases law reform bills passed in the 1830s drastically affected punishment. A far-reaching Upper Canadian act of 1833 reduced the number of crimes requiring the death sentence from about 150 to twelve. One area where the statute had an immediate effect was animal theft. A rural province like Upper Canada presented opportunities and temptations to steal livestock, but as in all rural societies Upper Canadian farmers set a high value on the animals they depended on for food, clothing, and motive power, and British law dealt harshly with rustlers. If convicted of stealing cattle, horses, or sheep, as Dennis Forbush and George Farrow were at the Kingston assizes in 1824, the penalty was hanging. Thirteen years later when John Whittington and John Davis, "coloured men," were convicted in Toronto of the same offence, they received the now-standard term of three years in the penitentiary.[36]

But it was serious acts of violence which, early and late, continued to have the most dire potential consequences. The crimes which in Upper Canada continued most often to result by statute in the death penalty were murder and rape. Extrapolating from a table published by Peter Oliver, the average number of persons charged with murder in the years between 1806 and 1840 was about 4.6 per year. No one has done a similar statistical estimate of the average rate of rape cases but a survey of the murder and rape cases for the same period in the Court of King's Bench minute books suggests that the incidence of rape may have been about the same as that of murder.[36] So, were nine or ten people hanged for murder or rape every year, along with the odd highway robber, also still subject to hanging in 1840? In a word, no. What the law prescribed and what actually happened were not always the same thing.

Let's back the legal process up a step. Not every sentence was carried out as the law directed, but of course before it came to that not everyone who was charged with a crime was found guilty. Leaning once again on Peter Oliver's early quarter sessions research, of ninety cases at that level, he found that thirty-two persons charged were acquitted.[38] A parallel exercise applied to the more serious offences tried in the Court of King's Bench totalling 104 cases produces twenty-nine "not guiltys," a similar result. Either way, if these samples are to be trusted, in Upper Canada a person charged with a crime, whether major or minor, had as much as a one-third chance of getting off (see table 6.13). The main reason why this was so was the jury system. Even though juries were then selected by the district sheriffs from among the supposedly intelligent and respectable adult male members of the community, they, like all juries, did not always reach the decision the prosecution, or the judge, wanted them to reach. As well, at the Court of King's Bench level defence counsels were usually present to put their client's case in the best possible light. In 1825, Judge William Campbell, reporting to the civil secretary on the western circuit of the Assizes, expressed the opinion that there had been too many acquittals which were "not proof of innocence," from "causes not infrequent in all small communities," in other words local juries could not always be persuaded to convict local people. The conviction-acquittal rate however, seems to have varied quite a lot depending on the offence involved. In general, people charged with moral offences, or with taking the property of

Table 6.13
Assizes verdicts where known, 1816–40

Crime	Number	Guilty	Not Guilty
Attempted Rape	7	3	4
Keeping a Disorderly House	1	1	0
Damning the King	1	0	1
Animal Theft	4	4	0
Larceny	24	21	3
Malicious Shooting	3	3	0
Receiving Stolen Goods	3	0	3
Murder	21	14	7
Passing Counterfeit Money	2	1	1
Infanticide	6	2	4
Disorderly	3	3	0
Rape	9	4	5
Aiding Prisoners to Escape	1	1	0
Breaking Gaol	1	1	0
Misdemeanour	1	1	0
Robbery	1	1	0
Manslaughter	2	2	0
Bigamy	1	1	0
Felony	2	2	0
Concealing Birth	4	3	1
Arson	3	3	0
Assault and Battery	3	3	0
Burglary	1	1	0
Totals	104	75	29

Sources: LAC, RG 5, A1, vols 30, 68, 74, 104, 170; AO, RG 22, Minute Books and Benchbooks.

others, whether by the theft of animals, burglary, robbery, or larceny, did not have a very good chance of acquittal, nor did those charged with felony, assault, malicious shooting, manslaughter, or murder. It should be noted though that even conviction on so serious a charge as murder could be avoided if the defence counsel could get the charge reduced. Hannah Cooper for instance, facing the death penalty for murder in 1836, instead received a six month sentence in the Newcastle District gaol for the lesser charge of manslaughter.[39]

The serious crimes which gave the accused by far the best chance of getting off or of having the charge reduced were rape, attempted rape, and infanticide. Even in straight rape cases the chances of acquittal appear to have been a bit better than 50 per cent. Alexander Greig, charged in 1834 with the attempted rape of Anne Bolton in her house on Yonge Street, was found guilty only of common assault and fined £50. Ethan Card was equally fortunate. He too was accused of attempted rape and like Greig was convicted only of assault. His fine was only £15 but as this was the second complaint made against him by Mary Switzer he was ordered "to find sureties for good behaviour toward Mary Switzer and ----- Switzer" for two years, "himself in £50 and two sureties in £25 each."[40]

Infanticide cases were relatively rare in Upper Canada. According to biographer Robert Fraser they rarely reached the courts and rarely resulted in a conviction when they did, though there were some exceptions (see table 6.13). Before a 1624 British statute was repealed in Upper Canada the death penalty could still be pronounced for infanticide, as it was in the well-documented cases of Angelique Pilotte and Mary Thompson in 1817 and 1824. When the lesser charge of concealing birth became available to the courts under a new statute (2 Wm. IV, C.1, 1831) the chances of conviction probably actually went up but at least the potential consequences of being found guilty were less dire. Susannah Drinkwater, convicted in 1837 in the Johnstown District of "concealing the birth of a small bastard child" was sentenced to a year at hard labour in the penitentiary. But by then even infanticide itself was viewed in a more lenient light. Ann Johnston of the Bathurst District was actually charged with the murder of her infant child in 1840. In a convoluted wording the jury found "that the prisoner was the mother of the child as charged in the indictment and was guilty of the birth thereof." Her sentence was only a year in the district gaol.[41]

The possibility of escaping all or some of the consequences of a guilty verdict did not end in the courtroom. Whether the sentence was death by hanging for murder or a fine of £20 for selling liquor without a licence it was always possible to appeal to higher authority for the reconsideration of a case. The lieutenant governor received a steady stream of petitions on behalf of people found guilty by the courts. A look at a sample of seventy-five such petitions covering the years 1814–40, drawn mainly from the Upper Canada Sundries series, confirms that such appeals were well worth making (table 6.14). For about 30 per cent of the petitions no outcome, either positive or negative, can be established, a distressingly high

Table 6.14
Results of some petitions, 1814–40

Result	Number	Percentage
Yes	29	38.6
No	23	30.7
Unknown	23	30.7
Total	75	100

Sources: LAC, RG 1, E3, vols 11, 30, 36a; RG 5, A1, vols 1a–260;
RG 7, G16C, vols 54–8; City of Toronto Archives, RG 1, B1,
Boxes 1–4.

proportion, but where the result is known the comparative figures are quite striking. The chances of some amelioration of a sentence were about 56 per cent in favour.

Petitioning then appears to have paid off more often than not, but over the whole period that statement needs some qualification. It was a common opinion in legal and journalistic circles before the law reform act of 1833 that because the penalties for so many crimes were so severe, the legal system was continually being undermined by the unwillingness of the courts to impose the full rigour of the law or by pardons and remissions of sentences granted quite freely by the executive. The deterrent effect of the prescribed penalties, it was argued, had been largely lost because an expectation had arisen that they would rarely be enforced. A major goal of the 1833 changes was to impose certainty. Because the number of capital crimes had been drastically reduced, all the laws were now to be enforced to the letter. A convicted criminal could no longer assume that the chances of not facing severe punishment were quite good. Penalties were to be applied without exception.[42]

An examination of clemency petitions presents a chance to test whether the new system worked as it was supposed to. The answer seems to be yes, to a degree. For the pitifully few petitions where a clear result is known up to 1833, the odds of success may have been as high as two to one in favour of some sort of lessened punishment. After 1833 the odds were only a little better than even, with about a 52.5 per cent chance of success (table 6.15). Still it is clear that the theory that the law would be applied in full to all miscreants was never realized. According to Peter Oliver, in the extreme case of rape, for which the punishment remained death after 1833, only one man was ever hanged during the entire Upper Canadian period

Table 6.15
Petition results and outcomes, 1814–40

A. Petition results and outcomes, 1814–33

Result	Number	Percentage
Yes	8	36.4
Commutation of Death Sentence: 3		
Full Pardon: 2		
Reduced Sentence: 1		
Remission of Fine: 2		
No	4	18.2
Unknown	10	45.4
Totals	22	100

B. Petition results and outcomes, 1833–40

Result	Number	Percentage
Yes	21	39.6
Commutation of Death Sentence: 1		
Full Pardon: 6		
Reduced Sentence: 3		
Remission of Fine: 4		
Conditional Pardon: 5		
Released on Bail: 2		
No	19	35.8
Unknown	13	24.5
Totals	53	99.9

Sources: LAC, RG 1, E3, vols 11, 30, 36a; RG 5, A1, vols 1a–260; RG 7, G16C, vols 54–8; City of Toronto Archives, RG 1, B1, Boxes 1–4.

and hangings for homicide were commuted for more than half of those sentenced.[43]

How was it possible to literally get away with murder, or with any other crime? In general the formula was to present a plausible case for innocence or mitigating circumstances or pure sympathy, and if possible to have the support of "respectable" local citizens, but each case was naturally different. A detour through some portions of Upper Canada's criminal past will demonstrate how it could be done.

Let's begin near the end of the period, and with the most serious circumstances. If the death sentence had been pronounced it was not even necessary for the condemned person to appeal, for by then such cases were automatically reviewed by the executive council. The 1840 trial of Philip and Mary Huffman, who lived in Raleigh

Township near Chatham, created a sensation. Both the Huffmans were convicted of murdering their eight-day-old child by drowning it in the Thames. The case was notorious because the Huffmans, though they lived together as man and wife, were not really married, he being already married and she in fact his young daughter, so the case was one of incest as well as infanticide. In this case the Executive Council, apparently not having fully subscribed to the intentions of the law reforms of 1833, expressed themselves "anxious to avoid inflicting capital punishment whenever possible." Nonetheless they allowed the death sentence pronounced on Philip Huffman to stand and he was hanged. Mary Huffman's sentence was commuted to transportation for life to Van Diemen's Land. Though Judge C.A. Hagerman, who presided at the trial, could not say "that one was more guilty than the other," the council evidently took the patriarchal view that Philip Huffman, as father and authority figure, was most to blame.[44]

Robert Fraser, who has made a study of infanticide in Upper Canada and has written the biographical entries in the *Dictionary of Canadian Biography* for two women, Angelique Pilotte and Mary Thompson, who were sentenced to death for infanticide but eventually pardoned, believes that these two women were exceptions because very few people were ever even convicted for the crime.[45] It is an ironic twist of circumstances that Philip Huffman, one of the few who was and was hanged, was a man.

Most appeals for softer treatment related less dramatic stories. In 1819 Margaret Willson of York approached the most influential woman in the land, Lady Sarah Maitland, wife of the lieutenant governor and daughter of the governor general, the Duke of Richmond, on behalf of her husband, in prison for theft. She had four points to make. Her husband had an exemplary record, having served for twenty years in Sir Isaac Brock's regiment, the 41st, including during the War of 1812 in Canada; no owners of the allegedly stolen articles had appeared in court to identify the goods; she was in distress because her husband, now out of the army and earning his living as a cordwainer, could no longer provide for her and their four children (and another on the way); and he had been convicted because of "want of council [sic] to instruct a country jury." Her petition to have her husband let out of gaol must have moved Lady Sarah, who in turn moved Sir Peregrine Maitland to order his early release.[46]

Mrs Isabella McCosh of Cornwall, fined £20 for selling liquor without a licence the same year, also tried the hardship argument in petitioning the lieutenant governor. She was a widow with three "helpless children" who had acted out of "hard pinching want." She was unable to pay the fine though she had tried "by all virtuous means" to raise the money. She also had supporters. Her petition was endorsed by eight local worthies including one sitting and one future MHA, five magistrates, and the Rev Alexander McDonell. Again Sir Peregrine Maitland, who has been described as a rather unbending man, gave in. Because of so many "respectable recommendations" he "has in your case deviated from his general determination to punish rigidly these infractions of the law."[47]

The 1824 "petition of the inhabitants of Kingston on behalf of Jane Maguire" may not have been signed by everyone in the town but covered in several pages a wide spectrum of "respectable" names, including such political enemies as Christopher Hagerman and the Bidwells. Mrs Maguire, in an unpremeditated "act of intemperate passion" during a quarrel with her husband, shot him in the hand "and deprived him of the use of it." She was convicted of "malicious shooting" and sentenced to hang. Not if the community had any say in it. She was well known and liked in Kingston, had "respectable connections," and had brought up her children "to the true precepts of the Christian religion." Unknown to her she had another invaluable advocate, Judge Campbell, who had presided at her trial. Campbell recommended the commutation of her sentence to banishment on two grounds. First, she had suffered severe and lengthy provocation. "For a long series of years" she had "experienced much ill treatment from her husband whose habits are extremely irregular." Second, the statute under which she had been convicted had always been "considered so highly penal that few executions have taken place under it." Campbell also advised banishment on practical grounds. Mrs Maguire and her husband were so at odds that "it is extremely probable she will murder him if they are living in the same country."[48]

Another numerously signed petition from "the inhabitants of Markham Township" presented a mixed case of innocence and insanity on behalf of Eliza McLean, convicted in 1836 of stealing a piece of calico with a value of ten shillings. The story advanced was that she had not directly stolen the cloth but had got it from a second party during one of her frequent "aberrations of intellect." The petitioners added that she was the mother of ten children, though whether that was meant merely as a plea for sympathy or an explanation of her "aberrations" was not made clear. At any rate her sentence was remitted.[49]

Jacob Briggs, a black man sentenced to hang for the rape in Windsor in 1840 of seven-year-old Frances Hazeltine, had no body of supporters to plead for a less severe sentence for him, but his case again illustrates how anxious the executive could be to find ways "to avoid inflicting capital punishment." On review they discounted the evidence of the child herself that "she felt something inside her" and of the midwife who examined her "within the hour" and testified that penetration had occurred "and that he had remained until he had satisfied his desires." Instead they relied on the opinion of Dr McIntosh, staff assistant surgeon to the Forces. Echoing a common piece of folklore about the sexual prowess of black men, it was his view "that it would have been impossible for a full grown man, particularly a Negro – note, the prisoner is a negro, the child a small child – to have entered the body of the last witness to the usual extent without leaving plain evidence of great injury." Briggs's sentence was commuted to transportation for life.[50]

The conviction and eventual pardon of Henry Cole, accused in 1839 with "assault with intent to ravish" eleven-year-old Margaret Kearney, adds another ingredient to the mix of factors which could contribute to the success of petitions, one which has already been seen in operation in a different context – persistence. The Cole trial caused quite a stir at the time because he was a person of some local prominence, a strongly partisan Tipperary Irish Protestant immigrant to Toronto Township who had been active in disrupting William Lyon Mackenzie's political meetings in the riding and who had done zealous service as a captain of the militia during the Rebellion period. As such he had his share of political and denominational enemies.

There was never much doubt about his guilt. Just before Christmas 1838, Cole and a man named Hugh Kearney, with Kearney's daughter Margaret in tow, had been on a cutter trip home which turned into a kind of rural pub crawl, ending at a tavern in the village of Springfield where they decided to spend the night. All accounts agreed that both Cole and Kearney were very drunk. Shortly after Margaret Kearney was put to bed, Cole went to her room where the assault took place. Margaret Kearney's testimony has an authentic ring. Cole said "give me a kiss and I will give you ten dollars. He immediately leaped into the bed and got on top of me and began to tear and pull me about. I hallooed and screamed and he pulled me out of bed onto the floor, pulled up my petticoats – tore my frock and abused me very greatly." Hugh Kearney came to his daughter's rescue and subsequently reported the incident. Cole was arrested, tried in May, 1839 and sentenced to two years in the penitentiary.

Then the petitioning began, led by Cole's wife Eliza, who not only repeatedly wrote to Lieutenant Governor Sir George Arthur on her husband's behalf but travelled personally to his office in Toronto to make a face-to-face appeal. She had vigorous support from Cole's partisans. According to his friends, the whole affair was a conspiracy concocted by his enemies. One of them wrote that Cole was "perfectly honest" and "a member of our Church of England" while Hugh Kearney, a Roman Catholic, was "inclined to dishonesty." At first the petitions were refused because no fault could be found with the verdict, but eventually Sir George Arthur, another lieutenant governor not famous for his soft heart, was worn down. His civil secretary admitted that Mrs. Cole's campaign was having its effect. "I cannot help wishing," he wrote, "that you would relieve the government from the importunities of one, who, by her frequent applications, is likely to weary us all." Henry Cole was released after serving half of his sentence, "under all circumstances."[51] David Murray has concluded that "knowledge of the legal process was much more widespread in the colonial period than it has subsequently become." Many people who got into trouble were evidently well aware of how to work the system and much of the time the provincial executive was prepared to play the game and to grant at least part of what was asked for. Just how some familiarity with the workings of the law, the courts, and the provincial executive was acquired, especially by people of little or no means or education, is something of a mystery. Some direct and indirect evidence points to the frequent friendly involvement of local people who had a measure of knowledge and influence, particularly lawyers. Of course in really serious court cases, such as those where the death penalty was a possibility, lawyers were inevitably involved as defence counsels and even if the accused had no lawyer the court could appoint one. In a number of capital cases examined by Robert Fraser and other writers, not one but two lawyers acted for the defence, including such prominent figures as W.H. Draper, R.B. Sullivan, Miles O'Reilly,

Simon Washburn, and the young John A. Macdonald. Most of the accused in these cases came from humble circumstances and it is unlikely that their lawyers earned much for their efforts except experience and reputation, good or ill. Washburn in particular has been said to have been "very kind and generous" on behalf of his clients, including black people, for whom "he almost certainly provided free legal aid."[52]

Lawyers were also involved in drawing up petitions and in collecting supporting signatures. A number of petitions have come to light which are definitely known to be wholly the work of someone other than the petitioner, such as a lawyer, law student, or notary, which were read to illiterate petitioners who then made their mark.[53]

Besides lawyers, many others – relatives, neighbours and friends – must have had a hand in appeals for clemency, especially when supporting signatures from the respectable citizenry were canvassed and collected. Some such petitions were massive tasks of organization, requiring the efforts of many people and much time, travel, and expense. The number of signatures collected in 1838 for the petitions on behalf of the convicted rebels Samuel Lount and Peter Matthews has been estimated at between 12,000 and 20,000. In at least one murder case involving an Irish immigrant the organizer of a petition bearing 174 names was a Roman Catholic priest.[54]

No matter how much support a petition received from others it must be remembered that petitions, like those of Lount and Matthews, did not always produce a happy result. As has been seen, petitions overall had at most about a fifty-fifty chance of even partial success. Neither the backing of large numbers of well wishers nor that of the locally prominent were always enough to make a difference. For the petitioner there was always one crucial unknowable factor, the opinion of the trial judge, whose recommendation was always sought by the executive. For a petition to succeed the judge had to be at least ambivalent. If he was strongly opposed to any softening of the sentence there was no hope.

The case for clemency presented by Julia Snow in 1838 on behalf of her husband had two weaknesses. She had not recruited any additional signatories as character witnesses to bolster her case, but even if she had, and unfortunately for her and her husband, the judge was evidently inflexible. Beverly Snow, a black immigrant from Washington DC, working as a waiter, was in Kingston Penitentiary, convicted of stealing from his employer. The evidence against Snow had been circumstantial and Mrs Snow was convinced that he was a victim of racial prejudice. By her account her husband had owned property in Washington, was not poor, and had no motive to steal. "In the minds of many," she wrote, "there unhappily exists a prejudice against coloured people" who did not believe that blacks could acquire means by "persevering industry." The Snows had come to "this country of equal and happy laws" to escape such bigotry. If Beverly Snow really was innocent they had been badly deceived for her petition failed. On the basis of the report from the judge the lieutenant governor could not "perceive any circumstances in the case to justify his interposition."[55] Jacob Briggs, convicted of rape, was saved from hanging because he was black. Beverly Snow may well have been convicted and refused clemency for the same reason.

The conviction of Elizabeth Mott and her daughter Anna Maria noted earlier was duly appealed. Mrs Mott had many friends in her home town of Belleville including the usual collection of politicians, magistrates, and merchants, such as Edward Murney, George Benjamin, A.H. Myers, and Henry Corby, who testified as to her good character, having, they said, known her for years and never having heard a word against her. Judge Jonas Jones was not impressed. "There is in my opinion no doubt of her guilt," he told the lieutenant governor, "she is a woman of ill fame and her daughter is an illegitimate child." The lieutenant governor had no choice but to reject her petition. Her supporters, he assumed, must have signed the petition "under the influence of kind feelings, without due inquiry into the true facts of the case."[56]

The stories in these thumbnail sketches by no means exhaust the range of rationalizations, explanations, and excuses employed by those who though found guilty sought still to evoke sympathy and compassion. Simple protestations of innocence, though common enough, were rarely enough to make a difference without additional proof or at least the benefit of influential assistance. A path much followed was to blame other persuasive but evil-minded people for leading the trusting petitioner away from the straight and narrow path of righteousness. Grace Smith, a young black girl convicted of arson in Toronto in 1839, had acted, according to her family, under the influence of a Mrs Morris, to whom she was apprenticed as a dressmaker. She was a mild and simple girl, "too compliant to the directions of Mrs. Morris," who could make her do anything.

(Mrs. Morris was never charged with any crime.)[57] Among those swept up as alleged rebels by loyal forces in the aftermath of the Mackenzie and Duncombe risings this defence was repeated over and over. Naive but otherwise blameless men had "been unjustly led into wrong paths" by "the smooth speaking" of "that John Rolph, being member of parliament," by "that retched rebel leeder," by "the artful machinations of the notorious Charles Duncombe," or just by "some evil minded men."[58]

Catharine Sharpley claimed, vainly, to be the victim of her own good nature. She was put in the Brockville gaol for stealing in 1823 because her side of the story, that it was all a mistake, was not believed, despite the fact that she was of "an old respectable family in Ireland" and her husband, who died at the Battle of Chippawa, had been sergeant and paymaster of the First Royal Regiment. Her version was that she had done a favour for someone else by selling clothes for a man who did not want it known that he needed to sell them. The clothes turned out to be stolen and the man disappeared to the United States, leaving Mrs Sharpley literally holding the bag. The conviction in 1827 of "Betsey, an Indian woman" who spoke no English for manslaughter came about in a more bizarre way. Lawyer Simon Washburn, who represented her at the trial, wrote afterwards to the civil secretary that one of the jurors had confessed to him that, unable to reach a decision, the jury had "tossed up" or "drawn lots" for a verdict. The case of Mary Dyer, found guilty of assault in Toronto in 1835, was a little more clear-cut. Her contention was that the seriousness of the incident had been greatly overblown, as it had been only "a little dispute with my neighbours." Her account differed sharply from the official, and decisive, one in which she had "inflicted a dreadful wound" and "exulted in the offence."[59]

Just as instructive as the narratives of those who claimed wrongful conviction are those of men and women, or often their relatives, who admitted guilt, but felt the need to explain why it was the criminal's or society's fault. As might be expected alcohol often played a featured part. In 1816 Lydia Evans thought her husband John should be spared the disgrace of a public whipping because he had been drinking when he committed theft. Thirty-six-year-old Margaret Hawley, the wife of a disabled pensioner of the 27th Regiment, stole a piece of linen from a shop on King Street in York in 1831 "while drunk." In the Henry Cole attempted rape case the strongest case for the defence that could be mustered was that he was too drunk at the time to have even attempted rape.[60]

Certainly alcohol and violence often mixed, sometimes fatally. Mary Cotter, in York Gaol in 1833 for assaulting her husband with the fire tongs, explained that he had brought it on himself "through his negligence and too unnecessary use of ardent spirits." He was "a votary of dissipation and vice and has frequently abused me and vitiated me almost to madness." The conviction of Margaret Kennedy's husband for manslaughter in Niagara in 1827 was the result of "a drunken quarrel in a tippling house on a Sunday." Robert Percy, just out of gaol in June 1839, wanted money from his wife who refused to give him any. He went out, "got money elsewhere" and returned in a drunken rage to murder his wife with an axe in front of the horrified downstairs neighbours.[61]

Isabella McCosh, who had her fine remitted on the grounds that she was too poor to pay, was not the only offender to plead poverty. In at least two other cases the same reason was given to excuse the same crime – selling liquor without a licence. Retailing cheap whiskey illegally was a common way for the very poor to make enough money to survive, especially if, like John and Ann Hall, they were also old and in ill health.[62]

Ignorance of the law, or just plain ignorance, were also used as excuses by offenders or by others on their behalf. Dennis Russell was charged in 1828 with carnal knowledge of a girl under the age of ten, the daughter of his employer, but Judge L.P. Sherwood thought that Russell might be pardonable because neither Russell nor the girl's parents were aware that the act "amounted to any offence punishable by law." The jury which found William Farnsworth guilty of setting fire to his employer's warehouse recommended mercy. In the jury's opinion Farnsworth, a former slave, showed "very little intelligence." He was partly excusable because of his "apparent ignorance and stupidity." Leonard March's bad behaviour was said by his mother to be the result of having been "kicked in the head." Mary Hall's husband was put in prison for six months in 1839 for "ill using" her, but she explained that the incident occurred because of "a total aberration of mind" due to the death of their only child. Robert Percy, the axe murderer, claimed that he was insane, though the judge and jury did not agree. Fifteen-year-old Mary Court set fire to the barn of James Cavers in Adelaide Township in 1838, though she was said to have borne him no grudge. Since she testified that she "put a coal into a sheaf of wheat to see how the straw would spark," she may simply not have been overly bright.[63]

To return to the discussion with which this chapter began, it is clear that Upper Canada was far from being a society largely innocent of criminal activity. Indeed the events of the late 1830s convinced some prominent Upper Canadians that crime was not just endemic in society but was reaching alarming levels. In 1839 Colonel Walter O'Hara, assistant adjutant general of the militia of Upper Canada, hired a sixteen-year-old girl named Mary Anne Fraser as a servant on a one month contract but she left the job before the month was up. Her explanation for leaving her employment was that she had been hired to look after the O'Hara children and to do light work but instead had been made to perform "drudgery," including digging potatoes and feeding pigs. Besides, she said, the quality of the food given to the servants was very poor. O'Hara took her to court for breach of contract where she was sentenced to a week in the Toronto gaol at hard labour but much to O'Hara's anger and disgust she was given early release in custody by a sympathetic magistrate, George Gurnett. The O'Haras, the colonel fumed, were left in "great hardship" with only one remaining servant to cope with seven children. "It is necessary" he wrote, that "the public should be protected against a class of persons who are under the assumption that they can violate contracts with impunity," otherwise "the mobocracy" of Toronto would prevail. Colonel O'Hara was not the only establishment figure to feel, as the 1830s drew to a close, that civilized society in Upper Canada was being threatened from below. The lieutenant governor himself, Sir George Arthur, in rejecting a pardon appeal in an arson case in November 1839 was evidently still shaken by the recent uprisings and border raids. "At this particular crisis," he believed, "it is of great importance to strike terror into criminals of this kind."[64]

The people who were involved in the judicial process from start to finish, the magistrates and judges who presided at trials and the lieutenant governor and his Executive Council who responded to subsequent appeals for clemency, had always known from experience that Upper Canada had a more or less permanent criminal class. Their working days were spent in judgment of people "of bad character" and "of dissolute and immoral habits of life" who were "a public nuisance," who "seemed to have no employment," were "very artful," and especially were "old offenders."[65]

As the Upper Canadian period ended, crime and perceived immorality were posing increasing problems in a colony experiencing difficulties in the integration of immigrants and the process of urbanization. Yet serious crime, especially crimes of violence, was decreasing, not increasing, in Upper Canada. What had increased somewhat was the reach and the efficiency of the state in enforcing the laws, particularly in the towns. More people were being apprehended, tried, and put into prison, but often for relatively minor offences, many of which had previously been undetected or ignored, if indeed they had even been on the statute books. Colonel O'Hara and Sir George Arthur were overreacting to what they perceived as serious threats to civic order. There is scant concrete evidence that the provinces' institutions were under siege by a "mobocracy."

The Upper Canadian state was in the process of tightening its grip on law breakers, but for those who found themselves in trouble with the law there were still quite a few options which could be pursued to avoid the full rigours of punishment. The state, after all, had a human side. The time-honoured practice of personal or collectively supported petitions to the executive continued to have a frequent mitigating effect.

7

Getting Help

The British traveller John Howison spent two and a half years in
Upper Canada, from 1818 to 1820, and in 1821 published his
impressions in a book called *Sketches of Upper Canada*. The province, he told his British readers, was "in many respects a delightful
place of residence." He was particularly struck by the absence of the
"famishing and healthless poor" he had been accustomed to seeing
in England. In Upper Canada, he wrote, "beggary, want, and woe,
never meet the eye. No care-worn anxious countenances, or fam-
ished forms, are to be seen among its inhabitants ... a man may travel
through her various settlements again and again, and never have his
mind agitated, nor his feelings harassed, by the voice of misery."[1]

Howison was badly deceived, or was not looking in the right
places. In 1817, the year before he arrived, the first formally organized charitable societies set up to provide relief to the poor in
Upper Canada appeared in the province's principal towns, Kingston
and York. The Kingston Compassionate Society initially provided
only outdoor poor relief but by 1821 had also opened a hospital for
the sick poor. The Society for the Relief of Strangers in Distress in
York was created specifically to cope with "much apparent and temporary distress" among recently arrived immigrants. Also in 1817
the town of York first dealt, though less charitably, with the problem
of homeless people. A number of the poor had built crude shelters
"on the government park lot adjoining the town" and had become
"a great nuisance." The sheriff was instructed to have them out
within eight days.[2]

It could be argued that there was not supposed to be any poverty
in Upper Canada. The provincial Parliament, meeting for the first

time in 1792, clearly ruled out any government provision for people in need, particularly excluding from the legal system "the laws of England respecting the maintenance of the poor," which since 1597 in England had provided assistance to the poor in each parish by means of local taxation known as the "poor rates." Just why the Upper Canadian government deliberately avoided the creation of any such system of relief has been a matter of quite a bit of speculation. It certainly was not because there were no precedents to follow. As well as in England itself, all of the other English-speaking British North American provinces had enacted laws setting up some version of the English poor law system, the last being New Brunswick, which legislated provision for the poor in 1786, only six years before Upper Canada's decision to do nothing official at all for the poor. David Moorman has pointed out that some extant plans drawn up by government surveyors for projected Upper Canadian towns prior to 1792 included a space set aside for housing the poor. Upper Canada then rejected both English and colonial normal practice, but on what grounds?[3]

For more than forty years Canadian social and legal historians have grappled with this question but no definitive answers have emerged. The most thorough investigation of the matter, by Russell C. Smandych, concludes with the admission that he just does not know: "the question of why the English poor law was not adopted in Upper Canada cannot be considered closed." The problem is that there is a serious lack of hard evidence to explain who was responsible for not adopting English policy and what their motives were.[4]

In the absence of evidence there has been no shortage of theories. There may have been a naive belief that in a new and developing province where land was free or cheap and workers would presumably always be needed there would be no problem of poverty that could not be dealt with by the charity of individuals or churches, and this may even have been largely true before the War of 1812. By 1792 the poor law in England itself had come under attack as being inefficient, unduly costly, and overly generous, allegedly discouraging the poor from actively seeking work. Such opinions about the system would have been known to and possibly shared by Upper Canada's first lieutenant governor, John Graves Simcoe, who may then have sought to avoid the supposed mistakes of the mother country. In any case a poor law system on the English model would not have been very practical in Upper Canada. Its small scattered population, lacking organized parishes, probably could not at first have provided a sufficient local tax revenue to support more than a few of the unfortunate. Cost was certainly a concern. If the poor were to be supported in Upper Canada, who should pay the bill? Perhaps while the colony was still finding its feet it should be the imperial government's responsibility to provide any needed help. Or if the province was responsible, how was the revenue to be raised?[5]

There is no record of a debate having taken place on the bill which excluded the English poor law, which might indicate a prior agreement among the Assembly, the Legislative Council and the lieutenant governor to avoid contention, for there was a real financial issue at stake. To raise revenue, some of which could have been spent on the poor, Simcoe wanted to impose "a county rate," that is a tax on land. The Assembly, composed primarily of landowners and land speculators, would have none of it, alleging that such a tax would discourage immigration. Instead they proposed a "rum tax bill," which would have placed "a Duty of six pence per gallon on all spirits and wine passing through the country." This bill passed in the Assembly but was killed by the Legislative Council, where Simcoe had more influence and where there was a strong merchant presence. The result was a saw-off. Nobody got what they wanted, with no revenue bill passing at all. So, no money, no poor law?

That money was a central concern is also suggested by the fact that along with the poor law, the English law on bankruptcy was also specifically excluded from the laws of Upper Canada. Like the poor law, the English law on bankruptcy had its detractors, as being too lenient, permitting debtors to avoid prison by paying only a part of their debts. In Upper Canada where debt was chronic, the mercantile element wanted every means possible to extract payment from debtors. There was to be no coddling of the poor or the indebted.

Finally, it has been argued that just because the Upper Canadian legislature did not put a system of poor relief in place in 1792 does not necessarily mean that they did not intend to enact appropriate legislation at a later date, but since no law of any sort relating to the poor was passed until forty-five years later and even then was never enforced, this seems a dubious explanation at best.[6]

Whatever the real reasons for the exclusion of the poor law from Upper Canada may have been, the result was the same. People who by bad luck or bad management suffered misfortune in Upper Canada had no agency of government to turn to. Yet when immigrants from the United Kingdom began to arrive in increasing numbers after 1815, more and more of them needed help.

The first immigrants, the Loyalists and post-Loyalist settlers, mostly had frontier experience, some funds and no long debilitating sea journey to make. Some were given or brought tools or even stock. They inevitably met difficulties but usually had the knowledge and skills to overcome them, or they had family, friends, or neighbours to lend a hand when needed. Besides, there simply were not all that many of them, nor, except for the 6,000 or so original Loyalists, did they come to the province all at once in very large groups. The newcomers after the war were different. Once immigration from the British Isles got under way it became a steady influx of people, few of whom had the same kind of resources or initial skills. The population before the War of 1812 has been estimated to be 76,984. By 1842, driven to a great extent by immigration, it had reached 487,053.[7]

Poverty in Upper Canada was always primarily a post-war immigrant problem. A couple of pieces of statistical evidence make this point immediately very clear. In a sample of eighty-six needy people who petitioned the lieutenant governor for financial or other aid between 1815 and 1840, 92 per cent identified themselves as British immigrants. A report giving a breakdown by place of birth of 681 men, women, and children to whom charitable relief had been afforded in Toronto in 1839 reveals an even higher immigrant proportion and points directly to the European origin of the problem of poverty. 95 per cent of them were Irish, English, Scottish, or "Foreign."[8]

Rainer Baehre, the leading historian of the immigrant poor in Upper Canada, has calculated that in the heaviest immigration years of 1831 to 1835, 154,400 immigrants from the British Isles arrived at Montreal, most of whom were going on to Upper Canada. At least one-fifth of these new arrivals were "utterly destitute." In other words, even before they set foot in Upper Canada they had no resources whatsoever with which to go on to begin their new lives. The problem of poverty did not necessarily end in Upper Canada but neither did it always begin there.

In Great Britain and Ireland the decades following the Napoleonic Wars times were hard for many people. "A combination of fluctuating markets, overpopulation, enclosure, poor harvests, the displacement of manual labour by machinery, child labour, dislocation, urban squalor, and declining wages among craftsmen," produced a restless population, looking for a way out. Emigration was one potential solution to bleak prospects at home. In the years between 1815 and 1840 there were a few quasi-public or privately funded assisted emigration schemes which helped the poor to get to the colonies, but the great majority of those who joined the swelling stream of emigrants to British North America had to find their own way. They did not begin as paupers, for it cost money to cross the Atlantic. The cheapest form of passage, in steerage, cost, with provisions, £10 to £15 a head, or £40 to £60 for a modest-sized family of four. Such a sum was totally beyond the reach of the really poor. The passage money was the greatest single expense, but not the only one. People who did not live in one of the ports of embarkation had the expense of transporting themselves and their belongings there. This cost too could be budgeted for in advance, but ships often did not sail on the advertised day and money set aside to be used for expenses after arrival at Quebec and beyond could be rapidly used up in board and lodging bills while waiting to embark. Any delay cost money. Elizabeth Jane Errington cites the case of a family who waited in lodgings in Liverpool for two weeks and had to borrow from family and friends to pay their bills even before they left port. They arrived in Quebec penniless. Their case was by no means unique. People of some but limited means amassed what they thought, or hoped, would be enough to take them to their final destination in Upper Canada. Too often their estimates of costs were sadly over-optimistic.[9]

Whether the immigrants were destitute on arrival or not there were still many difficulties ahead. The Upper Canada-bound again faced inevitable delays and added expense for transportation and lodging at Quebec, Montreal, and the various Upper Canadian ports. Men looking for immediate work found that jobs could be scarce and that employment fluctuated with the seasons. In the cholera years of 1832 and 1834, many passengers became sick on the crossing, and arrived, if they arrived at all, drained of strength and determination. A surprising number of families became separated after landing, usually because a father or other adult male went on ahead to look for work or land and did not reappear, leaving wives and children unsupported, ultimately dependent on the charity of strangers. Those wanting to become settlers as soon as possible had to deal with the expense, delays, and frustrations of the land-granting system, and after 1826 with the fact that land was no longer free. All the new settlers suffered from inexperience – with the techniques of clearing the land of massive trees, with the extremes of climate, and with the lack of nearby medical aid in case of illness or accident. Invariably they also met higher than anticipated initial costs and slower results in producing anything to eat or sell. In hindsight it is surprising that there were not even more destitute, desperate people in Upper Canada than there were.[10]

In lieu of any government-sanctioned means to assist the unfortunate in Upper Canada a variety of makeshift unofficial arrangements were resorted to in an attempt to take up the slack. Following the early examples provided by Kingston and York, other communities along the immigrant route such as Prescott, Brockville, and Cobourg eventually organized their own poor relief societies, led by the locally prominent and financed by voluntary donations. In 1836 Toronto became the first and only community during the Upper Canadian period to open an institution exclusively for the use of the poor. The House of Industry was also the creation of Toronto's leadership elite. At its inception the chairman of its board admitted what the legislature had tacitly denied in 1792, that poverty was inevitable in Upper Canada. "While it is desirable," he wrote, "to avoid the formation of large Alms-Houses, as having a tendency to encourage idleness ... it is obvious that there must be in all communities a class of aged and helpless poor, and of orphan children, who must be maintained at the public expense." The House of Industry was built and largely financed by volunteers, though it did receive modest grants from the province and the city, but which had to be re-applied for annually. Unofficially some public money was spent on the poor on an *ad hoc* intermittent basis by the magistrates in some districts. In 1800 the magistrates of the Home District refused to do anything for "a woman of the name of Page," who, with her children "were in great distress," on the grounds that "the laws of the Province did not authorize them to make use of public money" for such a purpose, but two years later, with no authorization, a differently constituted quarter sessions court ordered the district treasurer to pay £10 to "William Hunter, of the Town of York, Blacksmith" for the board and lodging for two months of "Mary Day (a pauper and insane person)" and approved spending a further sum "for the purpose of conveying the said Mary Day to the Province of Lower Canada, from whence she came." In 1803 the Home District magistrates found a new expedient to temporarily provide for the family of a terminally ill Markham Township man named Moses Martin, whose children "were naked and starving." The town wardens were instructed to seize "all the moveable property and chattels belonging to the said Moses Martin" to be sold to provide them with "food, clothing and other necessaries." What if anything the magistrates planned to do for them when the money ran out does not appear in the minutes.[11]

It has been assumed that the example of "the notorious pauper auctions" of New Brunswick, under which poor people were put "in the hands of the person who shall offer to keep them at the least expense" and which led to much abuse of the poor, was never followed in Upper Canada. In fact precisely the same system was used on occasion by the magistrates of the London District. In 1816 the district clerk of the peace was ordered "to advertise to the public the Widow of Samuel Wilson, and George Fisher, to be let to the lowest bidder." The magistrates also provided for destitute children by "binding them out" as servants until the age of twenty-one to someone willing to give them "the necessaries of life." All such strategies for relieving the poor during the early history of the Home and London districts were used only sporadically and no regular arrangements seem to have emerged.[12]

The magistrates of the Midland District apparently spent some public money on the poor prior to 1819, but in that year they resolved that no such funds would be appropriated in the future. The only district that has been so far found to have set up any actual system of ongoing poor relief was Niagara. David Murray's ground-breaking research has shown that in the 1820s the Niagara magistrates maintained a "pauper list" of individuals and families whose requests for assistance had been approved, after rigorous scrutiny, and who received small sums on a weekly or monthly basis. The list was reviewed quarterly, when names could be removed or added. David Murray rightly describes the amount of this support given to the poor as "niggardly." The sums granted ranged from ten shillings a month to five shillings a week, which on a yearly basis would have been £6 to £10, a good deal less than the likely average earnings of an unskilled labourer (see table 2.2) or even the minimum £20 per year pension given to disabled militiamen or the widows of militia privates. In any case the Niagara District pauper list was discontinued in 1830 on the grounds of expense and the doubtful legality of spending public money on the poor. Subsequently the Niagara District magistrates continued to make some maintenance payments in special cases but only on an *ad hoc* basis. In 1830 the pauper list had contained twenty-two names. By 1833–34 only two people were receiving aid. The increasing numbers of the needy exerted strong pressure on the magistrates however, and by 1840 the number of relief recipients had crept back up to fifteen, still the proverbial drop in a bucket in a total district population of 32,500.[13]

One group of unfortunate people in Upper Canada, the destitute insane, did receive a form of attention from the government, though it could hardly be called compassionate. Again in a hit-and-miss way such people were from time to time put into the district gaols for want of anything else to do with them, in inevitably unsatisfactory conditions. Though they were a constant irritation to the gaolers and the other prisoners, an act of the legislature of 1833 regularised the practice by officially allowing all the districts to use their gaols to house the insane. Peter Oliver found that in 1835 about 42 per cent of the expenditure on the Toronto gaol was for lodging the insane.[14]

It should be apparent by now that most people who fell on hard times in Upper Canada were not likely to receive help from any agency of government. If they got help at all it was from charitable individuals or societies. That however did not stop people in need from asking the government for help, usually in the familiar form of a petition to the lieutenant governor, though such petitions clearly represent only the tip of an iceberg. Many people must have needed and wanted help but only a few wrote to the lieutenant governor to tell him so. A striking illustration of this discrepancy can be seen in a comparison of the number of people known to be seeking aid at the end of the period at the recently opened House of Industry in Toronto with the number who actually petitioned for help. A roll of the inmates and out-pensioners of the House of Industry as of 20 January 1840 contained the names of 363 men, women, and children. In all of 1839–40 only twenty-four people petitioned for relief. What the petitions for help provide then is only a limited sample of hardship, but a sample is better than nothing. A look at such petitions permits at least a partial insight into the nature of poverty and distress in Upper Canada. So who were the petitioners and how did they come to be in a desperate state?[15]

Tables 7.1 and 7.2 suggest some initial statistical answers. Who they were, so far as their known origins are concerned, is pretty clear. They were mostly Irish, English, and Scottish, in that order, with the Irish consistently more numerous than the others. While table 7.1 does not actually tell us anything definite about immigration to Upper Canada, only about the situation on arrival at Quebec, Baehre's

Table 7.1
Overseas immigrant arrivals at the Port of Quebec by origin, 1829–41

Year	Ireland	England	Scotland	Europe
1829	9,614	3,565	2,643	0
1830	18,300	6,799	2,450	0
1831	34,133	10,343	5,354	0
1832	28,204	17,481	5,500	15
1833	12,013	5,198	4,196	0
1834	19,206	6,799	4,591	0
1835	7,108	3,067	2,127	0
1836	12,590	12,188	2,224	485
1837	14,538	5,580	1,509	0
1838	1,456	990	547	0
1839	5,113	1,586	485	0
1840	16,291	4,567	1,144	0
1841	18,317	5,970	3,559	0
Totals	196,883	84,133	36,329	500
Percentage	61.8	26.4	11.4	0.2

Source: Cowan, British Emigration to British North America, appendix B, table 2.

Table 7.2
Personal petitions for relief by origin, 1815–40

Ireland	England	Scotland	Thirteen Colonies	UE	BNA	Unknown	Total
40	28	11	11	11	2	163	266

Sources: LAC, RG 5, A1, vols 7–247; B6, vol. 6; C1, vols 1–43; City of Toronto Archives, RG 1, B1, Boxes 1–2; OAR (1912), 378–96.

research on the destination of immigrants after they left the port of Quebec clarifies the matter somewhat. Combined figures for the years 1832, 1833, and 1836 show that 23.3 per cent stayed in Lower Canada, 11.4 per cent went to the United States and 62.6 per cent went on to Upper Canada, but which national groups tended to go where, and in what proportions, is impossible to tell. Since the percentage of Irish immigrants arriving at Quebec was considerably higher than their share of the British-born ultimately recorded in the Upper Canada Census of 1842, it may be that they had a greater propensity to stay in Lower Canada or to move on to the United States.[16]

Sadly the great majority of the petitioners represented in table 7.2 did not provide an actual place of birth (and the temptation to make educated guesses about them has been resisted), but it is again pretty obvious that most were from the British Isles. The North American-born were few and none were from Upper Canada itself. Among those British immigrants in table 7.2 for whom a birthplace is known the Irish made up 50.6 per cent, the English 35.4 per cent and the Scots 13.9 per cent. Does this mean that the problem of poverty in Upper Canada was really mostly an Irish problem? Well yes and no. The Irish were a problem because there were so many of them, but, relying only on the evidence in the petitions, they were not a problem disproportionate to their actual numbers within the immigrant stream, or eventually within Upper Canada. When at the end of the period the population dust finally settled with the release of the Census of 1842, after more than twenty years of British immigration, the relative percentages among the British-born were: Ireland, 49.3 per cent; England, 25.6 per cent; Scotland, 25.1 per cent. In other words the percentage of Irish people who petitioned for relief was just about what it should have been, given their share of the population. The English in fact may have been more likely to ask for help than their numbers warranted, but if there was an anomaly, it was the Scots, whose petitioning numbers fell well below the level to which they were numerically entitled.[17]

Judging from these petitions, in avoiding hardship as in avoiding trouble with the law (see chapter 6) it was a considerable advantage to have been born and grown up in Upper Canada. This is not to suggest that no native-born Upper Canadians ever needed help, only that they were much less likely to do so. An 1839 report of the two-year-old House of Industry in Toronto concerning 681 people then receiving relief, by birthplace, listed: Ireland, 390 (58.2 per cent); England, 188 (27.6 per cent); Scotland, 45 (6.6 per cent); "Canada," 36 (5.3 per cent); and "Foreign," 22 (3.2 per cent). Leaving aside the question of whether "Canada" referred only to Upper Canadians, it is still apparent that the native-born were much more likely to have had family, accumulated resources, experience, and knowledge on their side, which some immigrants clearly lacked. Put another way, it is probable that "the first years were the worst years." Most of the immigrant petitioners were in fact recent arrivals who had yet to find their feet in their new home. The initial immigrant experience was by far the most difficult. If that could be survived (and some never did get through it) things were likely to get better, if only slowly. A related point has to do with children. Among fifty-two petitioners who mentioned their families, the average number of children works out to

5.9 per family, though the actual number varied between one and fourteen. It was often said that a settler could not have too many children to help with the arduous chores of clearing land and raising crops and livestock; in the short run however immigrant petitioners often pointed to their young children as extra burdens which made their lot in life more difficult and expensive, since young children had to be fed, clothed, and housed while they were not yet productive members of the family settlement or wage-earning unit. Children could be part of the problem, if eventually part of the solution.[18]

Another set of numbers of apparently significant size can be attached to petitioners divided on the basis of whether they were living in an urban or rural place at the time the petition was submitted. A classification of this kind has been possible for 216 of the 266 petitions, and the breakdown is: 119 rural, 97 urban. "Urban" meant mostly and increasingly York/Toronto or Kingston, with a few petitions from places such as Hamilton, Cornwall, or Perth. At first glance then it might seem that people were less likely to fall on hard times in urban Upper Canada, but of course these numbers on their own are misleading, since Upper Canada was an overwhelmingly rural province. Even at the end of the period the urban population was only about 12 per cent of the total, so that on the basis of population there should have been at most only thirty-two petitions from urban locations, rather than three times that many. Here again the lesson, after the fact, is apparent. One was better off in the countryside where, if one could get a start in farming, the ability to provide for oneself and a family could only increase. It was true that from 1817 on, the rudimentary charitable agencies in the principal urban centres, Kingston and York, provided short-term assistance to people in need, but the best long-term solution for newcomers was to get on the land. In many instances rural communal activity such as various kinds of "bees" and simple neighbourly helpfulness may also have been more effective than the grudging level of charity handed out to those considered deserving in the towns. Of course there were failures in the rural areas, and some of the urban petitioners said they had tried to be settlers but had been forced to give up. Some also professed a wish to become settlers but lacked the means to buy or get to land, and some of these probably got their wish in time. In general though distress was, in proportion to population, an urban phenomenon.[19]

The petitions for relief were also heavily unbalanced by gender. There were 215 male to 51 female petitioners, and these figures need little if any adjustment for population since men did not outnumber women in Upper Canada by very much. We should not conclude however that men therefore experienced misfortune more frequently than women. In fact the contrary was the case. Another look at the inmates and out-pensioners of the Toronto House of Industry, this time in January 1840, makes this point clear. There were twenty women (and thirty-six children) living in the institution and only six men. Among the out-pensioners there were seventy-two women (and 232 children) and only three men, only one of whom was accompanied by a child.[20]

The reason why most petitions for relief came from men was that the men applied for help for themselves, and if married, for their wives and children, and it is evident that in the patriarchal society of the time an adult male assumed that it was his duty and his right to take whatever initiatives were necessary, and it was expected that he would be the one who communicated with officers of the government. This was not because women did not have a legal right to petition the lieutenant governor. The daughters of Loyalists, whether married or unmarried, as has been seen, regularly petitioned for land. A number of well-born women submitted petitions asking for jobs for their husbands, including Susanna Moodie, who appealed to Sir George Arthur for a position for her husband without even telling J.W.D. Moodie she was doing so.[21] But these were exceptions. When women submitted petitions it was because they had no alternative, not because they were weak, helpless, or incompetent, but because to act otherwise would have been, in the social circumstances of the day, disturbingly unconventional. Of the fifty-one female petitioners, forty-three were widows, thirty-one of whom had children, and the remaining eight were single women. By contrast, out of the 215 male petitioners, only one identified himself as a widower and only eight said they were single fathers. Quite a few male petitioners (sixty-five) appear to have been single men, though it is not always possible to be sure that they did not have families, and the marital status of a further sixty-two men is so ambiguous that it has to be classed as unknown. Of the 266 petitions, 127 definitely concerned families, most of which included an adult male. To sum up, most of the petitioners were immigrants and most of the immigrants came in families, or to a lesser extent as single men. Without exception, women who petitioned for help did so in the absence of an adult male, and as far as is known, the women who were single mothers became so after coming to Upper Canada.

A final numerical subdivision of the petitioners, noteworthy on the basis of size alone, is a military one. There were seventy-three former British soldiers among the petitioners, sixty rank-and-file and thirteen officers, plus fifteen who had been on active service in the Upper Canadian militia in 1812–14 or 1837–38. Such a sizeable proportion (33 per cent) of the petitioners invites some speculative comment. A military career, especially of some length, spent in a variety of conditions, climates, and hazardous circumstances was likely to leave a former soldier with lingering disabilities – impaired health, a weakened constitution, a weakness for ardent spirits, or the actual loss of limbs or sight. Generally speaking, old soldiers did not make good settlers, a hard lesson learned for example by a large group of Chelsea Pensioners, who during the 1830s, on the urging of the imperial government, exchanged their pensions as wounded out-patients of Chelsea Hospital for the prospect of land in Upper Canada with almost invariably disastrous results. Whether incapacitated by wounds or not, having been in a high risk occupation the post-military careers of soldiers reflected their heightened vulnerability and inability to cope with conditions in which others prevailed. It is also possible that, for the private soldiers especially, long habits of dependency and subordination had left them ill prepared to adapt to new conditions and challenges in which they had to make their own way and make their own decisions. It is not surprising then to find so many of them among petitioners for relief. There was as well some natural affinity between former military personnel and the men to whom they sent their petitions, the lieutenant governors, all of whom had been military officers, some like Maitland and Colborne, at a senior level. This military connection was raised frequently in petitions, the contention being that British officers should not allow old soldiers who had suffered much and offered their lives for King and country, and their families, to starve in a British colony. "On claims of equity and justice," army widow Catharine Roberts believed, "she is entitled to some remuneration for the deeds of the dead." One or two men, one of whom was Thomas Robinson, formerly a private in the Buffs, claimed to have served under the lieutenant governor in the past. "Every man in your Briguad" [sic], Robinson assured Sir John Colborne, "would have went to their knees in fire for you." The records do not reveal whether Colborne was prepared to take equally heroic measures to help Robinson, whose money was "all dun."[22]

The matter of physical health, or rather the lack of it, of which many old soldiers complained, leads to some further general considerations, not about who the petitioner were, but about how they claimed to have wound up needing assistance, and it is not surprising to find that assorted forms of health problems were high on the list. The ultimate health problem, the death of a family member, especially of a father, has already been shown to have produced a total of fifty-two single parents, widows, and widowers among the petitioners, and another sixty-three people specified some kind of sickness affecting themselves, a spouse, children, or all of them as a cause of their problems, which means that 44 per cent of the petitions concerned death or illness within families. Many of these petitioners had been struck by death or sickness at a particularly bad time, shortly after arriving in Upper Canada or even during the ocean passage, and had used up their resources for medical care as well as board bills and provisions before being able to start new independent productive lives in the colony. In the 1830s the cholera years were particularly devastating, sometimes wiping out almost all of a family, or more capriciously, as in the case of widow Margaret O'Hare, leaving her husband dead and her solely responsible for nine dependent children.[23]

In addition to cholera and other kinds of disease, many other physical problems, some relating to military service, were cited as causes of distress. The lingering effects of wounds was mentioned eleven times, and twelve petitioners had suffered some form of amputation. Two were cripples, eight were blind or partially so, and ten reported disability due to accidents which had occurred while working for themselves or others, such as axe cuts, falling trees, cave-ins, or explosions, particularly during canal construction. Pierre Giroux of Penetanguishene was reduced to destitution as a result of having his fingers and toes amputated when his hands and feet were frozen while transporting fish on Lake Huron in weather so cold that both his horse and dog froze to death. Getting sick or injured was a critical factor in causing hardship in Upper Canada. If we add an additional unfavourable health hazard, old age, given as a cause of

distress by thirty-two people, the point becomes even more significant, and there was considerable overlap among those who were old,
sick, and infirm.[24]

For comparative purposes it is worth looking once again at the
situation in that microcosm of misery, the Toronto House of Industry.
Among the fifty-six people who were actually being cared for in the
building itself in January 1840 were ten who were classed as "sickly,"
"infirm," "convalescent," or "confined to bed," five as "a cripple" or
"paraletic," five as "incurable" or as an "idiot," and one as "deaf and
dumb," for a total of twenty-one, or 43 per cent of the total. (Three
of the "sickly" were also unusually old for the time, at eighty-eight,
ninety, and ninety-three years of age.) Among the seventy-five heads
of families receiving charity as out-pensioners for themselves and
their families there were eighteen who had "sick families," two who
were blind, two cripples or paraletics, two classed as an idiot or
lunatic, and four as very old, in this case making up 37 per cent of
the total. It is hardly necessary to draw the obvious conclusion.
Problems arising from sickness or disability were the largest single
cause of hardship in Upper Canada. And given that seventy-two of
the seventy-five out-pensioner heads of families were women, who
were supporting a total of 231 children, it is equally apparent that
the burden of destitution fell unequally on women and children.[25]

Among those who petitioned for relief a number of other factors
contributing to distress can be identified. Loss by fire of houses,
barns, or other buildings, stored crops and livestock was a fairly
common occurrence, with twenty-one cases reported, and could, or
so it was claimed, reduce even an established settler to penury.
Unemployment on the other hand, or rather the alleged inability to
find work of any kind, was relatively rare, only twelve petitioners
making this complaint. It was not necessarily true, as some Upper
Canadians believed, that there was always work in the colony for
anyone who was willing to take it, but the petitions suggest that the
inability to work through age or infirmity was likely more common
than the inability to actually find work. Failure to get work was
mentioned most frequently by people who claimed to be of more
than common birth or education, of whom there were about thirty
among the petitioners. The problem of finding work for such people
however was not always a lack of jobs *per se*, but of suitable jobs. As
one such "respectable" petitioner complained, he could not "get in
this country employment suitable to his habits and rank in life."

White-collar jobs, either in government or elsewhere, were scarce, and the only other easily accessible profession, teaching in the common or private venture schools, usually produced meagre returns.[26]

Serious or widespread crop failures did not happen very often in Upper Canada but when they did the result could be serious hardship for many people. The most dramatic case of this kind occurred in Glengarry County in 1816, "the year without a Summer." Unknown to the unsuspecting Glengarrians, an enormous volcanic eruption had happened at Mount Tambora in Indonesia in April 1815 and by the following year the dust from its immense ash cloud in the stratosphere had reached northeastern North America, in many areas causing a lack of sunlight and warmth. In Glengarry severe frosts in the summer of 1816 destroyed the crops planted that spring, even potatoes. According to the numerous petitions sent to the lieutenant governor and the legislature, some 550 families, including members of the four shiploads of Scottish immigrants who had just arrived late in 1815, were facing starvation, "till such time as God may bestow us favourable seasons." Twenty years later in 1836 an even more freakishly local occurrence of frost "early in the season" destroyed crops of wheat, oats, peas, and potatoes in the townships of Medonte, Oro, Flos, Vespra, Thorah, and Eldon, which lay west and east of Lake Simcoe, again producing numerous petitions describing much "destitution" or the likelihood of "positive starvation" leaving the children in one family "in a state of nudity." In each case it was the recently settled who suffered most from the loss of their crops, having little or no backlog of stored grain or other foodstuffs and lacking funds to buy seed or provisions. It is significant that the MHAs, magistrates, militia officers, and other established residents who wrote supporting letters recommending the impoverished settlers as fit objects of charity did not themselves complain of crippling loss, having presumably acquired sufficient means to be able to wait for better times.[27]

Needless to say there were many other individual alleged causes of calamity related by petitioners. Each petition represented a unique set of circumstances, but what they wanted from the government was always the same – some means of getting out of the mess they were in. For the majority it was simply money, in the form of short- or long-term funds, to get them through temporary hard times or to survive an otherwise very bleak old age. The appeal could be expressed in various ways such as "a small pecuniary assistance," or "a loan out of some fund." Some wanted military rations or other forms of provisions. A Mrs Leech of Lanark whose husband was in gaol for debt wanted to borrow a stove because her house was "insufficient" for the coming winter. Some petitioners could not bring themselves to beg outright on paper and asked for "some means of assistance," or "such aid as to your Excellency may seem meet." Ten petitioners asked for some means of free transportation to their land grants, but a greater number wanted a free ride of a different kind. Thirty-five disillusioned petitioners wanted no more of Upper Canada. They wanted free passage or funds to take them "home," usually to Ireland, England, or Scotland. Richard Pierpont, former slave, former pioneer in Butler's Rangers, and former private in Runchey's Coloured Corps in 1812–15, finding it "difficult to obtain a livelihood by his labour" in Upper Canada, asked in 1822 to be sent home to his native West Africa. Some made more modest requests, asking only for the means to get to an ocean port, either Quebec or New York. Finding themselves without family or friends, they wanted to go back to a place where they had left kin, friends, and familiar surroundings.[28]

What people in distress wanted from government is obvious, but what could the government actually do for them? By and large the answer is nothing. For settlers who were in the early stages of Loyalist or later British-sponsored settlement there were sometimes short-term rations, bedding, or tools provided from military stores, but to most petitioners the invariable answer was some variation of "the Lieutenant Governor regrets that he has no means of complying with your request," or "His Excellency much regrets that he has no funds at his disposal to provide for you." It was, in law, no more than the truth. There were no funds available, to the lieutenant governor or anyone else in the government, without specific legislation authorizing expenditure, which could be used to relieve the poor and helpless. The impoverished 1815 Glengarry immigrants, though they had come out "under the patronage of His Royal Highness the Prince Regent," were told that "the instructions of Gov't deprive His Excellency of the power of granting this request." Richard Pierpont never got to go back to Africa. Such relief as was extended personally by the lieutenant governor came from his own private purse. Not a few of the more pathetic petitions contain a marginal notation of the civil secretary such as "gave him a pound from the Lt. Govr."[29]

So what became of the 266 people who appealed to the lieutenant governor and his Executive Council to help them out of situations with which they themselves could not cope? In most cases the answer is that we shall simply never know. The beginning and the middle of a human story has been told; the end is forever lost. What we do know is tragic enough, and these glimpses of the petitioner's lives – their "stories so far" – help to convey, nearly two centuries after the event, some of the ingredients of misfortune in Upper Canada, "the poor man's country." It has to be admitted of course that, besides the cruelties of fate, troubles could also be largely self-inflicted by various forms of incompetence, ignorance, or pig-headedness, and that there were some petitioners who attempted to gain sympathy and handouts under false pretences. A man named Reuben Illingsworth, who claimed that intermittent blindness made it impossible for him to hold a job, was declared on investigation to be a fake, trying "to extend his system of imposition on the public." A more successful fraud was practised by a William H. Yelland, who in 1839 and 1840 extracted £10 from Sir George Arthur and in 1844 a further £5 from Sir Charles Metcalfe and ten shillings from Sir Richard Jackson, before investigation revealed that he was "not of the most abstemious habits" and was living with one of three sons-in-law that he had in Upper Canada, a prosperous merchant in Hamilton. "I was advised," he told Arthur, "to appeal to a popish priest for relief. I would suffer death rather than do so. I am not a bigot or a party man." A number of other claims for special treatment must also be treated with a degree of scepticism. When John MacIntyre of Dalhousie Township petitioned successfully in July 1828 to be given tools with which to clear his land on the grounds that he was too poor to buy them, no fewer than thirty other Lanark area settlers sent in similar petitions alleging their own inability to afford implements, though some of them had been on their land for as long as seven years. Francis Wyatt from Perth, a persistent seeker of cash or loans in the early 1820s who eventually abandoned his widowed mother and younger siblings to return to England, turned out to have a long history as a swindler and left debts behind him amounting to £500. Quite a few petitioners, such as William Pitt, also of the Perth area, were simply incompetent. He had got deep in debt due "to his own mismanagement and imprudence, being quite unfitted for the active duties of a farm, in which he threw away a large sum of money." Samuel Chearnley, "late of Cork ... gentleman, B.A. of Trinity College," arrived in Upper Canada in 1818 and was given a grant of land and the lease of a Crown reserve in Hallowell Township but believed himself entitled to more land and recognition. In the next years he bombarded the lieutenant governor's office with petitions for various form of compensation or assistance until executive exasperation set in, on the grounds that he did not have "the smallest cause of complaint." Meanwhile Chearnley abandoned his land and threw away his money on hired labour, rent in Picton, and a series of harebrained schemes. Eventually he too joined the ranks of the poor and did receive a measure of charity from the government, being allowed in 1827 to shelter in the largely burned out former parliament buildings in York, then acting as a temporary asylum for destitute immigrants.[30]

Such people were exceptions. Most of the petitioners were "deserving," that is their troubles were not of their own making, as some condensed versions of their appeals will demonstrate. Joseph Burton of York, an Irish immigrant and his wife and three small children, were reduced "to penury and want" after his house and all their possessions were lost in a fire in September 1814 and he then broke his leg in June 1815. Donald McPherson, a former soldier who came to Upper Canada from Scotland in 1822, lost all his possessions in a shipwreck on the St Lawrence on arrival. He was finally getting established on a farm in Monaghan Township when his entire crop of wheat was wiped out by a hailstorm in July 1829. Complaining of being old and infirm, he came to York in January 1830 to appeal to Sir Peregrine Maitland for "pecuniary assistance" for himself, his wife, and four children. James Doherty, also an 1822 immigrant, from Ireland, lost one eye and later the other as the result of an accident while working on the Rideau Canal. After settling in Ramsay Township, he lost everything, including his land deed, to fire in December 1830, leaving him destitute and unable to support his wife and five children, all girls, "who are unable to render him any assistants [sic] on his farm." He was told he could apply to the provincial secretary and the surveyor general for a copy of his deed, but that His Excellency "has no funds at his disposal to provide for him." James Cowley, like Doherty, was the victim of an industrial accident while working as "a miner all the time" on the Long Sault Canal, where in February 1837 he had his leg broken when "blown up by powder in a clay bank." Two of his sons were also injured in similar accidents, one being blinded. Unable to support a family of ten, he hoped the lieutenant governor would "consider our most grievous necessities." John Henderson came to Upper Canada from the United States in 1816 and married an Upper Canadian girl with whom he had five children. In 1833 he lost the use of his right hand when his fingers had to be amputated. He served in the Rebellion and received a wound in his left hand which "mortified," forcing the amputation of the whole arm in June 1838. His wife was left to support the family in Toronto "by industry and the kindness of several ladies of this city" until she fell and injured her leg in 1839 and was put into the Toronto Hospital. His petition, which needless to say was written for him by others, asked for "such relief as Your Excellency shall think proper."[31]

Men did most of the petitioning but it is worth repeating that the burden of hardship in Upper Canada fell particularly heavily on women and children, especially if they were widows and fatherless children. Of the twenty adult inmates of the Toronto House of Industry in 1840, fourteen were women, seven of whom were widows, five with children. Among the thirty-four children there were twelve who were orphaned or abandoned. Of the seventy-two female out-pensioners, forty-one were widows, thirty with children. As well seven women had been abandoned by their husbands and a further seven husbands were absent by virtue of being sick, or in the militia, or in prison. Of the female petitioners, as has been seen, the great majority, 84 per cent, were widows.[32]

Not much has been written about widowhood in Upper Canada. The major studies that have been done on widows concern urban women in Montreal and Ottawa in the late nineteenth century. The lives of such widows, these authors agree, were hard – "to survive as a widow in the nineteenth century was a continuous struggle" – because of the limited opportunities for women to make a living in a patriarchal world, but they were not necessarily helpless victims condemned to live on the charity of others. "Such women rarely gave up." Instead, within the limited options available to them, many widows used a variety of strategies to ensure the survival of themselves and their families. These strategies could include co-residence, raising domestic animals and keeping gardens, taking in boarders, running a business, taking paid work, or sending their children out to work.[33]

It is possible that some of the widows who petitioned the lieutenant governor or who were inmates or out-pensioners of the House of Industry eventually employed some or all of such means to support themselves and their families, but it is clear that most of them when they sought help had not reached that stage. The Montreal and Ottawa widows of a later time were not in the main new arrivals. They had homes and neighbours and friends and connections. Few of the widows suddenly left to fend for themselves in Upper Canada had those advantages. They were in a "distant country" on their own, far from familiar faces and surroundings and in desperate straits. They did not have time to make connections and develop strategies. They needed help immediately, which in most cases was not given, certainly not by the provincial government. The widows and female petitioners in general who appealed to the most powerful male figure in Upper Canada as a possible source of aid had no "strategies" to suggest. Instead, whatever their individual potential capabilities may have been, in the short run they stressed their womanly weakness, helplessness, and desperate need in the hope of a sympathetic response from the lieutenant governor. Margaret O'Hare, referred to earlier, whose husband died of cholera in 1832, had no relatives in Upper Canada and no means to support her nine children. She wanted to take the family home to England, "trusting that Your Excellency will think of something for us." The Governor could not "render her the least assistance" but wondered if she might get help from "private persons in the neighbourhood." Sarah McKechnie, who had arrived from Scotland in 1834, also wanted to go home. Her husband too had died, probably of cholera, on board ship in the St Lawrence. Her oldest son had drowned in the St Lawrence and her remaining six children had been sick during the two years they had been in Upper Canada. She asked for return passage or "such assistance in this country as to Your Excellency shall seem fit." Her petition was endorsed "no means of procuring her return." Catharine Roberts had followed her soldier husband to Madras, the Cape of Good Hope, and St Helena before he became one of the Chelsea Pensioners who commuted his pension in exchange for a new start in Upper Canada. Before he died, "in an unguarded moment," he sold his land for a soon-spent £4, leaving her "in a strange country" without friends. She professed to believe that "British liberality and generosity are proverbial over the world and she trusts some means will be granted to smooth her passage to the grave." Nancy Daley's husband, a Peter Robinson settler from Cork, froze to death crossing Rice Lake in the winter of 1825, leaving her with an infant child in need of "protection." Even widows of the respectable classes were not immune from difficulties. Harriet Hall's husband had served in the British Army for twenty-nine years before he was induced "by derangement of mind" to sell his commission as a captain in the 16th Regiment. When he died she was left with three children "nearly destitute in a foreign country." She petitioned for "a pension or some assistance to enable me to provide for my family and take me back to England." The husband of Rachel McCormick was not dead when she petitioned in 1833 but for practical purposes he might as well have been. Like seven of the women who were inmates or out-pensioners of the House of Industry in 1840, she and her four children had been abandoned by her husband. She was in a state of near starvation, "living this few days on one loaf of bread." She wanted permission to sell their land grant or "if Your Excellency would assist me to go to my land I would not part with it or on your directions to bind my children out as my husband has left me and I is not able to pay for my lodgings."[34]

A few women wanted the lieutenant governor to help them with a different kind of matrimonial problem, wife abuse, but judging by the available evidence, such women got no greater assistance and rather less sympathy than those who were suffering from poverty. Consider the cases of two Upper Canadian women whose stories begin in the Perth military settlement. Margaret Daverne and Eliza Richey make only brief and ineffectual appearances in the public records of Upper Canada, but the names of their husbands pop up very frequently. Daniel Daverne was an early English immigrant to Upper Canada, arriving before the War of 1812, in which he served successively as sergeant and ensign in the Prince Edward County militia, clerk, and then senior clerk in the Quartermaster General's Department. In 1816 he was chosen to be secretary and storekeeper at Perth, and shortly after arriving was also made superintendent of the settlement. Daverne, it turned out was a crook. In 1819 a court of inquiry was appointed to look into the administration of his offices, but he left town ahead of the law, allegedly taking with him money and supplies. Although there was strong evidence of "malservation of funds" he was never prosecuted, perhaps because he was thought to have left the country, but the land grants he had received, 800 acres plus two town lots in Perth, were cancelled "by order of His Grace the Commander of the Forces, July 14, 1819." In fact he turned up soon enough not very far away, in Adolphustown.[35]

In 1824 Margaret Daverne submitted the first of a series of petitions to Lieutenant Governor Maitland. She had been "compelled to fly from" her husband and her home in Adolphustown in 1821 because of the "inhuman" and "cruel and unrelenting treatment" she had received from him. She was trying to get Daverne to pay for her maintenance but without success. She wanted the land grants that had been given to him, but cancelled, transferred to her in trust for her children so that at least they would have some property. The lieutenant governor forwarded her petition to his Executive Council with a note to say that he would "concur in any measure for the relief of Margaret Daverne and family that the council can devise which will not break any regulations or form an embarrassing precedent." But Daverne's family could not be allowed to benefit from his misdeeds. (His brother Richard also tried for years to get his hands on the land.) The executive councillors could "find no means of relief for Margaret Daverne." The lieutenant governor's secretary wrote unhelpfully to Mrs Daverne that "with every feeling for your situation and every disposition to afford you relief," compliance with her request would be "incompatible with established usage and liable to be attended with important difficulties of a legal nature." Precedent was more important than people.

In 1826, after seeking legal advice, Margaret Daverne decided to try to obtain a divorce and again appealed to the lieutenant governor for help and advice. She could not possess any property, not even her clothing, which Daverne had kept, "until the separation actually takes place." Again the official reply was discouraging. There was no precedent for such a thing. "There is no instance on record," the governor's secretary wrote, "of any act of divorce having been passed by the legislature of this colony, and should such a bill pass the two houses there is no one here to signify the Royal Assent, which can in such case only be given by the King in Council." Needless to say Margaret Daverne did not get her divorce, but in the end she was legally separated from her husband when Daniel Daverne died at Adolpustown in March 1830.[36]

Eliza Richey made her appearance at Perth as the wife of a former officer, Lieutenant Alexander Cuppage of the 103rd Regiment, who served in Upper Canada during the War of 1812 but then sold his commission "due to unforeseen misfortunes and embarrassed circumstances" and settled at Perth. Inconveniently for his wife he died shortly after "from a fit of apoplexy," leaving her with three children under six. She had the apparent good fortune to be courted by her second husband, Wellesley Richey, an Irish immigrant and former sergeant in the 90th Regiment, now keeping a tavern in Perth, who became a widower sometime before 1825, by which date he and Eliza were married. Richey had been granted 200 acres and a town lot in Perth and now also got his hands on 500 acres awarded to Eliza Cuppage in trust for her son, but for unknown reasons he gave up the tavern and the prospect of settlement in the Perth area and spent the 1830s as a Crown land agent in the Lake Simcoe region, "subsisting, locating and employing emigrants in Oro, Medonte and Orillia." This is where Eliza comes in. Her 1834 petition to Lieutenant Governor Sir John Colborne told a sorry tale. She had separated from Wellesley Richey on the understanding that she was to have "the lot on Bass Lake she then lived upon" and that he would help to support and educate the children. She had been "anxious for a separation on any terms" because after "the many years of trials she had endured from his violent temper" she believed her life to be in danger. He had "plunged the point of a carving knife into her forehead," had given her "blows from a tomahawk and a gun barrel in the breast," and "caught her by the throat to finish his work which he was prevented from doing by the children and the servant woman." William Morris, MHA of Perth, who had known the Richeys there and "knows what she has suffered" had advised her to leave Richey "lest she suffer the same fate as his first wife who was sent to an untimely grave ere she attained her 17th year." The promise to help support the children had been broken "like every other he made." She had been forced to borrow money and was living in "a state of starvation." She needed help and also wanted title to the lot on Bass Lake. Eliza Richey got the usual bureaucratic response. The state could not interfere "to settle a misunderstanding between Mr. Richey and his wife." To add insult to injury, the commissioner of Crown lands reported that neither of the Richeys had any title to any land on Bass Lake.[37]

The petitions of Margaret Daverne and Eliza Richey in fact represent only the tip of an iceberg of Upper Canadian women who, for whatever reason, left their husbands. Elizabeth Jane Errington's research has revealed that "hundreds" of women left home, but "it was in all instances the husband who was considered the wronged partner." To quote Chief Justice William Campbell, "the law is decidedly hostile to the practice of wives running away from their husbands."[38]

The assorted glimpses of despair represented by these petitions to the lieutenant governor from both men and women are also merely representative of the much larger numbers who needed help at some point. Sir Francis Bond Head's secretary told a supplicant in 1836 that "the demands made on him for charitable aid are so numerous that he is obliged to confine his assistance to those who have a claim on his support. He therefore must decline to comply with your request." Most of the time the lieutenant governors simply said that there was nothing they could do, but the requests did not stop coming, partly because there was nothing to be lost by asking, and also often from a genuine belief that something could, and should, be done. The petitioners were not aware, as was John Smyth of Augusta Township, that the government had from the beginning set its face against poor relief and that there was "no provision in this country for the support of the poor," but rather looked to "that plan of universal benevolence for which the British government is so justly famed." They asked for relief "agreeable the laws of our province." or "a small supply of our government allowance," or "some of the charitable fund," or believed "that Your Excellency has it in his power to render me assistance and that I can be relieved by government." Others just made direct appeals to the generosity of the presumably well-to-do lieutenant governor in the hope that he would be "touched by the effects of human woe," or that "the representative of our Gracious Queen will not allow an old soldier to suffer." Some few female petitioners wrote during Sir Peregrine Maitland's term to Lady Sarah Maitland, in the hope that she, the daughter of the Duke of Richmond, might perhaps prove to be more charitable than most.[39]

In the end if help was provided to those in need it did not come in the main from any official source but from private citizens, organizations, and churches. It has been noted that societies for the relief of the poor appeared in Kingston and York as early as 1817, and subsequently in other Upper Canadian towns. A survey of the records of the civil secretary throughout the 1820s and 1830s produces other periodic references to charitable initiatives. "A few of the ladies at York," including Mrs Robinson, who donated "a strong cotton gown" worth five shillings, helped to support a widow Maloney through the winter of 1826–27, the same year that saw the founding of the Female Benevolent Society in Kingston to care for the sick poor. "An old black woman commonly called Black Betty," a former slave, lived "for years" on the charity of the congregation of the Church of England in Kingston. The treasurer's report of the Society for the Relief of the Sick and Destitute in York in 1829 noted that the sum of £192-6-0 had been collected from donors, but £201-0-4 had been expended, leaving a debt of £8-14-4. The society also recorded its thanks to local steamboat masters for giving free passage to many poor people "on the recommendation of the society." Widow Ann Edmonds, who in 1834 was "aged and feeble," had no support except that provided by the Roman Catholic clergy in Belleville "and other charitable individuals." Another widow, Anne Devlin, supported herself and her three children in Toronto in 1835 "by the pittance she receives from occasional employment in the houses of some few charitable families in this city."[40]

It should not be supposed that the poor people of Upper Canada were all helpless beggars who made no efforts to help themselves. Perhaps the most striking example of self-help was the persistent presence in York/Toronto of the homeless, who squatted on public land in small shelters or shanties, from, as has been seen, at least as early as 1817. Like the numerous women who walked away from unfortunate marriages these unofficial residents took the law into their own hands as a means of survival. By the time Toronto became a city in 1834, besides the presence of squatters' huts on the Don River a semi-permanent illegal community had grown up on the lakeshore at the foot of Yonge Street on the public "pleasure grounds" and in the space between the lake bank and the water. Concentrated mainly in the area south of Front Street between Yonge and York streets, this makeshift community of buildings "which disfigure the bayshore" became a cause of complaint, especially for people who owned substantial nearby homes facing the lake, including Rev John Strachan, G.H. Markland, and Mrs W.D. Powell. A report prepared for Mayor William Lyon Mackenzie listed a total of twenty-four structures, three of them "houses of entertainment." Most were described as small houses or shanties but one was a kind of cave dug into the bank, which housed two families. Though of course no one had any legal title to the buildings, they were bought and sold, in one case for £10, and two were rented at 12/6 a month. The mayor did not approve of public property being taken up "at the expense of the health and comfort of the citizens ... to some private purpose."[41]

The majority of the people who came to Upper Canada in increasing numbers succeeded to some degree and by various means in making the transition from newcomers to residents. The process can rarely have been easy, but it was got through and the result was at least some minimum level of comfort. In fact the records of even some of the most dedicated petitioners attest to this. Former Lieutenant William Vere Hunt fruitlessly petitioned lieutenant governors Colborne, Bond Head, and Arthur over a period of eight years for free land, a passage home to Ireland, or financial assistance, each time advising them of "my melancholy condition which I believe is unparalleled in this country" or of his "unexampled distress," but was finally able to get "a small overseership" through "the kindness of Major Bonnycastle." But most immigrants had to make their own way with no help from anyone in authority.[42]

Lest it be thought that the government of Upper Canada was totally indifferent to the needs of the swelling ranks of the poor, it must be noted that considerable debate on how to deal with the poor eventually took place among the public and in the legislature in 1836 and 1837, resulting in the passage of the contentious Houses of Industry Act. The legislature's solution was to download the cost and responsibility for the care of the poor onto the districts, who, by increasing the rates on taxable property, were required to build institutions, at a cost of not more than £1,000, to feed or house the unfortunate, but only after three successive grand juries had recommended such a step to the district magistrates. The houses of industry were designed for "all poor and indigent persons who are incapable of supporting themselves" but also for the committal of "all persons able of body to work and without any means of maintaining themselves, who refuse to or neglect to do so; all persons living a lewd, dissolute vagrant life or exercising no ordinary calling or lawful business sufficient to procure an honest living; all such as spend their time and property in Public Houses to the neglect of their lawful calling." In other words they were intended for the care of the deserving and the reform of the undeserving, who were to be "diligently employed in labour." The opposition in the legislature and in the press protested that the scheme would place too heavy a burden on the taxpayers, that it would provide a haven for the idle and profligate, and that it would "create a receptacle for the idle and worthless that are cast upon our shores." The law in any case became a dead letter. The requirement for a recommendation from three successive grand juries was never fulfilled in any district in Upper Canada. A presentment by a Niagara District grand jury in 1837 seems to have more accurately reflected the prevailing view. The jurors opposed holding out "inducements to the idle and profligate of becoming paupers, as we are of the opinion that all who are able to labour in this country, have the power of earning a subsistence if they have the will to labour." There were charitable and caring people in Upper Canada who did what they could, as individuals, as churches and through societies, to help people who could not help themselves. The government and the society as a whole were less inclined to be sympathetic.[43]

Appeals to the state for assistance from unfortunate Upper Canadians were very much "petitions of grace," for no law compelled anyone in the province to take any action on behalf of people who could not look after themselves. During the fifty years of Upper Canada's existence the opposite was the case, for the law prevented action from being taken. That so many Upper Canadians survived poverty and distress was due only to the courage and fortitude of those ordinary Upper Canadians who met and overcame the obstacles of hard times.

Conclusion

One of the hardiest misconceptions about Upper Canadian society, perpetuated even by otherwise reputable scholars, is the myth of self-sufficiency; the assumption that Upper Canadian farmers, who were the vast majority of the population, mostly lived a kind of isolated, "Robinson Crusoe" existence, largely independent of the world of commerce and finance. It needs only a little reflection to make it obvious that rural Upper Canadians would be "self-sufficient" only to the extent and for as long as they had to be. Few people ever really wanted to be entirely self-sufficient and no one ever really was. From the beginning people needed and wanted things they could not make or grow themselves – axes, ploughs, and other tools, pots and pans and crockery, boots and shoes, tea and sugar, and a range of other items, which had to be bought with cash, produce, or on credit.[1]

Just as Upper Canadians have been portrayed as economically self-sufficient, it has also been alleged that they lived their lives apart from, and indifferent to, the Upper Canadian state. "To most Canadians in the middle of the nineteenth century," a contemporary author has written, "government was as irrelevant to their day-to-day lives as it is today to the Mennonites, the Hutterites and Amish."[2] Assuming that Upper Canadian society had not undergone a really radical change in the ten years or so after a separate province called Upper Canada ceased to exist, it is again evident that such a statement is a considerable exaggeration.

It can hardly have been completely irrelevant to the entire adult male population that they were, willingly or not, automatically members of one of Upper Canada's militia regiments, which obliged them, at a minimum, to turn out once a year for training, and sometimes to leave their homes and families to risk, and possibly lose, life or limb in war or rebellion. Nor can it have been irrelevant, especially to men and women who were immigrant settlers, that a branch of government not discussed in this book, the steadily expanding postal service, brought precious news from "home" to families roughing it in the bush. Government was not irrelevant to families who sent their children to the common or grammar schools; to the men who did their compulsory statute labour on the roads; to the men, women, and children who were dependent on a government pension; to landowners who paid taxes or to those who had to take their turn as pathmasters, assessors, tax collectors, and township clerks; to people who got into trouble with the law or to the hundreds of magistrates and constables who had brought them to justice. Government was highly relevant to the thousands of Upper Canadians who gained some or all of their livelihood directly or indirectly from the state in a myriad of ways, if only by knitting socks for prisoners in the Kingston Penitentiary. Most dramatically, the awareness of the importance of government in their lives must have been brought forcefully home to the many thousands of land petitioners who found themselves being cross-examined in the Executive Council office by such august figures as chief justices William Dummer Powell and John Beverley Robinson, or by Hon. William Allan or Archdeacon John Strachan.

It seems reasonable then that David Murray's discovery that ordinary Upper Canadians knew more about the legal process than would be true of later generations might be broadened to include some knowledge of the workings of most other aspects of the government. Just how much they knew, and how they came to know it however are questions to which there is likely no definitive answer. Certainly the role of the personal petition was central to all relations with the state. It was the access key to what the state was obliged to give, and by extension, to what the state might be persuaded to give. Even before there was a Province of Upper Canada its people were taught by their imperial and colonial masters that if they appealed to the governor or the legislature in an appropriate written form, expressing sufficient deference and humility, they were almost certain to receive those boons, such as land and pensions, to which they were entitled by law or regulation, and might possibly be awarded other optional favours – jobs, compensation, licenses, full or partial forgiveness of their legal transgressions, and for the poor, possibly even "a pound from the Lt.-Gov'r."

General awareness that government should be formally approached in writing showing a sufficient degree of real or feigned respect was one thing, but government agencies operated within a complex set of laws and regulations which were subject to amendment, giving, for example, pensions to more or fewer people, higher or lower grants to school trustees, requiring pension applicants to produce more documentation, or tightening up or relaxing the settlement duties which had to be performed prior to land ownership. The government, to its credit, went to some lengths to disseminate information among the populace, probably most successfully through the newspapers, initially using the official *Upper Canada Gazette*, but more widely via the expanding network of local papers. Indeed, given the complexity of many of the procedures which the state imposed on those who had, for instance, to negotiate the baffling labyrinth of the land system or repeatedly meet all the requirements necessary for drawing a pension, it is remarkable how solid a grasp of government red tape most people seem to have had. The fact, to cite another instance, that only a very small proportion of Upper Canada's needy ever submitted petitions asking for help suggests that it was likely widely understood that there was "no provision in this country for the support of the poor." Still there were cases of people who, like Susannah Kendrick, only found out that the government had changed the rules when her pension payments stopped.

There is little evidence that during most of the Upper Canadian period there was much interest in finding means to improve the way in which the government operated or to make the relationship between the state and the people more congenial. Examples of tinkering with the system, such as the successful substitution of the township assessors for the clerks to take charge of counting the population, or the introduction of that costly and cumbersome bureaucratic entity the Heir and Devisee Commission to try to fix a land title problem which ought never to have arisen in the first place, were not common. It was only after the arrival of Sir George Arthur as lieutenant governor in 1838 that any attempt was made, by way of a commission of enquiry requested by the Assembly, to take any kind of comprehensive look at what went on in the various government departments, or to contemplate possible changes and efficiencies.

Sir George, perhaps influenced by his previous experience as governor of the penal colony of Van Diemen's Land where it was necessary to run a tight ship, and who was certainly concerned and alarmed by the possibility of a renewal of armed rebellion or invasion and the spectre of American democracy, not only wanted to know what went on in the central bureaucracy but also in the districts in matters of local government and education. One of the frequent responses he received from the mainly Tory-leaning district clerks and sheriffs who were canvassed was that administrative reform might be a preferable alternative to Lord Durham's recommendation of responsible government.[3] But of course the likelihood of any purely Upper Canadian remedial measures was abruptly swept aside by the union of Upper and Lower Canada in 1841.

Upper Canadians had from the beginning interacted with their government on many fronts and continued to do so in an increasing number of ways. Was the government, despite its ineptitudes, making some attempts to exert more sway over a population often seen from above as ignorant, lacking respect for the law, and potentially violent and disloyal? Was "state formation" happening in Upper Canada? Scholars have pointed to the appearance in Upper Canada of the Kingston Penitentiary and the Toronto House of Industry, and of the passage of legislation in 1839 to eventually establish a provincial asylum, as the beginning of a shift from local and piecemeal methods of dealing with crime, poverty, and mental illness to the use of large centralized government institutions in the face of increased poverty, perceived lawlessness, and gaols crowded with the mentally disturbed. Peter Oliver, as has been seen, believed he had detected an "astounding" surge in the level of moral offences, which was combatted in part by the incorporation of many municipalities with their paid constabularies.[4]

There is no doubt that the provincial executive had always had a centralizing bent. As early as 1796 John Graves Simcoe took the land-granting business out of the hands of the district land boards and magistrates and gave the Executive Council complete control over it. There were later attempts by the imperial government and the legislature to weaken the council's authority but in 1841 they were still busily at work accepting and considering a steady flow of land petitions. The lieutenant governor and his councillors wanted as much control over the affairs of the province as they could exercise because at bottom they had a profound distrust of its people, and even more distrust of their neighbour nation to the south. Their paranoia had some justification of course. The province began in revolution which provided a Loyalist base for the population, and in 1812–14 and 1837–38 their fears became reality, but their dread of "mobocracy" and concern for homeland security seems to have exerted a kind of pall over all their actions. Suspicious of possible fraud, they made the people literally come to them for land and pensions, taking a multitude of paperwork through incomprehensible and seemingly endless procedures whose main purpose appeared to be the collection of fees by as many officials as possible. They ran a suspicious, tight-fisted, penny-pinching administration which created ill will among large groups of the population such a common school teachers and trustees, War of 1812 and Rebellion losses and compensation claimants, and pensioners. The executive actions of government were cumbersome and slow, carried out by employees chosen on the basis of their loyalty, religious denomination and, especially on the basis of who they knew, and too little on their competence. The provincial executive was little concerned with modernization or innovation. They had a horror of doing anything "incompatible with established usage" and clung firmly to familiar precedent. Besides, since so much that was done was in imitation of British practices, it was close to unthinkable for the Upper Canadian bureaucracy that things could be done in any other way.

In the circumstances, a process of state formation, though undoubtedly in some degree getting underway, was facing an uphill battle in Upper Canada. The only purely state initiative undertaken late in the Upper Canadian period, the Kingston Penitentiary, did attempt to deal on a provincial scale with serious crime, but its value as an example of burgeoning government control over a yeasty population is mixed. Here Peter Oliver has argued that though it was "an essential instrument of social control," its founding was not an attempt to combat rising crime rates, because crime rates were not believed by the judiciary to be rising, nor was it intended by its most influential proponents to be a shining example (borrowed from American models) of up-to-date humane penal theory, but rather a means of bringing the certainty of punishment to serious offenders and a practical way of getting them out of the badly run, overcrowded, underfunded district gaols. In typical Upper Canadian fashion the penitentiary was itself chronically starved of funds by the legislature, poorly administered, and run on less than humane lines.[5]

The Toronto House of Industry has been said to have been a kind of milestone in a transition process leading to the institutional care of the poor in Upper Canada. According to historian Martina L. Hardwick, it "was used by the elites in an attempt to show the poor who exactly was in control."[6] It however was at best a quasi-state institution which received only partial support from government. More significantly, it was a model which was not replicated elsewhere in the province, and the legislative scheme proposed for that purpose by the Assembly in 1837 was firmly rejected in the province as a whole.

Knowledge is supposed to be power so the government's store of information about its own operations, expenses, and personnel should have increased as a result of the growing number of categories required to be filled in for the preparation of the Blue Books, but as has been seen these volumes were far from complete, and in any case were primarily prepared for British eyes. It is probably a fair assumption that the government of Upper Canada on its own might never have embarked on any such information-gathering project at all if not made to do so by their imperial supervisors, since the administrative apparatus of the Upper Canadian state was too underdeveloped to cope adequately with the task. It might also be added that from the historian's point of view "improvements" to statistics gathering in the Blue Books were not always for the better. In 1838 the prison statistics began to include as a separate category the small number of black prisoners, whose presence in Upper Canada was evidently seen as a growing problem, but at the same time no longer recorded the birthplace of any of the prisoners.[7]

In any case if the government of Upper Canada was on the path to centralization it was a path beset by setbacks. Executive responsibility for land matters was periodically chipped away at. Control of education was returned from elite to local hands when the General Board of Education, established in 1823 under the leadership of Anglican Archdeacon and executive councillor John Strachan, was abolished by the colonial secretary in 1833, following a representation from the House of Assembly "because it appears to be the people's wish that school lands and funds not be in exclusive control of the executive, and because the request is expressed moderately."[8] Upper Canada was at most, a state only partly formed.

As late as 1841, when Upper Canada ceased to exist, the province was still profoundly rural and agricultural. The government's head-counting system by township and district recorded that in that year there were 455,688 people in the province. Gilbert Stelter has calculated that 88.5 per cent of them, or more than 403,000 men, women, and children, were then living in rural areas.[9] Even allowing for the fact that some of these were small businessmen or tradesmen, it is obvious that the possession of land for farming was and had been from the beginning a central concern of most of the population. By 1841 the provincial government had already disposed of most of the potentially useful land in varying amounts to thousands of applicants. It is hardly necessary to express agreement with the conclusions of other writers on the subject of Upper Canadian land policy who have described it as a failure. But it was not just a failure as policy, it was a failure in human terms, a failure of the government's obligation to its people. Land was initially fairly easy for settlers to obtain from the district land boards but getting title to it was next to impossible while the executive spent four years figuring out a table of fees which various officials would eventually be allowed to charge for their involvement in the process, creating inconvenience to settlers and a legal tangle not rectified for many generations. When land granting was centralized in the capital inconvenience was compounded many times over at the petitioners' expense by delay, primarily due to the amount of red tape involved in making sure that eight different government officials, including the lieutenant governor himself, got their share of the fees on land. The backbreaking task of converting hardwood forest into productive farms was surely a sufficiently crushing load for pioneer families to have to endure. The aggravation of dealing with a slow, complex, costly bureaucracy need not have been imposed on hapless settlers to the extent that it was.

In the long run as well, the grossly inequitable distribution of land, which saw some 85 per cent of Crown land reserved or given away to "privileged" applicants (who became *de facto* speculators), added another layer of inconvenience and annoyance. Good land remained undeveloped and unused for many years, making rational settlement next to impossible, delaying much needed road building, and deferring tax revenue sorely needed by the districts. In the matter of land administration it is hard to conceive of a possible mistake that was not made by the imperial or provincial governments. It should be borne in mind that it was ordinary men, women, and children who suffered from the blunders of the state.

The fact that Upper Canada was an overwhelmingly rural province, as Susan Lewthwaite has pointed out, did not mean that it was a bucolic Eden, populated entirely by hard-working, honest, law abiding citizens. Especially in its early years law enforcement could be difficult and even dangerous, and violence, particularly in the form of assault and battery, was all too common. Nonetheless it is clear that it was among the small minority who lived in the province's growing urban communities that the problem of crime came to be most concentrated. It is clear also that the nature of criminal activity in Upper Canada changed significantly. Violence, once by far the leading form of crime, gave way to somewhat more sophisticated criminal activities, especially larceny. Upper Canadian society was never entirely peaceable, but by the end of this era was in fact becoming increasingly so. The Upper Canadian populace contained its due share of bad actors and malingerers but, the aberration of the Rebellion aside, crime was never a really serious problem and a "mobocracy" existed only in the minds of some members of the elite.

The Upper Canadian judicial system was never really draconian, probably because it did not need to be. The British penal code adopted by the legislature in 1792 included a wide range of quite savage penalties which went more and more unenforced to their full extent. The reforms of 1833 took most of these off the statute books in favour of a short list of severe penalties for a small number of serious offences, but even so enforcement was only marginally more rigorous. It was in the realm of petty crime, dealt with by the magistrates in quarter sessions and later also in the new municipal courts, where severe sentences had usually been rare and acquittals frequent, that a stiffening of attitudes toward minor violations can be detected. In the towns of Upper Canada especially, attention began to be paid at the end of the period to enforcing a host of local regulations, including to an extent "moral" offences, previously largely ignored. Queen Victoria had barely ascended the throne when Upper Canada's leaders began to try to impose the kinds of social values now associated with her reign on a reluctant citizenry.

Whether the judicial system was more or less lenient, errant Upper Canadians never ceased to look for ways to circumvent the course of the law or to mitigate its effects. Many people who got into trouble seem to have known, or were advised by others, of the possibilities which were available to them in order to avoid all or some of the strictures of the law. At the local level especially, of quarter sessions

in the largely rural areas, the courts were not all that unfriendly to
petty offenders. Neighbours quarrelled with neighbours, but neighbours and relatives also sat on juries and could be remarkably toler-
ant. Even at the more serious level of the assizes, as Chief Justice
Campbell observed, acquittal by a local jury was not necessarily
proof of innocence. As well, conviction did not always mean full or
any punishment. The efficacy of petitioning, whether by an individual or large numbers of sympathizers, was repeatedly demonstrated
in a large proportion of cases. Judges, executive councillors, and lieutenant governors were human too and could be moved by a convinc-
ing story, or successfully pestered into concessions by persistent
appeals. It was not that Upper Canadians did not have respect for
the law – contempt of court for example was a relatively rare
offence – but neither were they always simply submissive to whatever legal fate had been handed them. When the law seemed unfair
some Upper Canadians took the law into their own hands. Women
in large numbers left abusive marriages, or even, like Jane Maguire,
used guns on their brutish husbands, because they could find no legal
recourse. The poor of York/Toronto continually squatted on public
property, to the annoyance of the prominent, because the law made
no provision for their welfare.

The legal system was not the only area of state power that was
subject to some bending and adaptation by the people of Upper
Canada. The common schools, though supposedly run in accordance
with rules devised by the elite, were essentially taken over by the
interested parents of their area, who followed or ignored the regulations to fit their needs and circumstances. Many schools operated
without the requisite number of trustees, some women and Americans
were hired as teachers despite official disapproval, trustees were not
above fudging the attendance figures to qualify for the government
grant. Local government, though never a centre of great power or
influence, was also largely taken over by the landowners of the townships, who sometimes took upon themselves responsibilities that
were strictly speaking none of their business. At the township meetings, along with the usual slate of local officials, the assembled rate-
payers habitually chose their own constables, though this was legally
the task of the magistrates. The meetings also eventually became
occasions for wide-ranging debate on current provincial issues, and
could also be forums for criticism of the government and of political
rivalry. Whether these were really examples of grassroots democracy

or not, by the 1830s they were beginning to provide opportunities for the reform minded to have some local influence and to exercise the meagre powers of school and township offices.

Of course from the government's point of view allowing a certain amount of local licence was an acceptable price to pay for the enormous amount of official work that got done either cheaply or free. The schools may not have been run on entirely orthodox lines but the parents and trustees who built the schools and hired and supervised the teachers took on a thankless and difficult chore and kept the system operating as well as could be expected. The individuals selected by their peers to be assessors, collectors, clerks, poundkeepers, town wardens, pathmasters, and constables worked for little more than their expenses, and often for less than their expenses. Not all local officials were competent or even honest, but by and large the local government system also worked, and worked to the financial advantage of the state.

No administration wants to spend money unnecessarily or unwisely or without proper authorization. Yet it is possible to suspect that the Upper Canadian executive had a congenital antipathy to spending public money and frequently short-changed their constituency. The interminable foot dragging on the payment of losses claims; the reluctance to pay adequate, or any, compensation for work done or for harm inflicted by government actions; the periodic cutting back on pension payments; and the amount of delay, obfuscation and red tape involved in getting anything from government at all, bespeak the executive's ingrown reluctance to spend money, probably augmented from 1822 on by the British government's demand that they provide an annual account of their activities in the Blue Books.

Was the problem at bottom financial, that the Upper Canadian government was underfunded? It was true that Upper Canada's own sources of revenue were limited. Income from customs duties on goods coming from the United States was not substantial and returns from land rent, sales, and fees never reached hoped-for levels. An available source of steady income, quit rents, was abandoned, perhaps from a fear of dissent, before they were ever imposed. Upper Canada's chief source of revenue, a share of customs duties collected in Lower Canada on the flow of goods destined for the upper province, was sometimes interrupted by disputes over what proportion of the duties Upper Canada was entitled to, leaving temporary shortfalls in the treasury. The government however seems usually to have had enough funds to cope with its ordinary expenses, though paying large unexpected bills or undertaking major public projects were beyond the province's means. In 1825, at Attorney General John Beverley Robinson's urging, the province began to acquire a significant debt by lending the Welland Canal Company £25,000, and a further £27,000 in 1827, and in the 1830s Upper Canada, now strapped for funds, began to borrow large sums from British bankers and sent Receiver General J.H. Dunn off to London to negotiate terms with bankers Thomas Wilson & Co. (which failed in 1837), Baring Brothers and Glyn, Mills and Co. Nonetheless Douglas McCalla, who has closely examined the public finances of Upper Canada, has concluded that the province's debt was not excessive compared to comparable jurisdictions of the time and could safely have been higher. The point is that the executive was quite prepared to finance what Robinson called projects of "national" importance which most directly benefited the urban merchants and forwarders of Upper Canada but felt no great urgency in coping with the many unmet needs of the rural majority.[10]

The standard form of personal petition to the lieutenant governor in Upper Canada required the petitioner "in duty bound" to pray for the long life and health of His Excellency, the Lieutenant Governor. The people of Upper Canada were expected to be respectful, to follow correct procedures and not to make impertinent or unreasonable demands. It was their duty to form the militia, to pay their taxes, to obey the law, and to fill a lot of minor government offices, duties which, by and large, were discharged well enough, without excessive grumbling. The government had its own obligations: to provide for the defence of the province, for civil order and justice, for common education, to grant land to settlers and pensions to militia widows and disabled militiamen. Land was dispensed lavishly, if not efficiently, since it cost the state nothing, but those responsibilities which required expenditure were performed grudgingly and with a maximum of bureaucratic caution. It was the people's duty to beg, the government's to condescend.

Until 1824 the central government had no workable system for determining how many people there actually were in the province, and no more attempted to record all their names than they attempted to keep track of the names of the children who attended their common schools. Men who were members of the militia and taxpayers had their existence recorded, but only at the county and township levels. No census was taken until 1842, in the new integrated Province of Canada. Before that the antiquated autocratic government of Upper Canada had no way of knowing who all its people were, where they had come from, what they did for a living or what form of religion they adhered to. The civil registration of birth, marriage, and death began still later, in 1869. To the government of Upper Canada the people were an undifferentiated, amorphous mass. Women in particular, who made up some 48 per cent of the population, were mostly unseen and unheard, though not all women fitted that description. Women may have made up a minority of land seekers, criminals, government employees, and teachers but they stood out in two unlucky categories. Nearly half of all militia pensioners were widows, and the vast majority of people seeking relief, especially after the opening of the House of Industry in Toronto, were women.

"In these days of political economy," Anna Jameson wrote perceptively in 1838 in *Winter Studies and Summer Rambles in Canada*, "it is too much the fashion to consider human beings only in masses." She was aware, even if her husband the attorney general and his government colleagues may not have been, of the "wide frame of human society, with all its component elements variously blended." There were flesh and blood people in Upper Canada, with individual names and personal histories, comprising, by 1841, 236,797 men, 218,856 women, and 35 ambivalent respondents whose sex was "not given."[11] By fortunate accident however the government of Upper Canada and its successors, by preserving the massive numbers of land petitions and the lesser numbers of petitions and letters for jobs, pensions, pardons, compensation, or relief, unwittingly left open at least one avenue by which some measure of forgetfulness can be pushed back. Petitions and other personal documents of the time are not always all that revealing and none contain complete life stories, but they all touch on some aspects of a life in progress, such as where they came from and when, their age, their families and connections, their past employment and experience, their "merits and pretentions," their aspirations, their failures and misfortunes, and even their desperation. They lift a corner at least of the veil of obscurity that has shrouded so many lives. A last brief look at the fragmentary personal record left by some otherwise obscure Upper Canadians in contact with an often less than helpful government helps to reinforce the point.

To the humble petition of Allan Nixon of 1811 was appended two certificates attesting to the fact that he had joined the Royal Standard in New Jersey under Colonel Barton in 1777, served throughout the revolution and came to Upper Canada a bit late, in 1786. Other certificates of his good character were signed by Niagara-area notable William Crooks and Loyalist office-holders Robert and Abraham Nelles. His documents were submitted on his behalf by militia officer Titus Geer Simons. He wished to be put on the Loyalist list "in order that His Majesty's most gracious intentions to the U. E. Loyalists may be extended to your petitioner." He was told that he needed to produce his discharge papers and better proof of his service, which he evidently did not have. Without the right pieces of paper he never made it onto the list.

Eliza Hulet wrote a somewhat muddled petition from Norwich in Oxford County in July 1838 to plead for bail for her "partner," Nathan Town, an imprisoned convicted rebel, on the grounds that she was mostly confined to bed "the family needing his labour" and presumably his expertise, since he was an (unlicensed) doctor. Town was in fact granted bail that September, though whether her appeal had any effect in the matter is open to doubt since the great majority of the prisoners were all routinely released within the year. Her petition contained the usual protestations of loyalty and female frailty, but did add one additional curious detail. "Poor female petitioners," she wrote, "have been noticed sometimes when they come from the heart I know mine does ... I love my country and the English nation my father was an English man he died at Northumberland last year his name Sir David Wm Smith." She was, or claimed to be, the child resulting from the much rumoured "amour" the surveyor general had conducted with the woman hired to look after his motherless children, before he left Upper Canada for good in 1802.

Dugald Hamilton, formerly a soldier in the 71st Highlanders who in 1835 had cleared one and a half acres of his grant in Blanford Township and was living in the house he had built, had been discharged "agreeably to the regulations of 14 November 1829" with a quarterly gratuity of fifteen months' pay. His petition complained that it took him a week to travel to York to collect each quarterly instalment and wanted the remaining gratuity paid in a lump sum. The lieutenant governor, Sir John Colborne, agreed to break the rules and sanction the payment if the deputy commissary general confirmed that he was entitled to it.

Richard Collins, "a man of colour" and a widower "making a living as a labourer" in Port Hope in 1831, was caring for his eleven-year-old daughter who was crippled by a serious hip condition, and wanted to have her admitted to York Hospital for surgical treatment. His petition had the written support of the locally prominent, including three magistrates and a Church of England minister. Her admission was agreed to with the proviso that if her condition turned out to be incurable he would take her back so that she would not become a burden on the state.[12]

Do such bits and pieces of commonplace lives and the many others like them have any meaning? Do they matter? Do they simply represent the hazards and uncertainties of dealing with a sometimes mysterious and arbitrary government? Certainly these were not important people making important decisions: they were more likely to be on the receiving end of the decisions of others, but they were not "typical" Upper Canadians because there were no typical Upper Canadians. They each had their own unique personal life histories and these histories, to the extent that they can be recovered, have their own importance, and need to be known. We know a lot, in broad terms, about how and why people left their original homes and got to Upper Canada, how most of them eventually became established there, and about the routine cycle of their lives, but to get a deeper and more genuine picture of human reality it is necessary to come to grips with this enormous variety of individual experience. Actual people, living through the hazards of leaving home, of getting land or work, and of raising families in an unfamiliar and frequently inhospitable place, were always distinct. It made a difference to be English, Irish, Scottish, "foreign," or to be Upper Canadian; to be male or female; to be married or single; to be educated or illiterate. No two individuals were alike.

Upper Canadians and the Upper Canadian state existed in a particular, and in some ways, a special place and time, before the isolated inland province became permanently connected to the wider world through the miracles of the telegraph and the railroad, and before an administration largely controlled by a small group of well-meaning but self-satisfied and self-serving appointed officials suddenly had power wrenched away from them and from Toronto itself, and the province entered a process of political transformation which first thrust Upper Canada into a reluctant union with its sister province and culminated in the adoption of responsible government. Before 1841, Upper Canada was a different place, where changes in the relationship of the state to the people came slowly, if they came at all.

To explore the nature of that relationship it is still important to study the history of powerful people, of Upper Canada's economic, political, and administrative elite, for the conditions they established, the laws, rules, and regulations they devised and re-devised constantly touched the lives of ordinary Upper Canadians in ways which have not always been fully comprehended. But ordinary upper Canadians deserve their own history. Exploring the many ways in which real people interacted with and coped with the vagaries of government and administration brings us a bit closer to an answer to a basic question. What was it really like to live in Upper Canada?

Notes

INTRODUCTION

1 Robertson, *Landmarks of Toronto*, 3: 311.

2 Greer, "Canadian History: Ancient and Modern," 586.

3 The best known studies of this type are: Michael Katz, *The People of Hamilton, Canada West: Family and Class in a Mid-Nineteenth-Century City* (Cambridge, Mass.: Harvard University Press, 1975), and David Gagan, *Hopeful Travellers: Families, Land, and Social Change in Mid-Victorian Peel County, Canada West* (Toronto: University of Toronto Press, 1981).

4 Errington, *Wives and Mothers*, xiv–xv.

5 A selection of articles of this type published in *Ontario History* in the past ten years or so might include: K. Brennah, "The Role of Women in the Children of Peace" and P. Brock, "Accounting for Difference: the Problem of Pacifism in Early Upper Canada" (Spring, 1998); D. McCalla, "Upper Canadians and Their Guns: an Exploration via Country Store Accounts, 1808–1861" (Autumn, 2005); K.S. Frost, "Black Men and Women Engage Slavery in Upper Canada, 1793–1803" (Spring, 2007); J. Roberts, "The Games People Played: Tavern Amusements and Colonial Social Relations" and J.W. Paxton, "Merrymaking and Militia Musters: (Re)Constructing Community and Identity in Upper Canada" (Autumn, 2010).

6 Wilton, *Popular Politics and Political Culture in Upper Canada, 1800–1850*, chapters 1 and 2.

7 Johnson, "'Claims of Equity," 219–220.

8 *OAR* (1905), cix.

9 Greer and Radforth, eds., *Colonial Leviathan*, 10–11.

10 Major works on English state formation include: P. Corrigan and D. Sayer, *The Great Arch: English State Formation as Cultural Revolution* (Oxford: Blackwell, 1985) and M.J. Braddick, *State Formation in Early Modern England, c.1550–1700* (Cambridge: Cambridge University Press, 2000). Major examples of the many contributions of Bruce Curtis to this field are: "Representation and State Formation in the Canadas, 1790–1850," *Studies in Political Economy* 28 (1989): 59–87, *True Government by Choice Men? Inspection, Education and State Formation in Canada West* (Toronto: University of Toronto Press, 1992), and *The Politics of Population: State Formation, Statistics and the Census in Canada, 1840–1875* (Toronto: University of Toronto Press, 2001). As the title implies all ten articles in the collection edited by Greer and Radforth, *Colonial Leviathan: State Formation in Mid-Nineteenth-Century Canada* assume the post-1840 origin of state formation in Canada.
11 Curtis, "The Canada Blue Books," 535–55.
12 Baehre, "Imperial Authority and Colonial Officialdom," 207. On the other hand in her PhD thesis "Segregating and Reforming the Marginal: The Institution and Everyday Resistance in Mid-Nineteenth-Century Ontario," Martina Hardwick stresses the degree of resistance to the institutionalisation of the poor, the insane, criminals and the Native Peoples at mid-century, but argues (p. 18) that "the state in the 1830s was only beginning to come into itself."
13 The standard work is: Gates, *Land Policies*.
14 Craig, *Upper Canada*, xiii.

CHAPTER ONE

1 Craig, *Lord Durham's Report*, 119; *OAR* (1920), 236, 238; G. Wilson, *The Clergy Reserves of Upper Canada*, 140: Gates, *Land Policies*, 230; Read, "Unrest in the Canadas," plate 23; Moorman, "The First Business of Government," 68.
2 Craig, *Lord Durham's Report*, 118; Read, "Unrest in the Canadas"; Wood, *Making Ontario*, 94.
3 Moorman, "The First Business of Government," 61–3.
4 Darroch and Soltow, *Property and Equality in Victorian Ontario*, 176–8.
5 Gates, *Land Policies*, chapter 2.
6 Moorman, "The District Land Boards," 36, 1992, 101; *OAR* (1905), lxx, lxxiii, 16–17.
7 *OAR* (1905), 16; Moorman, "The District Land Boards," 90, 117, 158.
8 Moorman, "The First Business," 25–6.

9   Ibid., "The First Business," 25–6.
10 Ibid., "The First Business," 26–7; Gates, *Land Policies*, 45.
11 Gundy, "The Family Compact at Work," 129–46.
12 Gates, *Land Policies*, 333.
13 Gundy, "The Family Compact at Work," 131; Moorman, "The First Business," 27.
14 Mealing, "John Graves Simcoe," 755–6; Gates, *Land Policies*, 30–2; OAR (1920), 67–8.
15 Moorman, "The First Business," 47, 49, 150, 163, 168–9.
16 Ibid., "The First Business," 88.
17 Ibid., "The First Business," 158, 165; OAR (1905), cix (1930), 60, 132; LAC, RG 1, L 3, vol. 224a, H4/107, vol. 384, N14/19, vol. 450a, S4/25.
18 Moorman, "The First Business," 152.
19 Ibid., "The First Business," 82–4, 152, 169; Strachan, *A Visit to the Province*, 204; LAC, RG 5, A1, vol. 40, 18868–71.
20 The description that follows is based on: P. Kennedy, "Deciphering the Upper Canadian Land Books and Land Petitions," LAC unpublished paper, 1978, 1–6, illustrations 1–9.
21 Moorman, "The First Business," 123, 129, 134, 242; Firth, *The Town of York*, 1: 55, 2: 330.
22 Moorman, "The First Business," 255–62.
23 Gates, *Land Policies*, 130; Moorman, "The First Business," 311.
24 Gates, *Land Policies*, 172, 179.
25 Moorman, "The First Business," 283; OAR (1920), 147, 149, 171; Gates, *Land Policies*, 174; LAC, RG 7, G16C, vol. 53, 12.
26 Gates, *Land Policies*, 173; OAR (1920), 164, 180.
27 Glazebrook, *Life in Ontario: A Social History*, 43; Strachan, *A Visit to the Province*, 135; Howison, *Sketches of Upper Canada*, 236; Wood, *Making Ontario*, 96; HAJ (1831), appendix.
28 See for example, Hamil, *Lake Erie Baron*; Carr, *The Canada Land Company*; Cameron and Maude, *Assisting Emigration to Upper Canada*.
29 LAC, RG 1, L3, vols 1–4, 111–112, 223, 224a, 336a, 337a, 460a, 466, 537–538.
30 York *Gazette*, 8 Feb. 1812.
31 Moorman, "The First Business," 118.
32 LAC, RG 1, L3, vol. 385, N19/13, N20/14, N20/19, N21/12, vol. 386, N1/3.
33 LAC, RG 5, A1, vol. 10, 4302.
34 Firth, *The Town of York*, 1: 82–3, 137, 186; Armstrong, "Andrew Mercer," 509–510.

35 Hodgetts, *Pioneer Public Service*, 15.

36 LAC, RG 7, G16C, vol. 14, 79, RG 1, L3, vol. 223, H2/124.

37 LAC, RG 5, A1, vol. 1a, 413–4, RG 1, L3, vol. 2, A4/47, 48, A4/50, A2/31, vol. 1, A1/7, A1/15, vol. 224a, H4/45; Firth, "John White," 766–7.

38 LAC, RG 1, L3, vol. 224, H3/59, 60.

39 LAC, RG 1, L3, vol. 177, E13/3, vol. 178, E16/4, vol. 181, E2/18; RG 1, L1, Land Book N, 59, 434, 473.

40 LAC, RG 7, G14, vol. 3, 1105–6.

41 LAC, RG 1, L1, Land Book Q, 436, L3, vol.112, C17/141, vol. 385, N19/5.

42 LAC, RG 1, L3, N22/19.

43 LAC, RG 1, Land Book P, 297, Land Book Q, 181, 436, RG 1, L3, vol. 224, H3/59.

44 LAC, RG 1, L3, vol. 111, C17/71, C17/92, vol. 384a, N17/2, N17/24, vol. 385, N19/543; RG 5, A1, vol. 26, 11813–4.

45 LAC, RG 1, L3, vol. 537, W22/51.

46 LAC, RG 1, L3, vol. 268, K2/17, K2/18, K3/28, 40, vol. 273, K15/49, vol. 409, P20/36; Reid, *The Loyalists of Ontario*, 170; OAR (1931), 192.

47 Craig, *Early Travelers*, 287–97; Campney, *The Scottish Pioneers of Upper Canada*, 129; Cameron, "Till we get tidings from those who are gone," 1–16.

48 Craig, *Early Travelers*, xix; Howison, *Sketches of Upper Canada*, 242.

49 Strachan, *A Visit to the Province*, 55, 203–9.

50 Ridout's report was published in: Public Archives of Canada, Manuscript Division, *Preliminary Inventory, Record Group 1*, 24–6.

51 OAR (1905), 16, 17; LAC, RG 1, L3, vol. 381a, N1, 16; Armstrong, *Handbook of Upper Canadian Chronology*, 226.

52 LAC, RG 1, L3, vol. 383, N12/29.

53 For a discussion of the consequences of success or failure in settlement see: Clarke, *The Ordinary People of Essex*, 429–30.

CHAPTER TWO

1 LAC, RG 1, E3, vol. 69, 107; McCalla, *Planting the Province*, 302.

2 McCalla, *Planting the Province*, 123, 163, 167, 305–6.

3 LAC, RG 1, E13 (Blue Books), vols 143, 155.

4 Craig, "The American Impact on the Upper Canadian Reform Movement Before 1837," 333–52; B. Curtis, "The Canada Blue Books," 535–65; Hodgetts, *Pioneer Public Service*, 12.

5 Armstrong, *Handbook of Upper Canadian Chronology*.

6 LAC, RG 1, E13 (Blue Books) vol. 141.

7 McCalla, *Planting the Province*, 166–7.

8 Russell, "Wage Labour Rates," 73, 77; McCalla, *Planting the Province*, 105; Craven, "The Law of Master and Servant in Mid-Nineteenth Century Ontario," 192–4.

9 LAC, RG 1, E13, vol. 141; Russell, "Wage Labour Rates," 64–5, 78; Moorman, "The First Business of Government," 194; Strachan, *A Visit to the Province*, 89.

10 Robertson, *Landmarks of Toronto*, 3: 170.

11 Webber, "Labour and the Law," 108–12; Johnson, *Becoming Prominent*, 62–64.

12 8 George III, C. VII (1827); LAC, RG 68, General Index to Commissions, pt 2a, 484–508; Talbot, *Five Years Residence in the Canadas* 1: 413–14; Johnson, *Becoming Prominent*, 65.

13 LAC, RG 1, E13, vol. 155.

14 47 George III, C. XI (1807).

15 37 George III, C. VII (1797); 59 George III, C. VII (1819); 4 George IV, C. VII, (1823); 6 George IV, C. (1825).

16 LAC, RG 1, E13, vol. 155; 46 George III, C. I (1806); 57 George III, C. VII (1817); Johnson, *Becoming Prominent*, 42.

17 Armstrong, *Handbook of Upper Canadian Chronology*, 162–190; OAR (1932), 172–3.

18 LAC, RG 1, E13, vols 141, 145, 146, 155; Gundy, "The Family Compact at Work," 129–146.

19 *HAJ* (1837–38), app., 289–90; LAC, RG 1, E3, vol. 35, 161.

20 LAC, RG 1, E14, vol. 11; E3, vol. 59A, 56–8.

21 Johnson, "A Lady Should Have Nothing to do with Risks," 85–101.

22 LAC, RG 1, E3, vol. 48B, 192–3, vol. 35, 161, vol. 53, 458–9, vol. 63, 114–5.

23 LAC, RG 5, A1, vol. 19, 8120, vol. 148, 80878–9; RG 1, E13, vol. 141; E3, vol. 2, 2–3, vol. 48B, 189–93, E14, vols 11, 13; Firth, *The Town of York*, 2: 18.

24 Armstrong, "The Carfrae Family," 163–4, 181.

25 LAC, RG 1, E3, vol. 48B, 188–93, vol. 50, 218–9; *HAJ* (1837–38), app., 289–90; Baldwin and Baldwin, *The Baldwins and the Great Experiment*, 58.

26 Johnson, "A Lady Should Have Nothing to do With Risks," 90–91; Nish, *Debates of the Legislative Assembly of United Canada*, 1: 186; LAC, RG 1, E3, vol. 49, 24, RG 5, A1, vol. 115, 64909–10.

27 Firth, *The Town of York*, 2: 305; Smith, *Young Mr. Smith of Upper Canada*, 16, 24; Bonnycastle, *The Canadas in 1841*, 1: 174.

28 *HAJ* (1825), app., (1828), app., (1839), app. 2, pt. 1; *OAR* (1932), 121; Firth, *The Town of York*, 2: 67; Bonnycastle, *The Canadas in 1841*, 1: 174.

29 Fingard, "The Winter's Tale," 70.

30 LAC, RG 1, E13, vol. 155; MacRae and Adamson, *Cornerstones of Order*, 13, 21.

31 Oliver, *Terror to Evil-Doers*, 38–41, 62–3; *OAR* (1932), 9, 23, 26, 51, 64, 121, 196, (1933), 57, 196; Pringle, *Lunenburgh*, 65, 68; *HAJ* (1839), app. 2, pt.1.

32 39 George III, C. III (1799). They also appear to have acted as advocates for the poor and they were asked on occasion to attempt to curb "indecency and impropriety" on Sundays. *OAR* (1932), 6, 37; Murray, *Colonial Justice*, 122–3.

33 Crawford, *Canadian Municipal Government*, 25–6; Glazebrook, "The Origins of Local Government," 44; Canniff, *The Settlement of Upper Canada*, 481–2.

34 Canniff, *The Settlement of Upper Canada*, 454, 471–4, 481, 493; Ontario, Legislative Assembly, *Sessional Papers*, vol. 30, pt. 7; Thompson, "Local Authority," 142; LAC, MG 9, D8–28.

35 Fairley, *Selected Writings*, 48–9; Robertson, *Landmarks of Toronto*, 3: 86; Firth, *The Town of York*, 2: lxix.

36 Cruikshank, *The Correspondence of Lieut-Governor John Graves Simcoe*, 2: 53–4.

37 *OAR* (1932), 7; *HAJ* (1839), app. 2, pt. 1; Roberts," Women, Men and Taverns in Tavern-keeper Ely Playter's Journal," 383.

38 *OAR* (1932), 5, 14, 19, 31–2, 34; (1933), 89; Gourlay, *Statistical Account of Upper Canada*, 178; *HAJ* (1839), app. 2, pt. 1.

39 Thompson, "Local Authority," 171, 177–8, 184, 190, 193; 46 George III, C. V (1806); *HAJ* (1839), app. 2, pt. 1.

40 59 George III, C. VII (1819); *OAR* (1932), 56; Lockwood, *Beckwith*, 235.

41 *OAR* (1932), 5–6, 32; Firth, *The Town of York*, 1: 69.

42 *OAR* (1932), 24, 31–2, 69, 104.

43 *OAR* (1933), 156, 172.

44 Firth, *The Town of York*, 1: 89–91, 2: lxxxii; Canniff, *The Settlement of Upper Canada*, 454–5; 4 George IV, C. VII (1824).

45 Thompson, "Local Authority," 143, 165; Canniff, *The Settlement of Upper Canada*, 454, 474, 482, 493.

46 *OAR* (1932), 159, 178; LAC, MG 9, D8–28; Fairley, *Selected Writings*, 48; Canniff, *The Settlement of Upper Canada*, 454, 474, 482; Boyce, *Historic Hastings*, 52.

47 Firth, *The Town of York*, 2: lxix.

48 Thompson, "Local Authority," 170; Canniff, *The Settlement of Upper Canada,* 154, 481; Reid, *The Loyalists in Ontario.*

49 Boyce, *Historic Hastings,* 260; Canniff, *The Medical Profession in Upper Canada,* 427–8.

50 Canniff, *The Settlement of Upper Canada,* 454–5; Lockwood, *Montague,* 589; LAC, MG 9, D28–23; OAR (1933), 102; Thompson, "Local Authority," 166.

51 LAC, RG 5, B7, vol. 2; A1, vol. 22, 9229–30.

52 LAC, RG 5, A1, vol. 101, 58219–26, vol. 194, 108112–4, B7, vol. 2.

53 LAC, RG 5, A1, vol. 162, 88541–4; Armstrong, *Toronto of Old,* 18; HAJ (1836–37).

54 LAC, RG 5, A1, vol. 196, 109164–5, vol. 261, 142196.

55 LAC, RG 5, B7, vol. 2; Armstrong, *Handbook of Upper Canadian Chronology,* 170, 176.

CHAPTER THREE

1 Craig, *Upper Canada,* 156–8; Wylie, "Poverty, Distress and Disease," 9, 12, 14; Johnson, "Col. James FitzGibbon and the Suppression of Irish Riots in Upper Canada," 147; Palmer, *Working Class Experience,* 22, 37.

2 Wylie, "Poverty, Distress and Disease," 9, 15; Bleasdale, "Class Conflict on the Canals of Upper Canada in the 1840s," 9–39.

3 Dale, "The Palaces of Government," 18.

4 Gentilcore and Donkin, *Land Surveys of Southern Ontario,* 39–86; OAR (1905), 320, 322, 328.

5 Palmer, *Working Class Experience,* 22; OAR (1905), 323–4, 328–9; Widdis, "Speculation and the Surveyor," 444–5.

6 OAR (1910), 97; Gates, "Roads, Rivals and Rebellion," 238, 241.

7 Cruikshank, *The Correspondence of the Honourable Peter Russell,* 3: 292; Dawe, *"Old Oxford is Wide Awake,"* 22; OAR (1909), 313, 391, 480, (1911), 313, (1912), 63; Hind et al, *Eighty Year's Progress,* 109–10; HAJ (1839), app. 2, pt. 1; Cross, "The Stormy History," 8–9.

8 HAJ (1839), app. 2, pt. 1.

9 HAJ (1839), app. 2, pt. 1; Hind et al, *Eighty Year's Progress,* 124; Bouchier, "A Broad Clear Track in Good Order," 103; Schrauwers, *Awaiting the Millenium,* 97, 159, 181.

10 HAJ (1839), app. 2, pt. 1.

11 Cross, "The Stormy History," 5–6.

12 Arthur, *From Front Street to Queen's Park,* 40–43; Armstrong, *Handbook of Upper Canadian Chronology,* 50; Dale, *The Palaces of Government,* 8,

10; *HAJ* (1837–38), app., (1839), app. 2, pt. 1; Preston, *Kingston Before the War of 1812*, 180a; LAC, RG 5, A1, vol. 22, 9250.

13　*HAJ* (1837–38), app., (1839), app. 2, pt. 1; *OAR* (1911), 109.

14　Firth, *The Town of York*, 2: lxxxiv, 128–9; MacRae and Adamson, *Cornerstones of Order*, 44; Harper, *Painting in Canada*, 108; Jameson, *Winter Studies and Summer Rambles* 1: 110.

15　*HAJ* (1839), app. 2, pt. 1.

16　G. Sheppard, *Plunder, Profit and Paroles*, 176, 221; LAC, RG 5, A1, vol. 19, 8002–6, RG 19, E5A, vol. 3742, no. 174, vol. 3744, nos 268, 367, vol. 3755, no. 1508; Johnson, "A Lady Should Have Nothing to do With Risks," 344.

17　Brode, "James Gordon Strobridge," 741–2; 9 George IV, C. XI (1828); 1 Wm. IV, C. CXXI (1831); *HAJ* (1833–34, 1835, 1836, 1836–37, 1838); Upper Canada, Legislative Council, *Journals*, 1833.

18　Gundy, "Hugh Christopher Thomson," 772–4; LAC, RG 1, E3, vol. 64, 306–8, RG 5, A1, vol. 150, 82029–30, B3, vol. 6, 1097–8, RG 7, G16C, vol. 51, 249; *HAJ* (1835, 1836, 1839–40); 7 Wm. IV, C. CII (1837).

19　*HAJ* (1836–37); LAC, RG 1, E3, vol. 34A, 101–2, RG 5, A1, vol. 27, 12409–10.

20　LAC, RG 5, A1, vol. 46, 22735–9, vol. 47, 23304, vol. 48, 24009, vol. 49, 24159–61, vol. 50, 24637.

21　LAC, RG 1, E3, vol. 59A, 83–5, vol. 88, 72–5, E13, vol. 31.

22　LAC, RG 1, E3, vol. 69, 104–114, RG 19, E5A, vol. 3756, no. 1617; Christie, "Prideaux Selby," 749–50.

23　LAC, RG 5, A1, vol. 22, 9650, vol. 227, 124084–5.

24　City of Toronto Archives, RG 1, Box 3, Files 2, 12, Box 4, File 4.

25　*OAR* (1932), 30, 87, 109, 157; LAC, RG 1, E3, vol. 27, 45–7, 113–6, vol. 83, 189–92, vol. 96, 96–103, 176.

26　*HAJ* (1839–40), app. vol. 2; LAC, MG 24, I3, vol. 3; RG 5, B9, vols 53, 55, 57; AO, RG 22, Home District Quarter Sessions Minutes, 1832.

27　Johnson, "Gerald Craig's Upper Canada," 126–7; Roberts, *In Mixed Company*, 11–13.

28　*HAJ* (1829), app.

29　*HAJ* (1836–37), app.; Lockwood, "Temperance as Ethnic Subterfuge," 60.

CHAPTER FOUR

1　Riddell, *The Life of William Dummer Powell*, 140; LAC, RG 1, E3, vol. 144, RG 5, A3, vol. 19, 8106–7.

2 Zaslow, *The Defended Border*, 334; Sheppard, *Plunder, Profit and Paroles*, 4; William Gray in *Soldiers of the King*, 8, makes a case for higher Upper Canadian participation rates in the militia and in the fighting.

3 Gray, *Soldiers of the King*, 13, 248–84; LAC, RG 8, C703, 1A–40.

4 53 George III, C.IV (1813).

5 LAC, RG 5, A1, vol. 91, 50743–6; *HAJ* (1825–26), app.; Splane, *Social Welfare*, 216–18.

6 55 George III, C. VI (1815), 56 George III, C. XVII (1816); Gray, *Soldiers of the King*, 249–84.

7 2 George IV, C. IV (1821).

8 LAC, RG 5, A1, vol. 30, 13877–80; 2 George IV, C. IV(1821).

9 LAC, RG 1, E13, vol. 141; *OAR* (1913), 268; McCalla, *Planting the Province*, 40, 167; Sheppard, *Plunder, Profit and Paroles*, 210, makes the debatable claim that the cost of the pensions forced the government to begin a pattern of borrowing "which eventually drove the province into bankruptcy."

10 7 Wm. IV, C. 103 (1837), 1 Vic., C. XLIII (1838), 1 Vic., C. XLIV (1838).

11 3 Vic., C. XXVII (1840), 3 Vic., C. XXVIII (1840).

12 Phillips, "Educated to Crime," 259; 41 George III, C. XII (1802); *OAR* (1913), 199, (1914), 686, (1932), 36.

13 Kingston *Gazette*, 23 Feb. 1813; 7 George IV, C. II (1826); Greer, "The Pattern of Literacy," 327; Sheppard, *Plunder, Profit and Paroles*, 280–1.

14 LAC, RG 5, A1, vol. 18, 7413, vol. 23, 10173, 10422; Gray, *Soldiers of the King*, 268.

15 Gray, *Soldiers of the King*, 250, 260, 264, 267, 270, 275, 278.

16 2 George IV, C. IV (1821).

17 LAC, RG 8, C200, 85–90, C202, 52, 108.

18 LAC, RG 8, C197, 128–32.

19 LAC, RG 5, A1, vol. 38, 17878, vol. 32, 9227.

20 LAC, RG 5, A1, vol. 49, 24487–8, A2, vol. 6, RG 8, C703C, 15, RG 9, 1B4, vol. 1, 51–3, 101; Dougall, "George Ryerson," 795; Gray, *Soldiers of the King*, 145, 196.

21 LAC, RG 5, A1, vol. 27, 12169–71, vol. 34, 16566; *OAR* (1912), 206, 219, 269; 2 George IV, C. XX (1821), 2 George IV, C. XXIV (1822), 4 George IV, C. XXVIII (1824); Gray, *Soldiers of the King*, 265, 267; Forman, *Legislators and Legislatures of Ontario*, 1: xi.

22 *OAR* (1912), 503, (1914), 46–7, 70; Johnston, "Jean-Baptiste Rousseaux," 723–5.

23 *OAR* (1912), 504, (1913), 22, 42, 511.

24 *HAJ* (1839–40), app.; LAC, RG 1, E13, vol. 155; 1 Vic., C. XLIII (1838); Otto, *Maitland*, 33.

25 LAC, RG 1, E13, vol. 155, RG 7, G16C, vol. 51, 249.

26 LAC, RG 5, A1, vol. 216, 118669–70, vol. 230, 126122–34.

27 LAC, RG 5, A1, vol. 227, 124616, vol. 231, 126473, C2, vols 1, 25.

28 LAC, RG 1, E13, vols 154, 155, RG 5, A1, vol. 219, 120504.

29 LAC, RG 5, A1, vol. 245, 133848–53, vol. 246, 133967–9, vol. 233, 127387–96.

30 LAC, RG 7, G16C, vol. 54, 32, RG 1, E3, vol. 52, 234–258; AO, RG 22, Court of Queen's Bench Minute Books, Home District, 2, 25 Nov. 1839.

31 1 Vic., C. XLVI (1838), 3 Vic., C. LXV (1840); LAC, RG 1, E13, vol.154; *HAJ* (1837–38), app. (Petitions of Elinor Davis and Sarah Wright); Guillet, *The Lives and Times of the Patriots*, 80.

32 LAC, RG 1, E3, vol. 19, RG 5, A1, vol. 202, 112061, vol. 214, 117162, vol. 222, 22054–6; Boyce, *The Rebels of Hastings*, 72–3.

33 LAC, RG 5, A1, vol. 224, 122814–5, vol. 241, 132077; 2 Vic., C. LXVI (1839), 3 Vic., C. LXVI (1840).

34 3 Vic., C. LXIV (1840); Firth, *The Town of York*, 2: 7; Johnson, "A Lady Should Have Nothing to do With Risks," 93–6; for an example of a former public servant without pension see: Johnson, "John Joseph," 444–5.

35 LAC, RG 1, E13, vol. 155; *HAJ* 3, 19, Feb. 1830: 2 George IV, C. XVII (1830); Brock, *History of Middlesex County*, 120; Fahey, *In His Name*, 214–5.

36 Splane, *Social Welfare*, 216–7.

37 LAC, RG 5, A1, vol. 42, 20172, vol. 48, 23934–5; *HAJ* (1839–40), app.; *OAR* (1914), 270, 289, 371.

38 LAC, RG 5, A1, vol. 138, 75662–3, vol. 140, 76515, vol. 149, 81452, vol. 151, 83100, vol. 156, 85697, vol. 164, 89496, vol. 170, 92872, C2, vol. 1, 186–7.

39 Gray, *Soldiers of the King*, 252, 279, 282.

40 McCalla, *Planting the Province*, 302, 304; Ireland, "John H. Dunn and the Bankers," 83–100.

41 56 George III, C. XII (1816).

42 LAC, RG 5, A1, vol. 42, 20172, vol. 46, 22782.

CHAPTER FIVE

1 A survey of writing on education in Upper Canada can be found in Taylor, *Canadian History*, 222–4.

2 47 George III, C. VI (1807), 56 George III, C. XXXVI (1816), 60 George III, C. VII (1820), 4 Wm. IV, C. LCI (1833).

3 Gidney, "Elementary Education," 169–85.

4 LAC, RG 5, B11, vols 2–6; *HAJ* and apps., 1826–40; LAC, MG 24, I3 (McGillivray Papers), vol. 39, 205–254. All of the references to Eastern District schools that follow are from this source.

5 Fahey, *In His Name*, 225; James, "John Rae," 605–8.

6 Hodgins, *Documentary History*, 1: 102–4; LAC, RG 5, B11, vol. 2, no. 21.

7 LAC, RG 5, A1, vols 243–4, 133035, vol. 170, 93076–7, vol. 115, 64669–70, vol. 78, 42540–1, B11, vol. 5, no. 470, C1, vol. 7, no. 842, MG 24, K12; Mealing, *Statistical Account of Upper Canada*, 291; Gidney, "Elementary Education," 182; Hodgins, *Documentary History*, 2: 119; Russell, *Attitudes to Social Structure*, 9.

8 Craig, *Upper Canada*, 182; LAC, RG 5, A1, vol. 115, 64669–70, vol. 170, 93076–7, vol. 86, 47450–1, vol. 94, 52194, vol. 48, 2395–7, vol. 111, 63137–8, C2, vol. 42, no. 2201.

9 Love, "The Professionalization of Teachers," 109; *HAJ* (1831, 1832–33, 1835, 1838, 1839), apps. (School Reports); Wilson, "The Teacher in Early Ontario," 219–23.

10 *HAJ* (1839), app. 2, pt. 1; LAC, MG 24, I3, vol. 3, 206, 254.

11 Gidney, "Elementary Education," 179.

12 Houston and Prentice, *Schooling and Scholars*, 68.

13 LAC, RG 5, A1, vol. 240, 131472–3, vol. 58, 30387–8, RG 1, E1, vol. 57, 313–4, MG 24, I3, vol. 3, 230–254; Curtis, *Building the Educational State*, 64, 66–7; *HAJ* (1838), app.

14 *HAJ* (1838), app.

15 See table 5.4. The district figures are from Canada, *Census*, vol. 4, 1871, 122; Gidney, "Elementary Education," 173; Firth, *The Town of York*, 2: 148.

16 LAC, MG 24, I3, vol. 3, 244, 250, 254, RG 5, B11, vol. 6, (no. missing); Reid, *The Loyalists in Ontario*, 75.

17 *HAJ* (1826–7, 1828, 1830, 1831–2, 1838, 1839), apps.; LAC, RG 5, B11, vol. 6, (no. missing), vol. 4, no. 345, vol. 5, no. 470, MG 24, K12; Greer, "The Pattern of Literacy," 327; fragmentary contrary evidence from the Bathurst District shows two of the three female teachers there with more boys than girls in their schools in 1827, and the only two female teachers in 1831 both had more boys than girls.

18 Gidney and Millar, *Inventing Secondary Education*, 106; LAC, RG, B11, vol. 3, no. 143; *HAJ* (1839), app.

19 Firth, *The Town of York*, 2: 50; Spragge, "The Upper Canada Central School," 171–91; Wilson, "Thomas Appleton," 11–12; LAC, RG 5, B11, vol. 2, no. 140, vol. 3, nos 87, 132, vol. 4, no. 378, vol. 5, nos 507, 508, 633.

20 LAC, RG 1, E3, vol. 96, 109–10, 125–7, 133–9; Houston and Prentice, *Schooling and Scholars*, 66; Firth, *The Town of York*, 2: 153.

21 LAC, RG 5, B11, vol. 2, nos 87, 140.

22 LAC, RG 1, E3, vol. 96, 109–10, 125–7, 133–9.

23 *HAJ* (1828), app.; LAC, RG 5, B11, vol. 2, no. 151; Firth, *The Town of York*, 1: 204.

24 Gidney and Millar, *Inventing Secondary Education*, 178–89; Firth, *The Town of York*, 1: 202–3; LAC, RG 5, A1, vol. 65, 34299–302, B11, vol. 3, no. 54, vol. 4, no. 279, vol. 5, nos 470, 471.

25 LAC, RG 5, B11, vol. 5, no. 426.

26 LAC, RG 1, E3, vol. 69, 134–5.

27 LAC, RG 5, B11, vol. 3, nos 54, 151, vol. 4, no. 297, vol. 5, nos 470, 49; *HAJ* (1828), app.

28 Houston and Prentice, *Schooling and Scholars*, 45, 47; Wilson, Stamp and Audet, *Canadian Education*, 200; Curtis, *Building the Educational State*, 22.

29 Craig, *Discontent in Upper Canada*, 28.

30 LAC, MG 24, I3, vol. 3, 205–54 (The discussion and statistics relating to the Eastern District trustees which follows is based on this source), vol. 7, 25–64; RG 9, 1B5, vol. 3; RG 68, General Index to Commissions, pt. 2a, 410–86; Armstrong, *Handbook of Upper Canadian Chronology*, 33–47, 59–74; Gray, *Soldiers of the King*, 53–8, 101–5.

31 *HAJ* (1839), app. 2, pt. 1. The identity of Eliza Phelps can only be guessed at but she may have been the wife of Richard Phelps, a Methodist minister who served in the Simcoe circuit in 1837–38. Cornish, *Cyclopedia of Methodism in Canada*, 1: 125, 299.

32 Read, "The London District Oligarchy in the Rebellion Era," 195–205; *HAJ* (1839), app. 2, pt. 1; Brock, *History of the County of Middlesex*, 72–4; Johnston, *The Valley of the Six Nations*, 116; Chadwick, *Ontarian Families*, 2: 171; Dawe, "Old Oxford is Wide Awake," 48; Armstrong, "George Jervis Goodhue," 217–32.

33 LAC, MG 24, I3, vol. 3, 205–54; Johnson, *Becoming Prominent*, 101–2, 174, 176, 181, 208, 225.

34 Firth, *The Town of York*, 2: 145–9; Johnson, *Becoming Prominent*, 203, 217; Romney, "A Struggle for Authority," 22.

35 Read, *The Rising in Western Upper Canada*, 52, 223; Armstrong, "George Jervis Goodhue," 219–20, 223–5.

36 Hathaway, *Jesse Ketchum and His Times*, 256; Carroll, *My Boy Life*, chapter 36; Houston and Prentice, *Schooling and Scholars*, 52–4.
37 LAC, RG 5, A1, vol. 191, 106543–7.
38 Gidney, "Elementary Education," 179

CHAPTER SIX

1 Discussions of the nature of crime in Upper Canada may be found in: Oliver, *Terror to Evil-doers*; Bellomo, "Upper Canadian Attitudes"; Murray, *Colonial Justice*; Weaver, *Crimes, Constables, and Courts*; Beattie, *Attitudes Towards Crime and Punishment in Upper Canada*; Matthews, "The Myth of the Peaceable Kingdom," 383–401; Baehre, "Imperial Authority and Colonial Officialdom in Upper Canada."
2 Lewthwaite, "Violence, Law and Community in Rural Upper Canada."
3 Fyson, *Magistrates, Police, and People*, 201.
4 Cross, "The Shiner's War"; Oliver, *Terror to Evil-Doers*, 92; Craig, *Discontent in Upper Canada*, 18–19, 63–8.
5 Murray, *Colonial Justice*, 136–53; Weaver, *Crimes, Constables, and Courts*, 33–50; Wood, *Making Ontario*, 73–4; Oliver, *Terror to Evil-Doers*, 93.
6 Curtis, "The Canada Blue Books," 541, 544.
7 Oliver, *Terror to Evil-Doers*, 48–60; Romney, "Rebel as Magistrate," 327.
8 Wood, *Making Ontario*, 73–4.
9 Lewthwaite, "Violence, Law and Community," 364–6.
10 Calculated from Canada, *Census*, vol. 4, 1871, vol. 4, and Stelter, "Urban Development," table 2.
11 Stelter, "Urban Development," table 2.
12 LAC, RG 5, A1, vol. 145, 79466.
13 *HAJ* (1836), app., vol. 1.
14 Roberts, *In Mixed Company*, 59.
15 Oliver, *Terror to Evil-Doers*, 93; Weaver, *Crime, Constables, and Courts*, 44; Murray, *Colonial Justice*, 136–7; Akenson, *The Irish in Ontario*, 11.
16 Fyson, *Magistrates, Police, and People*, 211–12.
17 Murray, *Colonial Justice*, 147.
18 LAC, RG 5, B27, vols. 1&2
19 Johnson, *Becoming Prominent*, 117–19, 147–8; Russell, *Attitudes to Social Structure*, 116–22.
20 Baehre, "Paupers and Poor Relief in Upper Canada," 58–80.
21 LAC, RG 5, A1, vol. 155, 85145. A similar view expressed by Chief Justice John Beverley Robinson is cited in Oliver, *Terror to Evil-Doers*, 103.

22 LAC, RG 5, B27, vol. 2.

23 Johnson, *Becoming Prominent*, 62–4. The quarter sessions minutes for the Upper Canadian period are in AO, RG 22, Series 7.

24 Oliver, *Terror to Evil-Doers*, 93.

25 AO, RG 22, Ms. 82, 251.

26 Oliver, *Terror to Evil-Doers*, 93–4.

27 Murray, *Colonial Justice*, 143; Weaver, *Crimes, Constables, and Courts*, 46.

28 Oliver, *Terror to Evil-Doers*, 93.

29 AO, RG 21, Ms. 518, 610, 618; City of Toronto Archives, Series 507, files 1, 2.

30 Oliver, *Terror to Evil-Doers*, 16–20.

31 AO, RG 22, Ms. 82, 251; RG 21, Ms. 518, 610, 618.

32 LAC, RG 5, B27, vol. 2; Toronto *British Colonist*, 6 Nov. 1839.

33 AO, RG 22, King's Bench Minute Books, Johnstown District, 11 Sept. 1824.

34 AO, RG 22, King's Bench Minute Books, Gore District, 25 Aug. 1835.

35 LAC, RG 5, A1, vol. 165, 89936–7; AO, RG 22, King's Bench Minute Books, Victoria District, 16 Sept. 1840.

36 AO, RG 22, King's Bench Minute Books, Midland District, 2 Oct. 1824; Toronto *British Colonist*, 6 Nov. 1839.

37 Oliver, *Terror to Evil-Doers*, 31, table 1.2; AO, RG 22, King's Bench Minute Books, 1824–40.

38 Oliver, *Terror to Evil-Doers*, 18.

39 LAC, RG 5, A1, vol. 74, 39296; AO RG 22, King's Bench Minute Books, Newcastle District, 28 Sept. 1836.

40 LAC, RG 5, A1, vol. 147, 80012–30; AO RG 22, King's Bench Minute Books, Home District, 21 Oct. 1834, 2 June 1840.

41 Fraser, *Provincial Justice*, 327–31, 351–4; AO, RG 22, King's Bench Minute Books, Johnstown District, 9 Oct. 1837, Bathurst District, 24 Apr. 1840.

42 Oliver, *Terror to Evil-Doers*, 97–9.

43 Ibid., 30. Oliver cites the hanging of a Robert McIntyre for rape in 1820 as the only such case but at least one other man was hanged for rape, William Brass, in 1837. See Fraser, *Provincial Justice*, 293–5.

44 LAC, RG 5, A1, vol. 243, 132654–5, RG 1, E3, vol. 36A, 225–231; AO, RG 22, King's Bench Minute Books, Western District, 13 Apr. 1840, Bench Books of Judge C.A. Hagerman, 17 Apr. 1840.

45 Fraser, *Provincial Justice*, 354.

46 LAC, RG 5, A1, vol. 43, 20862–4.

47 LAC, RG 5, A1, vol. 44, 2133941.

48 LAC, RG 5, A1, vol. 68, 36177–81, B3, vol. 6, 255–6.

49 LAC, RG 5, A1, vol. 163, 88962–4.

50 LAC, RG 1, E3, vol. 11, 27–32; AO, RG 22, King's Bench Minute Books, Western District, 13 Apr. 1840.

51 LAC, RG 5, A1, vol. 214, 117141–2, vol. 222, 122054–6, vol. 241, 13260–71, RG 1, E3, vol. 19, 11; AO, RG 22, King's Bench Minute Books, Home District, 29 May 1839; Peel, "Switzer of Streetsville and Mackenzie," 136.

52 Murray, *Colonial Justice*, 220; Fraser, *Provincial Justice*, 284, 293, 307, 323, 327, 333.

53 Fraser, *Provincial Justice*, 307, 330; LAC, RG 5, C1, vol. 19, no. 8; Phillips, "Educated to Crime," 362–3.

54 Read and Stagg, *The Rebellion of 1837*, xc; Weaver, *Crimes, Constables, and Courts*, 307.

55 LAC, RG 5, A1, vol. 184, 10306–7.

56 LAC, RG 5, A1, vol. 248, 134990–4, C2, vol. 2, 3–4.

57 LAC, RG 5, A1, vol. 68, 36311–14, vol. 85, 40115–6, vol. 90, 49920–6, vol. 163, 88962–4; Johnson, "Gerald Craig's Upper Canada," 122–4.

58 LAC, RG 5, A1, vol. 181, 99971–2, vol. 184, 102844, vol. 186, 103788–91, vol. 189, 105564, vol. 194, 107971, vol. 199, 110379–80, RG 5, B3, vol. 6, 1308.

59 LAC, RG 5, A1, vol. 62, 33323–6, 36180–1, vol. 86, 46906–11, vol. 149, 91710–15, RG 7, G16C, vol. 13, 94.

60 LAC, RG 5, A1, vol. 27, 12460, vol. 115, 64906–7.

61 LAC, RG 5, A1, vol. 131, 72447–60, RG 1, E3, vol. 42A, 125–6, vol. 65, 101–4.

62 LAC, RG 5, A1, vol. 44, 21339–41, vol. 155, 85145.

63 LAC, RG 5, A1, vol. 90, 49920–6, vol. 167, 91050–2, vol. 272, 121641; AO, RG 22, Bench Books of Judge C.A. Hagerman, London District, 31 March 1840.

64 LAC, RG 5, A1, vol. 232, 127009–27, RG 1, E3, vol. 86, 26.

65 LAC, RG 5, A1, vol. 1A, 447–51, vol. 151, 82955–6, vol. 153, 83808–13, vol. 199, 110478–82; AO, RG 22, King's Bench Minute Books, Gore District, 25 Aug. 1835, Bench Books of Judge C.A Hagerman, London District, 31 March 1840.

CHAPTER SEVEN

1 Howison, *Sketches of Upper Canada*, 264–5.

2 Malcolmson, "The Poor in Kingston, 1815–1850," 291–2; Baerhe, "Paupers and Poor Relief," 59; LAC, RG 5, A2, vol. 5.

3   Baerhe, "Paupers and Poor Relief," 58; Greenhous, "Paupers and Poorhouses," 68; Moorman, "The First Business of Government," 32.

4   Smandych, "William Osgoode," 119.

5   Firth, *The Town of York*, 2: 180; Smandych, "William Osgoode," 101–3.

6   Smandych, "William Osgoode," 99–129.

7   Stelter, "Urban Development," table 2.

8   Johnson, "Claims of Equity," 229; LAC, RG 5 A1, vol. 238, 130073.

9   Baehre, "Pauper Emigration," 339–40; Errington, *Emigrant Worlds*, 58, 111.

10 Fingard, "The Winter's Tale," 65–94; Errington, *Emigrant Worlds*, 111–28.

11 Splane, *Social Welfare*, 72; Baehre, "Paupers and Poor Relief," 63; Baehre, "Pauper Emigration," 354; Carter-Edwards, "Cobourg," 68–9; City of Toronto Archives, Fonds 1035 (House of Industry) Description Display, 2; *OAR* (1932), 36–7, 51.

12 Greenhous, "Paupers and Poorhouses," 106; *OAR* (1933), 154, 168, 175.

13 Angus, "Health, Emigration and Welfare," 125; Murray, *Colonial Justice*, 109–25.

14 Oliver, *Terror to Evil-Doers*, 44–5.

15 *HAJ* (1839–40), app.; Johnson, "Claims of Equity," table 1.

16 Baehre, "Pauper Emigration," 348.

17 Canada, *Census*, vol. 4, 1871, 136. The "pre-eminence" of the Scots in another crucial area, agriculture, is discussed in Clarke, *The Ordinary People of Essex*, 447–8.

18 LAC, RG 5, A1, vol. 238, 130073.

19 Stelter, "Urban Development," table 2.

20 *HAJ* (1839–40), app.

21 Gray, *Sisters in the Wilderness*, 138.

22 Johnson, "The Chelsea Pensioners in Upper Canada," 271–89; LAC, RG 5, A1, vol. 199, 116307–9, vol. 108, 61393–4.

23 LAC, RG 5, A1, vol. 126, 69640–1.

24 LAC, RG 5 C1, vol. 4, no. 303.

25 *HAJ* (1839–40), app.

26 LAC, RG 5, C1, vol. 19, no. 76.

27 LAC, RG 5, A1, vol. 30, 13693–5, 13699–702, vol. 31, 14509–13, vol. 175, 96204, vol. 207, 114495; RG 5, C1, vol. 3, no. 302; MacGillivray and Ross, *A History of Glengarry*, 36–9.

28 LAC, RG 5, A1, vol. 58, 30116; Fraser, "Richard Pierpont," 697–8.

29 LAC, RG 5, A1, vol. 30, 13695.

30 Russell, *Attitudes to Social Structure*, 88; LAC, RG 5, A1, vol. 61, 32209–10, vol. 65, 34241–3,vol. 86, 47450–1, vol. 89, 49431, vol. 90,

50228–71, vol. 91, 50323–50809, vol. 135, 74351, vol. 243, 133442; RG 8, C510, 234–5; Johnson, "Gerald Craig's Upper Canada," 125–6.

31 LAC, RG 5, A1, vol. 24, 10657–8, vol. 98, 55033–4, vol. 109, 6252–3, vol. 205, 113506; RG 5, C1, vol. 19, no. 8.

32 *HAJ* (1839–40), app.

33 McLean, "Single Again," 127; Bradbury, *Working Families*, 182–213. See also Bradbury, "The Fragmented Family," "Pigs, Cows and Boarders," "Surviving as a Widow in Nineteenth-Century Montreal," "Widowhood and Canadian Family History," and *Wife to Widow*.

34 LAC, RG 5, A1, vol. 76, 40690, vol. 100, 56785–6, vol. 126, 69640–1, vol. 136, 74738–9, vol. 152, 83570–1, vol. 199, 110307–9.

35 LAC, MG 9, D27; RG 1, L1, Land Book M, 121; Turner, *Perth*, 32.

36 LAC, RG 1, L3, vol. 157, D14/142, vol. 165, pt. 1, D2/15, RG 5, A1, vol. 79, 42643–8, vol. 83, 44856, RG 7, G16C, vol. 17, 89, 102.

37 LAC, RG 5, A1, vol. 49, 24341, vol. 61, 32478, 32554, vol. 71, 37577–84, vol. 144, 78773–5, MG 9, D27; *HAJ* (1835), app.

38 Errington, *Wives and Mothers, School Mistresses and Scullery Maids*, 44–47.

39 LAC, RG 7, G16C, vol. 37, 250, RG 5, A1, vol. 29, 13212–5, vol. 28, 12994–7, vol. 101, 57637, vol. 94, 52194, vol. 162, 88695, vol. 154, 84605, vol. 24, 10657–8, vol. 80, 43436–7, vol. 82, 44186; C1, vol. 41, no. 2191.

40 LAC, RG 5, A1, vol. 80, 43386–7, vol. 87, 47904–6, vol. 97, 54331–4, vol. 141, 77308–9, vol. 156, 85441–2; Angus, "Health, Emigration and Welfare," 126–7.

41 Firth, *The Town of York*, 2: lxxxiv; LAC, RG 5, A1, vol. 141, 77206–7.

42 LAC, RG 5, A1, vol. 141, 77223–4.

43 Splane, *Social Welfare*, 70–71; Murray, *Colonial Justice*, 199.

CONCLUSION

1 McCalla, "A World Without Chocolate," 4, note 19, tables 1–7; The Robinson Crusoe image may have originated with Catharine Parr Trail's novel, *Canadian Crusoes: A Tale of the Rice Lake Plains*.

2 Gwyn, *John A.*, 68.

3 Wilton, "Administrative Reform," 105–25.

4 Bellomo, "Upper Canadian Attitudes," 11–20; Baehre, "Paupers and Poor Relief," 57–80; Hardwick, "Segregating and Reforming the Marginal," chapter 3; Oliver, *Terror to Evil-Doers*, 93–4.

5 Oliver, *Terror to Evil-Doers*, 105–6, 141–9, 181–4.

6 Hardwick, "Segregating and Reforming the Marginal," 104.

7 Curtis, "The Canada Blue Books," 544; David Murray, in his study of crime in the Niagara District, concludes that Blacks were regularly the victims of discrimination both as victims of, and alleged perpetrators, of crime. Murray, *Colonial Justice,* 169–74.

8 LAC, MG 11, CO43, vol. 43, Goderich to Colborne, 5 July 1832.

9 Stelter, "Urban Development," table 2.

10 Brode, *Sir John Beverley Robinson,* 120–1; Ireland, "John H. Dunn and the Bankers," 84–100; McCalla, *Planting the Province,* 169.

11 Canada, *Census,* vol. 4, 1871; A.B. Jameson, *Winter Studies and Summer Rambles,* 1: 171.

12 LAC, RG 1, L3, vol. 381A, N miscellaneous 1788–1802/67; RG 5, A1, vol. 204, 113050, vol. 149, 81452, vol. 107, 60740–1.

Bibliography

PRIMARY SOURCES

Library and Archives Canada

RG 1, E1, Upper Canada Executive Council Minutes
RG 1, E3, Upper Canada State Papers
RG 1, E13, Blue Books
RG 1, E14, Executive Council Correspondence
RG 1, L1, Minutes of the Land Committee of the Executive Council
RG 1, L3. Upper Canada Land Petitions
RG 5, A1, Upper Canada Sundries
RG 5, A2, Civil Secretary's Office, Drafts
RG 5, B3, Petitions and Addresses
RG 5, B9, Licences and Certificates
RG 5, B11, Miscellaneous Records Relating to Education
RG 5, B27, Gaol Returns
RG 5, C1, Provincial Secretary's Correspondence
RG 5, C2, Letter Books
RG 7, G14, Miscellaneous Records
RG 7, G16C, Letter Books, Upper Canada
RG 8, C Series, Militia Pensions
RG 9, 1B4, Pensions and Land Grants
RG 19, E5a, Board of Claims for War Losses
RG 68, General Index to Commissions
MG 9, 98–27, Perth Military Settlement
MG 24, A40, Colborne Papers
MG 24, I3, McGillivray Papers
MG 24, K12, Report on London District Common Schools

Archives of Ontario

RG 21, Municipal Records
RG 22, Quarter Session Minutes; Court of King's (Queen's) Bench, Minute
Books and Bench Books

City of Toronto Archives

RG 1, Council Papers
RG 7, Mayor's Letterbook

Printed Primary Sources

Bonnycastle, Richard H. *The Canadas in 1841*. 2 vols. London: Henry
Colburn, 1841.
Canada. *Census*. Vol. 4. 1871.
Craig, Gerald M., ed. *Lord Durham's Report*. Toronto: McClelland and
Stewart, 1963.
Cruikshank, E.A., ed. *The Correspondence of Lieut-Governor John Graves
Simcoe*. 5 vols. Toronto: The Ontario Historical Society, 1923–31.
– *The Correspondence of the Honourable Peter Russell*. 3 vols. Toronto:
The Ontario Historical Society, 1932–36.
Fairley, Margaret, ed. *The Selected Writings of William Lyon Mackenzie,
1824–1837*. Toronto: Oxford University Press, 1960.
Hodgins, J. George, ed. *Documentary History of Education in Upper
Canada*. 28 vols. Toronto: Warwick Bros. and Ritter, 1894–1910.
Howison, John. *Sketches of Upper Canada*. Edinburgh: Oliver and Boyd,
1821.
Jameson, Anna B. *Winter Studies and Summer Rambles in Canada*. 3 vols.
London: Saunders and Otley, 1838.
Mealing, S. R., ed. *Statistical Account of Upper Canada*. By Robert
Gourlay. Toronto: McClelland and Stewart, 1974.
Nish, Elizabeth, ed. *Debates of the Legislative Assembly of United
Canada*. 13 vols. Montreal: Presses de L'Ecole des hautes études com-
merciales, 1970–1993.
Ontario Archives Reports.
Strachan, James [John]. *A Visit to the Province of Upper Canada in 1819*.
Aberdeen: D. Chalmers & Co., 1820.
Talbot, Edward Allen. *Five Years' Residence in the Canadas*. 2 vols.
London: Longman, Hurst, Rees, Orme, Brown and Green, 1824.
Upper Canada, House of Assembly. *Journals and Appendices*.

Upper Canada, Legislative Council. *Journals.*
Upper Canada. *Statutes.*

Newspapers

Kingston *Gazette*
Toronto *British Colonist*
Upper Canada (York) *Gazette*
York *Patriot*

SECONDARY SOURCES

Akenson, Donald Harmon. *The Irish in Ontario.* Montreal and Kingston: McGill-Queen's University Press, 1984.
Angus, Margaret. "Health, Emigration and Welfare in Kingston, 1820–1840." In D. Swainson, ed., *Oliver Mowat's Ontario*, 120–35. Toronto: Macmillan, 1972.
Armstrong, Frederick H. "Andrew Mercer," *DCB.* Vol. 10. 509–10.
– "The Carfrae Family: A Study in Early Toronto Toryism." *OH* 54 (1962): 161–81.
– "George Jervis Goodhue: Pioneer Merchant of London, Upper Canada." *OH* 63 (1971): 217–32.
– *Handbook of Upper Canadian Chronology.* Toronto: Dundurn Press, 1985.
Armstrong, Frederick H., ed. *Toronto of Old.* By Henry Scadding. Toronto: Oxford University Press, 1966.
Arthur, Eric. *From Front Street to Queen's Park: The Story of Ontario's Parliament Buildings.* Toronto: McClelland and Stewart, 1979.
Baehre, Rainer. "Imperial Authority and Colonial Officialdom of Upper Canada in the 1830s: The State, Crime, Lunacy and Everyday Social Order." In L.A. Knafla and S.W.S. Binnie, eds., *Law, Society and the State: Essays in Modern Legal History*, 181–214. Toronto: University of Toronto Press, 1995.
– "Pauper Emigration to Upper Canada." *Hs/SH* 14 (1981): 339–68.
– "Paupers and Poor Relief in Upper Canada." *CHA Historical Papers* (1981): 58–80.
Baldwin, R.M., and J. *The Baldwins and the Great Experiment.* Don Mills: Longmans, 1969.
Beattie, J.M. *Attitudes Towards Crime and Punishment in Upper Canada, 1830–1850: A Documentary Study.* Toronto: Centre of Criminology, 1977.

Bellomo, J. Jerald. "Upper Canadian Attitudes Towards Crime and Punishment." *OH* 64 (1972): 11–26.

Bleasdale, Ruth. "Class Conflict on the Canals of Upper Canada in the 1840s." *L/LT* 7 (1981): 9–39.

Bouchier, Nancy B. "'A Broad Clear Track in Good Order': The Bytown and Nepean Road Company - Richmond Toll Road, Ottawa, 1851–1875." *OH* 76 (1984): 103–27.

Boyce, Betsy D. *The Rebels of Hastings.* Toronto: University of Toronto Press, 1992.

Boyce, Gerald E. *Historic Hastings.* Belleville: Hastings County Council, 1967.

Bradbury, Bettina. "The Fragmented Family: Family Strategies in the Face of Death, Illness and Poverty, Montreal, 1860–1885." In Joy Parr, ed., *Childhood and Family in Canadian History.* Toronto: McClelland and Stewart, 1982.

– "Pigs, Cows and Boarders: Non-Wage Forms of Survival Among Montreal Families, 1861–1891." *L/LT* 14 (1984): 9–46

– "Surviving as a Widow in Nineteenth-Century Montreal." *Urban History Review* 17 (1989): 148–60.

– "Widowhood and Canadian Family History." In Margaret Conrad, ed., *Intimate Relations: Family and Community in Planter Nova Scotia, 1759–1800*, 19–41. Fredericton: Acadiensis Press, 1995.

– *Wife to Widow: Lives, Laws and Politics in Nineteenth-Century Montreal.* Vancouver: UBC Press, 2012.

– *Working Families: Age, Gender and Daily Survival in Industrializing Montreal.* Toronto: McClelland and Stewart, 1993.

Brock, Daniel, ed. *The History of Middlesex County.* Belleville: Mika Studio, 1972.

Brode, Patrick. "James Gordon Strobridge." *DCB.* Vol. 6. 741–2.

– *Sir John Beverley Robinson: Bone and Sinew of the Compact.* Toronto: The Osgoode Society, 1984.

Cameron, Wendy. "'Till we get tidings from those who have gone': Thomas Sockett and Letters from Petworth Emigrants, 1832–1837." *OH* 85 (1993): 1–16.

Cameron, Wendy, and M. Maude. *Assisting Emigration to Upper Canada: The Petworth Project, 1832–1837.* Montreal and Kingston: McGill-Queen's University Press, 2000.

Campney, Lucille H. *The Scottish Pioneers of Upper Canada, 1784–1855.* Toronto: Natural Heritage Books, 2005.

Canniff, William. *The Medical Profession in Upper Canada, 1783–1850.* Toronto: William Briggs, 1894.

– *The Settlement of Upper Canada*. Toronto: Dudley and Burns, 1869.

Carr, Clarence. *The Canada Land Company*. Toronto: The Ontario Historical Society, 1974

Carroll, John. *My Boy Life*. Toronto: William Briggs, 1882.

Carter-Edwards, Dennis. "Cobourg: A Nineteenth-Century Response to the Worthy Poor." In J. Petryshyn, ed., *Victorian Cobourg: A Nineteenth Century Profile*, 167–81. Belleville: Mika Publishing, 1976.

Chadwick, Edward M. *Ontarian Families*. Toronto: Rolph, Smith and Co., 1894.

Christie, Carl. "Prideaux Selby." D C B. Vol. 5. 749–50.

Clarke, John. *The Ordinary People of Essex: Environment, Culture, and Economy on the Frontier of Upper Canada*. Montreal and Kingston: McGill-Queen's University Press, 2010.

Cornish, George H. *Cyclopaedia of Methodism in Canada*. Vol. 1. Toronto: Methodist Book and Publishing House, 1881.

Cowan, Helen I. *British Emigration to British North America, the First Hundred Years*. Toronto: University of Toronto Press, 1967.

Craig, Gerald M. "The American Impact on the Upper Canadian Reform Movement Before 1837." CHR 29 (1948): 333–52.

– *Upper Canada: The Formative Years, 1783–1841*. Toronto: McClelland and Stewart, 1963.

Craig, Gerald M., ed. *Discontent in Upper Canada*. Toronto: Copp Clark, 1974.

– *Early Travellers in the Canadas*. Toronto: Macmillan, 1955.

Craven, Paul. "The Law of Master and Servant in Mid-Nineteenth-Century Ontario." In D.H. Flaherty, ed., *Essays in the History of Canadian Law*, vol. 1, 175–211. Toronto: The Osgoode Society, 1981.

Crawford, Kenneth G. *Canadian Municipal Government*. Toronto: University of Toronto Press, 1954.

Cross, Michael S. "The Shiner's War: Social Violence in the Ottawa Valley in the 1830s." CHR 54 (1973): 1–26.

– "The Stormy History of the York Roads." OH 54 (1962): 1–24.

Curtis, Bruce. *Building the Educational State: Canada West. 1836–1871*. London, Ont.: Althouse Press, 1988.

– "The Canada Blue Books and the Administrative Capacity of the Canadian State, 1822–67." CHR 74 (1993): 535–65.

Dale, Clare A. *"The Palaces of Government": A History of the Legislative Buildings of the Province of Upper Canada and Ontario, 1792–1992*. Toronto: Ontario Legislative Library, 1993.

Darroch, Gordon, and L. Soltow. *Property and Inequality in Victorian Ontario*. Toronto: University of Toronto Press, 1994.

Dawe, Brian. *"Old Oxford is Wide Awake!": Pioneer Settlers and Politicians in Oxford County, 1793–1853*. N.p.: n.p.,1990.

Dougall, Charles. "George Ryerson." *DCB*. Vol. 11. 795.

Errington, Elizabeth Jane. *Emigrant Worlds and Transatlantic Communities*. Montreal and Kingston: McGill-Queen's University Press, 2007.

– *Wives and Mothers, School Mistresses and Scullery Maids: Working Women in Upper Canada, 1790–1840*. Montreal and Kingston: McGill-Queen's University Press, 1995.

Fahey, Curtis. *In His Name: The Anglican Experience in Upper Canada, 1791–1854*. Ottawa: Carleton University Press, 1991.

Fingard, Judith. "The Winter's Tale: Contours of Pre-industrial Poverty in British North America." *CHA Historical Papers* (1974): 65–94.

Firth, Edith G. "John White." *DCB*. Vol. 4. 766–67.

Firth, Edith G., ed. *The Town of York*. 2 vols. Toronto: The Champlain Society, 1962–66.

Forman, Debra. *Legislators and Legislatures of Ontario*. Vol. 1. Toronto: Legislative Library, 1984.

Fraser, Robert L. "Richard Pierpont." *DCB*. Vol. 7. 697–8.

Fraser, Robert L., ed. *Provincial Justice: Upper Canadian Legal Portraits*. Toronto: The Osgoode Society, 1992.

Fyson, Donald. *Magistrates, Police, and People: Everyday Criminal Justice in Quebec and Lower Canada, 1764–1837*. Toronto: The Osgoode Society, 2006.

Gates, Lillian F. *Land Policies of Upper Canada*. Toronto: University of Toronto Press, 1968.

– "Roads, Rivals and Rebellion: The Unknown Story of Asa Danforth Jr." *OH* 76 (1984): 233–54.

Gentilcore, Louis, and K. Donkin. *Land Surveys of Southern Ontario*. Toronto: York University Department of Geography, 1973.

Gidney, Robert D. "Elementary Education in Upper Canada: A Reassessment." *OH* 65 (1973): 169–85.

Gidney, Robert D., and W.P.J. Millar. *Inventing Secondary Education: The Rise of the High School in Nineteenth-Century Ontario*. Montreal and Kingston: McGill-Queen's University Press, 1990.

Glazebrook, G.P. de T. *Life in Ontario: A Social History*. Toronto: University of Toronto Press, 1968.

– "The Origins of Local Government." In F.H. Armstrong et al, eds., *Aspects of Nineteenth-Century Ontario*, 36–47. Toronto: University of Toronto Press, 1974.

Gray, Charlotte. *Sisters in the Wilderness*. Toronto: Penguin Books, 1999.

Gray, William. *Soldiers of the King: The Upper Canadian Militia, 1812–1815*. Erin, Ont.: Boston Mills Press, 1995.

Greenhous, Brereton. "Paupers and Poorhouses: The Development of Poor Relief in Early New Brunswick." *Hs/SH* 1 (1968): 103–28.

Greer, Allan. "Canadian History: Ancient and Modern." *CHR* (1996): 575–87.

– "The Pattern of Literacy in Quebec, 1745–1899." *Hs/SH* 11 (1978): 293–335.

Greer, Allan, and I. Radforth, eds. *Colonial Leviathan: State Formation in Mid-Nineteenth-Century Canada*. Toronto: University of Toronto Press, 1992.

Guillet, E.C. *The Lives and Times of the Patriots*. Toronto: University of Toronto Press, 1968.

Gundy, H.P. "The Family Compact at Work: The Second Heir and Devisee Commission of Upper Canada, 1805–1841." *OH* 66 (1974): 129–46.

– "Hugh Christopher Thomson." *DCB*. Vol. 6. 722–4.

Gwyn, Richard. *John A.: The Man Who Made Us; The Life and Times of John A. Macdonald*. Vol. 1. Toronto: Random House Canada, 2007.

Hamil, Fred C. *Lake Erie Baron: The Story of Colonel Thomas Talbot*. Toronto: Macmillan, 1955.

Hardwick, Martina L. "Segregating and Reforming the Marginal: The Institution and Everyday Resistance in mid-Nineteenth-Century Ontario." PhD Thesis, Queen's University, 1998.

Harper, Russell. *Painting in Canada: A History*. Toronto: University of Toronto Press, 1977.

Hathaway, E.J. *Jesse Ketchum and His Times*. Toronto: McClelland and Stewart, 1929.

Hind, Henry Y., et al. *Eighty Years Progress in British North America*. Toronto: L. Nichols, 1865.

Hodgetts, J.E. *Pioneer Public Service*. Toronto: University of Toronto Press, 1955.

Houston, Susan E., and A. Prentice. *Schooling and Scholars in Nineteenth-Century Ontario*. Ontario Historical Studies Series. Toronto: University of Toronto Press, 1988.

Ireland, John [Max Magill]. "John H. Dunn and the Bankers." *OH* 62 (1970): 83–100.

James, Warren. "John Rae." *DCB*. Vol. 10. 605–8.

Johnson, J.K. *Becoming Prominent: Regional Leadership in Upper Canada, 1791–1841*. Montreal and Kingston: McGill-Queen's University Press, 1989.

- "The Chelsea Pensioners in Upper Canada." *OH* 53 (1961): 273–89.
- "'Claims of Equity and Justice': Petitions and Petitioners in Upper Canada." *Hs/SH* 28 (1995): 219–40.
- "Col. James FitzGibbon and the Suppression of Irish Riots In Upper Canada." *OH* 58 (1966): 139–55.
- "Gerald Craig's Upper Canada: The Formative Years and the Writing of Upper Canadian History." *OH* 90 (1998): 117–34.
- "John Joseph," *DCB*. Vol. 8. 444–5.
- "'A Lady Should Have Nothing to do With Risks': A Case of Widowhood in Upper Canada." *OH* 88 (1996): 85–101.
Johnston, Charles M. "Jean-Baptiste Rousseaux." *DCB*. Vol. 5. 723–5.
Johnston, Charles M., ed. *The Valley of the Six Nations*. Toronto: The Champlain Society, 1964.
Kennedy, P. "Deciphering the Upper Canadian Land Books and Land Petitions." LAC unpublished paper, 1978.
Lewthwaite, Susan. "Violence, Law and Community in Rural Upper Canada." In Jim Phillips et al, eds., *Crime and Criminal Justice*, 353–86. Toronto: The Osgoode Society, 1994.
Lockwood, Glenn J. *Beckwith: Irish and Scottish Identities in a Canadian Community*. Carleton Place: Township of Beckwith, 1991.
- *Montague: A Social History of an Irish Township, 1783–1980*. Kingston: Mastercraft Printing, 1980.
- "Temperance as Ethnic Subterfuge." In C.K. Warsh, ed., *Drink in Canada*, 43–69. Montreal and Kingston: McGill-Queen's University Press, 1993.
Love, James. "The Professionalization of Teachers in mid-Nineteenth-Century Upper Canada." In N. McDonald and A. Chaiton, eds., *Egerton Ryerson and His Times*, 109–28. Toronto: Macmillan, 1978.
Malcolmson, Patricia E. "The Poor in Kingston, 1815–1850." In G. Tulchinsky, ed., *To Preserve and Defend: Essays on Kingston in the Nineteenth Century*, 281–98. Montreal and Kingston: McGill-Queen's University Press, 1976.
Matthews, W.T. "The Myth of the Peaceable Kingdom: Upper Canadian Society During the Victorian Period." *Queen's Quarterly* 94 (1987): 383–401.
McCalla, Douglas. *Planting the Province: the Economic History of Upper Canada, 1784–1870*. Ontario Historical Studies Series. Toronto: University of Toronto Press, 1993.
- "A World without Chocolate: Grocery Purchases at Some Upper Canadian Country Stores, 1801–1861." Paper presented to the Canadian Historical Association Annual Meeting, Halifax, 2003.

MacGillivray, Royce, and E. Ross. *A History of Glengarry*. Belleville: Mika Publishing, 1979.

McLean, Lorna. "Single Again: Widow's Work in the Urban Family Economy, Ottawa, 1871." *OH* 83 (1991): 127–50.

McNairn, Jeffrey L. *The Capacity to Judge: Public Opinion and Deliberative Democracy in Upper Canada, 1791–1854*. Toronto: University of Toronto Press, 2000

MacRae, Marion, and A. Adamson. *Cornerstones of Order: Courthouses and Town Halls of Ontario, 1784–1914*. Toronto: The Osgoode Society, 1983.

Mealing, S.R. "John Graves Simcoe." *DCB*. Vol. 5. 755–6.

Moorman, David. "The District Land Boards: A Study of Early Land Administration in Upper Canada, 1784–1794." MA Thesis, Carleton University, 1992.

– "'The First Business of Government': The Land Granting Administration of Upper Canada." PhD Thesis, University of Ottawa, 1997.

Murray, David. *Colonial Justice: Justice, Morality and Crime in the Niagara District, 1791–1849*. Toronto: The Osgoode Society, 2002.

Oliver, Peter. *"Terror to Evil-Doers": Prisons and Punishments in Nineteenth-Century Ontario*. Toronto: The Osgoode Society, 1998.

Otto, Stephen A. *Maitland: "A Very Neat Village Indeed."* Erin, Ont.: Boston Mills Press, 1985.

Palmer, Bryan D. *Working-Class Experience*. Toronto: Butterworth & Co., 1983.

Peel, Bruce. "Switzer of Streetsville and Mackenzie." In D. Duncan and G. Lockwood, eds., *1837 Rebellion Remembered*, 133–50. Toronto: The Ontario Historical Society, 1988.

Phillips, John D. "Educated to Crime: Community and Criminal Justice in Upper Canada, 1800–1840." PhD Thesis, University of Toronto, 2004.

Preston, Richard A., ed. *Kingston Before the War of 1812*. Toronto: The Champlain Society, 1959.

Pringle, J.F. *Lunenburgh, or the Old Eastern District*. Cornwall: Standard Printing, 1890.

Public Archives of Canada, Manuscript Division. *Preliminary Inventory, Record Group 1*. Ottawa: The Queen's Printer, 1953.

Read, Colin F. "The London District Oligarchy in the Rebellion Era." *OH* 72 (1980): 195–209.

– *The Rising in Western Upper Canada*. Toronto: University of Toronto Press, 1982.

– "Unrest in the Canadas." In R.L. Gentilcore, ed., *Historical Atlas of Canada*, vol. 2, plate 23. Toronto: University of Toronto Press, 1993.

Read, Colin F., and R.J. Stagg, eds. *The Rebellion of 1837*. Toronto: The Champlain Society, 1985.

Reid, William D. *The Loyalists of Ontario*. Lambertville, NJ: Hunterdon House, 1973.

Riddell, William R. *The Life of William Dummer Powell*. Lansing, Mich.: Michigan Historical Commission, 1924.

Roberts, Julia. *In Mixed Company: Taverns and Public Life in Upper Canada*. Vancouver: UBC Press, 2009.

– "Women, Men and Taverns in Tavern-keeper Ely Playter's Journal." *HS/SH* 72 (2003): 371–406.

Robertson, J. Ross. *Landmarks of Toronto*. Vol. 3. Toronto: Toronto Evening Telegram, 1898.

Romney, Paul. "Rebel as Magistrate: William Lyon Mackenzie and his Enemies." In Jim Phillips et al, eds., *Crime and Criminal Justice*, 324–52. Toronto: The Osgoode Society, 1994.

– "A Struggle for Authority: Toronto Society and Politics in 1834." In V.L. Russell, ed., *Forging a Consensus: Historical Essays on Toronto*, 9–40. Toronto: University of Toronto Press, 1984.

Russell, Peter A. *Attitudes to Social Structure and Mobility in Upper Canada, 1815–1840*. Queenston: Edward Mellen Press, 1990.

– "Wage Labour Rates in Upper Canada, 1818–1840." *HS/SH* 16 (1983): 61–80.

Schrauwers, Albert. *Awaiting the Millenium: The Children of Peace and the Village of Hope, 1812–1899*. Toronto: University of Toronto Press, 1993.

Sheppard, George. *Plunder, Profit and Paroles: A Social History of the War of 1812 in Upper Canada*. Montreal and Kingston: McGill-Queen's University Press, 1994.

Smandych, Russell C. "William Osgoode, John Graves Simcoe, and the Exclusion of the English Poor Law From Upper Canada." In L.A. Knafla and S.W.S. Binnie, eds., *Law, Society and the State: Essays in Modern Legal History*, 99–129. Toronto: University of Toronto Press, 1995.

Smith, Mary L., ed. *Young Mister Smith in Upper Canada*. Toronto: University of Toronto Press, 1980.

Splane, Richard B. *Social Welfare in Ontario, 1791–1893*. Toronto: University of Toronto Press, 1965.

Spragge, George W. "The Upper Canada Central School." *OH* 32 (1937): 171–91.

Stelter, Gilbert A. "Urban Development in a Frontier Region: The Towns and Cities of Upper Canada, 1784–1851." Paper Presented to the Canadian Historical Society Annual Meeting, Saskatoon, 1979.

Taylor, John H. *Ottawa: An Illustrated History*. Toronto: Lorimer, 1986.

Taylor, M.B. *Canadian History: A Reader's Guide*. Vol. 1. Toronto: University of Toronto Press, 1994.

Thompson, Frances A. "Local Authority and District Autonomy: The Niagara District Magistracy and Constabulary, 1828–1841." PhD Thesis, University of Ottawa, 1996.

Turner, Larry. *Perth: Tradition and Style in Eastern Ontario*. Toronto: Natural Heritage/Natural History Inc., 1998.

Weaver, John C. *Crimes, Constables, and Courts: Order and Transgression in a Canadian City, 1816–1970*. Montreal and Kingston: McGill-Queen's University Press, 1995.

Webber, Jeremy. "Labour and the Law." In P. Craven, ed., *Labouring Lives: Work and Workers in Nineteenth-Century Ontario*, 105–203. Ontario Historical Studies Series. Toronto: University of Toronto Press, 1995.

Widdis, Randy W. "Speculation and the Surveyor: An Analysis of the Role Played by the Surveyors in the Settlement of Upper Canada." *Hs/SH* 15 (1982): 443–58.

Wilson, Alan. *The Clergy Reserves of Upper Canada*. Toronto: University of Toronto Press, 1968.

Wilson, J. Donald. "The Teacher in Early Ontario." In F.H. Armstrong et al, eds., *Aspects of Nineteenth-Century Ontario*, 218–36. Toronto: University of Toronto Press, 1974.

– "Thomas Appleton." *DCB*. Vol.6. 11–12.

Wilson, J. Donald, et al, eds. *Canadian Education: A History*. Scarborough: Prentice-Hall, 1970.

Wilton, Carol. "Administrative Reform: A Conservative Alternative to Responsible Government." *OH* 78 (1986): 105–25.

– *Popular Politics and Political Culture in Upper Canada, 1800–1850*. Montreal and Kingston: McGill-Queen's University Press, 2000.

Wood, J. David. *Making Ontario*. Montreal and Kingston: McGill-Queen's University Press, 2000.

Wylie, William N.T. "Poverty, Distress and Disease: Labour and the Construction of the Rideau Canal." *L/LT* 11 (1983): 61–83.

Zaslow, Morris, ed. *The Defended Border: Upper Canada and the War of 1812*. Toronto: Macmillan, 1964.

Index

Page numbers in italics refer to figures and tables.